MAY 27 '92	DATE DUE	

The Union League Movement in the Deep South

The Union League Movement in the Deep South

Politics and Agricultural Change During Reconstruction

Michael W. Fitzgerald

Louisiana State University Press   *Baton Rouge and London*

98 97 96 95 94 93 92 91 90 89 5 4 3 2 1

Designer: Patricia Douglas Crowder
Typeface: Linotron 202 Janson
Typesetter: The Composing Room of Michigan, Inc.
Printer: Thomson-Shore, Inc.
Binder: John H. Dekker & Sons, Inc.

Library of Congress Cataloging-in-Publication Data

Fitzgerald, Michael W., 1956–
    The Union League movement in the Deep South: politics and
agricultural change during Reconstruction / Michael W. Fitzgerald.
    p. cm.
    Bibliography: p.
    Includes index.
    ISBN 0-8071-1526-6 (alk. paper)
    1. Afro-Americans—History—1863–1877.   2. Reconstruction.   3. Union League
of America—History—19th century.   4. Southern States—Politics and government—
1865–1877.   5. Afro-Americans—Southern States—Politics and government.
6. Agriculture—Southern States—History—19th century.   I. Title.
E185.2.F54   1989
975'.00496073—dc20   88-38406
                                                                                           CIP

This publication has been supported by the National Endowment for the
Humanities, a federal agency which supports the study of such fields as history,
philosophy, literature, and languages.

The paper in this book meets the guidelines for permanence and durability of the
Committee on Production Guidelines for Book Longevity of the Council on
Library Resources. ∞

To my Mother and Father

Contents

Acknowledgments

In writing a book, one accumulates a substantial number of obligations. Among the most pressing of these is to acknowledge the individuals who made my research trips pleasant. I would like to thank Mimi C. Jones, Joe Caver, and Jackie Hines Pouncey at the Alabama Department of Archives and History, and Michelle Hudson and Charles Pearce at the Mississippi Department of Archives and History. At the National Archives in Washington, D.C., Sara Jackson and Michael Musick were also helpful. I should also mention Gordon Cotton of the Old Court House Museum in Vicksburg, in particular to praise his hospitality. Extended research far from home can be stressful—especially on a limited budget—but these individuals helped keep my spirits high.

The staffs of the following institutions were also of assistance: the Library of Congress, the University of North Carolina, Duke University, Louisiana State University, the New-York Historical Society, the New York Public Library (especially the Schomburg Center), the University of Alabama, the University of Mississippi, the University of Virginia, and the University of California. The librarians at UCLA deserve special mention for having borne substantial demands on their time. Finally, I wish to thank the facilities that furnished materials by mail, particularly the Boston Public Library, Bowdoin College, and the ITC Gammon Archives at Atlanta University.

Several institutions provided financial support. I would like to thank the University of California at Los Angeles for the Chancellor's Intern Fellowship and the Rosecrans memorial fellowship. The Carter G. Woodson Center at the University of Virginia assisted with a postdoctoral fellowship. Finally, St. Olaf College aided the preparation of the manuscript with various grants.

Margaret Fisher Dalrymple and Barbara Phillips at LSU Press provided needed help in guiding me through the publication process. Alexander Saxton read the manuscript with meticulous care and was the very model of consideration in all our dealings. Jonathan Wiener, Eric Foner, Steven Hahn, Lawrence Powell, and Armstead Robinson read it as well and provided much-needed criticism. Also reading portions of the manuscript were Edward Ayers, Margaret Creel, Robert A. Hill, Larry Lipin, Jonathan McLeod, and Jill Watts, all of whom have my deepest thanks.

My friends in Los Angeles also deserve kind mention for having made my years at UCLA pleasant ones. Thanks to Jackie Braitman, Michael Furmanovsky, Charles Hixson, Rebecca Kugel, Parke Skelton, and others who provided support and entertainment during my stay. My colleagues at St. Olaf College also deserve mention, particularly for providing needed advice during the publication process. Finally, my wife, Judy A. Kutulas, read and critiqued the entire text, and she contributed more to its completion than I can say.

The Union League Movement in the Deep South

Introduction

In the course of the nineteenth century, legal servitude was abolished throughout the Western Hemisphere, and the bound population of African descent became formally free. Emancipation shared certain social characteristics everywhere, as landowners strove to control the labor of the freed people while the former slaves attempted to extend their autonomy. In the southern portion of the United States, however, this process had one distinctive attribute: the former slaves soon acquired full civil and political rights—or at least black males did.[1] During Radical Reconstruction, southern freedmen gained access to substantial political power.[2] In response to this opportunity, a ground swell of political agitation swept the region, encompassing diffuse aspirations and giving them partisan direction. The initial organized response of the former slaves to enfranchisement was a unique episode in southern history. It illuminates the social order that emerged from the turmoil of the era.

1. David Brion Davis, *The Problem of Slavery in the Age of Revolution, 1770–1823* (Ithaca, 1975); Eric Foner, *Nothing But Freedom: Emancipation and Its Legacy* (New York, 1970); Eric Foner, *Reconstruction: America's Unfinished Revolution, 1863–1877* (New York, 1988); John Hope Franklin, *Reconstruction: After the Civil War* (Chicago, 1961); Eric J. Hobsbawm, *The Age of Revolution, 1789–1848* (London, 1962); Eric J. Hobsbawm, *The Age of Capital, 1848–1875* (New York, 1979); Kenneth M. Stampp, *The Era of Reconstruction, 1865–1877* (New York, 1965).

2. The term *freedmen* is employed here and elsewhere, rather than a more gender-inclusive term, because the League limited formal participation to males.

The Union League (or Loyal League) was the first Radical Republican organization in the southern states. It originated in the North during the Civil War as a patriotic club supporting the Lincoln administration. The organization was secret and oath-bound, with a ritual reminiscent of the Masons and clearly political in character. After the war the League spread among white yeomen in many regions of the South; it appealed to anti-Confederate sentiment in the hill country and supplanted existing Unionist clubs there. Once Congressional Reconstruction began, national Republican leaders used this existing structure to evangelize among the now-enfranchised freedmen. Paid organizers traveled through the southern states, initiating freedmen into the order. The response was dramatic: thousands joined the League during the summer of 1867, and it immediately became a major factor in the political situation. Militant actions were commonplace under League auspices, and black militias proliferated as tension escalated in the countryside. For two years, longer in some areas, the League constituted the Republican party's southern organizational arm. It controlled nominations for office, influenced policy, and essentially functioned as a Radical machine within the party. Although the League went into decline by 1869—having been battered by the Ku Klux Klan—its importance transcended its brief life. The League helped establish a tradition of black Republican voting that lasted for decades.

Most of the scholarly work on the Union League dates from just after the turn of the century, when the Dunning or Columbia school featured the secret clubs as an important aspect of Reconstruction. William A. Dunning himself wrote, "In the first elections under the reconstruction acts the leagues were the chief factors in giving coherence and efficiency to the majority party." Dunning and his followers depicted the League as malign, and they emphasized it prominently in their overall indictment of Radical Reconstruction. They stressed the clandestine character of the body, seeing its oaths and mysteries as means by which white Republicans manipulated the credulous freedmen. A later scholar described the League as "one of the most diabolical organizations in American history." This condemnation differed only in degree from most of the older assessments of the League; much of this work appears biased or downright racist by modern standards.[3]

The most prolific writer on the League was Walter Lynwood Fleming, who exemplified this approach. Fleming edited two collections of League documents and included a full chapter on the League in his *Civil War and Reconstruction in Alabama* (1905). A hostile tone characterized this writing, and in one typical passage Fleming commented: "In order to understand the absolute control exercised over the blacks by the alien adventurers . . . it will be necessary to examine the workings of the secret oath-bound society popularly known as the 'Loyal League.' The iron discipline of this order wielded by a few able and unscrupulous whites held together the ignorant negro masses for several years." Fleming emphasized the rituals; he viewed black superstition as largely responsible for the League's growth and depicted the organization's imposing ceremonies as central to its appeal. Fleming even described the League as a criminal conspiracy, observing that "some of the methods of the Loyal League were similar to those of the later Ku Klux Klan." For Fleming, the Union League summed up the evils of the Radical experiment.[4]

The reinterpretation of Reconstruction that gathered steam in the 1960s affected the League's reputation in an odd fashion, for more recent scholars tended to downplay the organization's importance. Because the Dunning school had emphasized the League for polemical purposes, modern revisionists seemed vaguely embarrassed by the secret club. It interfered with their rehabilitation of Radical Reconstruction. They referred to the League sympathetically, but they generally contented themselves with a curt dismissal of the existing literature as inadequate. For instance, W. E. B. Du Bois's seminal *Black Reconstruction in America* (1935) devoted only two para-

3. William Archibald Dunning, *Reconstruction: Political and Economic* (New York, 1907), 116; Susie Lee Owens, *The Union League of America: Political Activities in Tennessee, the Carolinas and Virginia, 1865–1870* (Ann Arbor, 1947), 6.

4. Walter Lynwood Fleming (ed.), *Union League Documents*, Documents Relating to Reconstruction, No. 3 (Morgantown, W. V., 1904); Fleming (ed.), *Documentary History of Reconstruction: Political, Military, Social, Religious, Educational and Industrial: 1865 to 1906* (1906–1907; rpr. Gloucester, Mass., 1960), II, 3–29; Fleming, "The Formation of the Union League in Alabama," *Gulf States Historical Magazine*, II (1903), 73–89; Fleming, *Civil War and Reconstruction in Alabama* (New York, 1905), 553, 565.

graphs to the League, noting merely that it was not a black version of the Klan. Likewise, Kenneth M. Stampp, in *The Era of Reconstruction* (1965), touched on the League only in passing. In the past few years, little has appeared on the subject. The last dissertation on the League in the South dates from the late 1950s, and it seems in some respects a throwback to the Dunning interpretation. Several historians describe the League's importance as overrated. For instance Thomas Holt, in *Black Over White* (1977), stated that the League has received "too much credit" for the growth of the Republican party in South Carolina. In avoiding serious treatment of the League, some revisionist historians tacitly accepted the negative portrayals established by earlier scholars.[5]

Thus, both the older writings and the newer discussions of the Radical organization present an inadequate assessment. Dunning's followers distorted the data badly, and their work certainly needs revision; but most later writing about Reconstruction, in de-emphasizing the League's importance, fails to meet this need. The League insurgency was one of the largest black social movements in American history, and its relative neglect seems unjustified. Union League proselytizing helped plant Republicanism among freedmen, and the League became one of the Ku Klux Klan's major targets—evidence in itself of significance and effectiveness. As Allen W. Trelease observed in *White Terror* (1971), "The League is in need of a historian, but it has been treated in summary fashion by almost every historian of the Reconstruction period."[6]

As important as the League movement was in the political arena, it also exercised a significant social influence, particularly upon the relationship between the planters and their labor force. Works by Leon Litwack, and many others, document tremendous ferment on the plantations during the immediate postwar period. After Ap-

5. W. E. B. Du Bois, *Black Reconstruction in America: An Essay Toward a History of the Part Which Black Folk Played in the Attempt to Reconstruct Democracy in America, 1860–1880* (1935; rpr. New York, 1971), 680; Stampp, *The Era of Reconstruction*, 156, 166; Clement Mario Silvestro, "None But Patriots: The Union Leagues in Civil War and Reconstruction" (Ph.D. dissertation, University of Wisconsin, 1959); Thomas C. Holt, *Black Over White: Negro Political Leadership in South Carolina During Reconstruction* (Urbana, 1977), 30.

6. Allen W. Trelease, *White Terror: The Ku Klux Klan Conspiracy and Southern Reconstruction* (New York, 1971), 426.

pomattox, planters tried to conduct cotton cultivation much as they always had. Their work force was now free, but they hoped to keep using gang labor, overseers, physical coercion, and women and children in the fields, and maintain a high degree of control over the freedmen's lives. Under President Andrew Johnson's plan of Reconstruction, planters also utilized state power through the Black Codes to bolster the labor discipline they sought to preserve. The freedmen resisted this scheme, seeing it as an attempt to resurrect slavery. An impasse of several years' duration resulted, as planters gradually determined that they had to rent land to the freedmen—either to individual families or to multifamily squads. The freedmen's restiveness helped force concessions, and thus came about the decentralized tenant farming that was to be so prominent a feature of southern life.[7]

Most of the recent work in this area has focused on economic aspects of the transition, ignoring the political context within which economic changes actually occurred. Widespread partisan organizing in the black community weakened planters' control over the labor force. Vast numbers of cotton planters abandoned gang labor precisely at the height of the Radical upsurge, just prior to the arrival of the Ku Klux Klan. Given the social turbulence the League provoked, the presence of the organization could only have complicated the landowners' already acute managerial problems. Various social and

---

7. Dan T. Carter, *When the War Was Over: The Failure of Self-Reconstruction in the South, 1865–1867* (Baton Rouge, 1985); Ronald L. F. Davis, *Good and Faithful Labor: From Slavery to Sharecropping in the Natchez District, 1860–1890* (Westport, Conn., 1982); Herbert Gutman, *The Black Family in Slavery and Freedom, 1750–1925* (New York, 1976); Jacqueline Jones, *Labor of Love, Labor of Sorrow: Black Women, Work, and the Family from Slavery to the Present* (New York, 1985); Peter Kolchin, *First Freedom: The Responses of Alabama's Blacks to Emancipation and Reconstruction* (Westport, Conn., 1972); Leon F. Litwack, *Been in the Storm So Long: The Aftermath of Slavery* (New York, 1979); William S. McFeely, *Yankee Stepfather: General O. O. Howard and the Freedmen* (New York, 1968); Edward Magdol, *A Right to the Land: Essays on the Freedmen's Community* (Westport, Conn., 1977); Michael Perman, *Reunion Without Compromise: The South and Reconstruction, 1865–1868* (Cambridge, England, 1973); Lawrence N. Powell, *New Masters: Northern Planters During the Civil War and Reconstruction* (New Haven, 1980); James L. Roark, *Masters Without Slaves: Southern Planters in the Civil War and Reconstruction* (New York, 1977); Michael Wayne, *The Reshaping of Plantation Society: The Natchez District, 1860–1880* (Baton Rouge, 1983). The term *decentralized tenant farming* includes sharecropping, other forms of family-based tenantry, and also the multifamily "squad system." The terminology highlights the contrast between these arrangements and the preceding norm on plantations, gang labor with coercive management.

economic causes contributed to the disruption of gang labor, but conflict between the work force and the landowners lay at the heart of the process. In Alabama and Mississippi, the Union League focused labor force resistance to planter dominance. League-related strikes and boycotts frequently pressured planters to grant their work force greater autonomy. Political organizing among blacks varied in intensity from one locality to another, but it was clearly enmeshed in the wider social and economic turmoil of the Reconstruction period.[8]

The League mobilization must be understood within this larger context, for it represented both a political movement and an agrarian upsurge. The same quest for land and autonomy visible in other aspects of freedmen's behavior manifested itself through this organization. The League's egalitarian rhetoric attracted the freedmen largely because of the impasse in plantation agriculture, and their militancy sprang from the resemblance their condition bore to slavery. The League appeal addressed agricultural concerns, and not surprisingly the League often functioned like a nascent labor organization. The Union League was a major catalyst in planters' recognition that freedmen would no longer work under conditions resembling servitude; to this extent, it paved the way for the transition to decentralized tenant farming. This whole issue has been underemphasized in the historical literature, for the black response to

---

8. Among the major contributions to this body of writing are: Stephen J. DeCanio, *Agriculture in the Postbellum South: The Economics of Production and Supply* (Cambridge, Mass., 1974); DeCanio, "Sharecropping in History and Theory," *Agricultural History*, XLIX (1975), 426–40; Robert Higgs, *Competition and Coercion: Blacks in the American Economy, 1865–1914* (Cambridge, England, 1977); Gerald David Jaynes, *Branches Without Roots: Genesis of the Black Working Class in the American South, 1862–1882* (New York, 1986); Roger L. Ransom and Richard Sutch, *One Kind of Freedom: The Economic Consequences of Emancipation* (Cambridge, England, 1977); Joseph D. Reid, *Agriculture in the Postbellum South* (New Haven, 1975); Ralph Shlomowitz, "The Transition from Slave to Freedman: Labor Arrangements in Southern Agriculture, 1865–1870" (Ph.D. dissertation, University of Chicago, 1978); Shlomowitz, "The Squad System on Postbellum Cotton Plantations," in Orville Vernon Burton and Robert C. McMath, Jr. (eds.), *Toward a New South? Studies in Post–Civil War Southern Communities* (Westport, Conn., 1982), 71–102; Gavin Wright, "The Strange Career of the New Southern Economic History," *Reviews in American History*, X (1982), 164–80; Jonathan M. Wiener, "Class Structure and Economic Development in the American South," *American Historical Review*, LXXXIV (1979), 970–1006; Wiener, *Social Origins of the New South: Alabama, 1860–1885* (Baton Rouge, 1978); Harold D. Woodman, "Post–Civil War Southern Agriculture and the Law," *Agricultural History*, LIII (1979), 319–37.

political events does bear directly on economic trends during the period.

A final point should be made briefly, the matter of generalizing from these findings to the rest of the region. There seems little reason to regard the League's social mobilization in Alabama and Mississippi as unique, for the movement possessed a similar following in all the Reconstructed states. Moreover, the two states were typical of the structural evolution of cotton culture. As Gerald David Jaynes points out, "The gang system on cotton plantations was an institution of the past by 1868." Throughout the cotton South, the abandonment of gang labor thus accompanied, or followed hard upon, the politicization of the freedmen with Congressional Reconstruction. If one accepts the intermingling of political and economic impulses among the freedmen, then their partisan mobilization must have enhanced their capacity to resist the planters. The data show that this occurred through the League in Alabama and Mississippi. Given the pervasive reports of League activity, and the typicality of these two states' economic evolution, it seems likely that the movement showed similar characteristics elsewhere. Other scholars' research indicates analogous developments throughout the cotton belt.[9]

My goal, then, is twofold: to provide a more accurate historical account of the Union League as a political movement and also to illuminate the social impact of the Radical upsurge in Alabama and Mississippi. The emergence of decentralized tenant farming was a crucial result of the tumult of early Reconstruction. The cause was not economic forces in isolation, but a complex mixture of economic, social, and political factors. The politicization of the freedmen developed from their acute dissatisfaction with planters' efforts to maintain a regime reminiscent of slavery. This movement immediately

9. Jaynes, *Branches Without Roots*, 173; Silvestro, "None But Patriots," 265–300; Richard H. Abbott, *The Republican Party and the South, 1855–1877* (Chapel Hill, 1986), 59–65, 88–92, 105–23. For the interaction between political agitation and agricultural change in various Deep South states, see Julie Saville, "Grassroots Reconstruction in South Carolina"; Joseph P. Reidy, "The Currency of Freedom: Wages and Ballots in Reconstruction Georgia"; and Stephen M. Miller, "Plantation, Workshop, and Ballot Box: Politics and Labor Organization in Reconstruction Mississippi" (Papers delivered at Southern Historical Association meeting, November, 1987, New Orleans).

strengthened blacks' abilities to resist the wishes of the landowners, thus intensifying the struggle for autonomy already under way. Neither the Ku Klux Klan nor Redemption itself could reverse the agricultural changes resulting in large part from black pressure during this period. The decentralized tenant farming system was one outcome, and this proved a critical transformation. As C. Vann Woodward put it, "The sharecropping and lien system was to prove an economic trap for black as well as white croppers, but the system was indeed new and not a continuity of the older order." The politicization of the freedmen bore directly on this major development in southern history.[10]

10. C. Vann Woodward, Review of Fraser and Moore (eds.), *From the Old South to the New*, in *American Historical Review*, LXXXVIII (1983), 188.

ONE

※ ❧ ※

Origins of the Union League:
North and South

Prior to the advent of Military Reconstruction, several forces converged that contributed to the later growth of the League. These factors established the context for the Union League and influenced the organization's political character. There were three basic causes for the growth of the League in the South. First, the National Council of the League—along with the Republican congressional leadership—decided to devote resources to a southern organizing campaign, and to direct the movement those funds helped create. Second, the growth of Unionist sentiments among mountain yeomen during the Civil War created a substantial Republican following and group of activists among southern whites. Third, black dissatisfaction with the aftermath of emancipation, and especially with postwar plantation agriculture, established a huge social constituency for a Radical movement; out of this anger grew community and social organizations that laid the groundwork for the League's expansion. These developments came together in the spring of 1867, creating an explosive growth of the Union League as soon as Congress passed the Reconstruction Acts; they determined its hierarchical nature and institutional characteristics. In particular, these causes explain why the League maintained relatively moderate policies despite the militant inclinations of the black community and also of the white mountain yeomanry.

The National Council of the Union League had contradictory

goals for the movement in the South during Congressional Reconstruction. Washington officials encouraged the politicization of the freedmen, but also strove to restrain their militancy. These white leaders urged caution upon the black insurgency they were helping to build. Members of the National Council responded more to the concerns of Republican congressmen than to those of the freedmen. They wanted to establish as broad a southern Republican party as possible, and they particularly hoped to avoid extreme measures that would damage the party in the North. Thus the organization's resources were used to direct freedmen toward a more moderate course than they might otherwise have taken. The League in Alabama and Mississippi developed in a radical direction by contemporary standards, but militant public demands for land redistribution and similar measures seldom materialized. The pressure of the National Council was largely responsible for this cautious approach by the black-dominated local leagues.

The actual beginnings of the League movement are obscure. Several northern localities had had white patriotic clubs by that name since early in the Civil War. As one scholar observed, "The variety of origins attributed to the Union League suggests that it was a general movement . . . rather than one society with a single origin." The National Council was established late in 1862; Republicans had suffered reverses in the congressional elections that year, and administration partisans redoubled their efforts in the face of this defeat. Activists adopted the secret order, vaguely Masonic in ritual, as suitable for mass agitation in support of the war. The League and its adjunct, the Loyal Publication Society, distributed quantities of tracts to the people of the North. The League possessed a diverse constituency. It had a following among patriotic native-born workingmen and was closely associated with the patrician Union League Clubs of New York, Philadelphia, and Boston. By 1864, the organization was potent enough to play a role in the reelection of President Lincoln. In the words of one of its leaders, the League became "powerful and controlling" in several of the contested northern states.[1]

1. Guy James Gibson, "Lincoln's League: The Union League Movement During the Civil War" (Ph.D. dissertation, University of Illinois, 1957), 2 and *passim*; G. Bliss and L. G. B.

The Republican party leadership directed the National Council, and according to one account the creation of the national body was suggested by President Lincoln himself. Many of the leaders were federal employees, and the three individuals involved with day-to-day operations held "lucrative" posts under Lincoln, as a League report put it. These officers were relatively obscure Republican activists. Judge James M. Edmunds, the organization's president from 1862 to 1869, served as commissioner of the General Land Office for years; he also held a variety of government and party positions during the late 1860s and 1870s, but beyond this, little is known of him. Such Washington bureaucrats used League activities to justify receipt of federal patronage. For example, Thomas G. Baker, the long-time national secretary, wrote that though his work in the League was not directly compensated, "*indirectly* of course I was well paid in being retained in the public service for so long." This pattern of motivation meant that League leaders followed the policies of the Republican officials who subsidized them. Moreover, the National Council was eager to enhance its importance by spreading the League into the South. As the crisis atmosphere ebbed in the North with victory, these leaders did not want simply to watch their organization disintegrate. They now hoped to be of further use to the Republican cause by marshaling the loyalist constituency of the South.[2]

Even before the end of hostilities the League moved southward. Most organizing centered on yeoman Unionists and Federal soldiers,

---

Cannon to Edwin B. Stanton, December 1, 1863, in Ira Berlin, Joseph P. Reidy, and Leslie S. Rowland (eds.), *The Black Military Experience*, Freedom: A Documentary History of Emancipation, 1861–1867, Ser. 2 (Cambridge, Mass., 1982), 107–108; Union League of America, *Proceedings of the Annual Meeting of the Grand National Council, Union League of America, Held at Washington, December 13th, 1865*, p. 7, hereinafter cited as ULA, *Proceedings, 1865*; Henry W. Bellows, *Historical Sketch of the Union League Club of Philadelphia: Its Origin, Organization, and Work, 1863–1879* (New York, 1879), 32, 36, 52–53, 58, 66–67; *Chronicle of the Union League Club of Philadelphia* (Philadelphia, 1902), 41, 70. For a recent account of the wartime League, see Frank L. Klement, *Dark Lanterns: Secret Political Societies, Conspiracies, and Treason Trials in the Civil War* (Baton Rouge, 1984), 34–63.

2. Union League of America, *Proceedings of the National Council of the Union League of America, at its Sixth Annual Session, Held in the City of Washington, D.C., on Tuesday and Wednesday, March 2d and 3d 1869*, p. 8, hereinafter cited as ULA, *Proceedings, 1869*; Gibson, "Lincoln's League," 16–28; Baker to Bryant, September 9, 1886, in John Emory Bryant Papers, William R. Perkins Library, Duke University, Durham.

but freedmen were also admitted as early as 1865 in South Carolina. This activity remained at a modest level for months after Appomattox as the Washington leadership puzzled over an appropriate response to Johnson's southern moves. The League's annual report of December, 1865, found it "impolitic" to discuss Reconstruction at that time, for the National Council would formulate a definite position as events unfolded. In the spring of 1866 the national organization stepped up agitation, especially among southern Unionists. Edmunds later recalled, "For a full year before any plan of restoration had been adopted by Congress [in March, 1867], the League was actively pushed into the South, for the double purpose of resisting Rebel outrages, and of laying the foundation for a truly Republican policy." The League leaders—by now being purged by Johnson from their federal jobs—prepared for an expanded role. A Washington office was opened and a League newspaper, the *Great Republic*, started with Edmunds as editor. In Alabama, where yeoman Unionists were plentiful, the League also set up a State Council, and John C. Keffer of Philadelphia arrived in Montgomery with a commission as state secretary of the order. The limiting factor during this period was largely financial—the League was deeply in debt by year's end. As Edmunds phrased it, only money was needed to organize "the whole loyal element of the South."[3]

The passage of Military Reconstruction in March, 1867, represented a major opportunity for the organization. Edmunds approached leading congressmen, arguing that because of its secretive character the League constituted the perfect means to spread Republicanism among the newly enfranchised freedmen. The case was persuasive in view of the dangers the former slaves faced, but for some weeks the Republican leadership withheld organized aid, so the burden fell to individuals. Edmunds secured a commitment of two hundred dollars a month from Senator William Sprague, of Rhode Island. Sprague, one of the richest men in Congress, was apparently interested in using the League to further the presidential ambitions of his father-in-law, Chief Justice Salmon P. Chase. In

---

3. ULA, *Proceedings, 1865,* pp. 8–9; Silvestro, "None But Patriots," 235; ULA, *Proceedings, 1869,* p. 9.

return, Edmunds assured Sprague of his support for Chase and of his opposition to a "Military head" for the national ticket. At all events, Sprague "came to the rescue," and the League was soon able to "prosecute the work with so much system and vigor" that party leaders were obliged to furnish assistance.[4]

By the early summer of 1867, the Union Republican Congressional Executive Committee (URCEC) had assumed oversight of party activities in the South. The URCEC soon agreed that the League was an excellent means to reach the freedmen. "I think the Congressional Committee is getting daily more friendly, and I know the League is daily getting stronger," observed Edmunds. The League was promised aid, and nearly $2,700 was given outright by the URCEC and congressional donors—primarily Sprague. This sum represented over half the League's 1867 budget of $4,600, and several thousand more came indirectly as subsidies for the *Great Republic*. In addition, the committee provided "any number, almost" of free political documents to party activists, and one leaflet circulated so extensively in councils, it was referred to as the Loyal League Catechism. Buttons and badges also arrived in bulk. Overall, as a League report stated, "cooperation of the League with the Union Republican Congressional Committee . . . added greatly to the efficiency of both organizations."[5]

Party financial aid allowed the League to expand operations drastically. During 1867, for example, almost 56,000 free copies of the *Great Republic* were sent southward. More important, many of the 118 speakers the URCEC hired that summer were themselves League organizers, and in both Alabama and Mississippi the com-

4. J. M. Edmunds to W. P. Sprague, July 26, August 7, 1867, both in William Sprague Papers, Rare Book and Manuscript Library, Columbia University, New York; Susie Lee Owens, "The Union League of America: Political Activities in Tennessee, the Carolinas, and Virginia, 1865–1870" (Ph.D. dissertation, New York University, 1943), 480. The League's proceedings for 1867 have disappeared from the Library of Congress, but Owens reprints most of the text as an appendix.

5. Edmunds to Sprague, August 7, 1867, in Sprague Papers, Columbia University; Washington *Chronicle*, November 27, 1867; Owens, "The Union League of America," 478–82; Washington *Chronicle*, July 23, 1867; Montgomery *State Sentinel*, May 22, 29, 1867; Montgomery *Advertiser*, July 12, 1867; T. L. Tullock to Chandler, October 12, 1867, T. O. Glascock to Chandler, October 3, 1868, both in William E. Chandler Papers, Library of Congress; Washington *Great Republic*, May 5, July 26, 1867.

mittee subsidized several prominent League activists.[6] Assisted by the URCEC, the League's National Council also hired traveling organizers, white and black; one of these, former Freedmen's Bureau official Thomas W. Conway, took an extended journey through the formerly rebellious states. By July, Conway could report a vast increase in the number of League members. As many as 300,000 members had enrolled in 3,000 League councils in the South.[7]

It is difficult to judge the accuracy of such figures. The National Council itself admitted that the actual strength of the order was "unknown," so rapid had been the spread of councils into the South. The overall trend was clear, however; the National Council's efforts assisted the League's rapid expansion. Within a matter of weeks, the Union League had become the organizational nucleus of a massive movement. In the words of one black Leaguer, "The greatest interest exists among the colored men everywhere. They are wide awake."[8]

While the League's success in the South was welcome, it was not viewed as an unalloyed blessing, for the freedmen's political enthusiasm rather alarmed the Republican leaders. The fear was that too Radical a position on civil rights would discourage southern white accessions. As Richard H. Abbott has pointed out, the northern Republicans most active in the southern drive were in the "moderate wing of the party," and this was evident in the URCEC membership. The chairman, Robert C. Schenck, was not a conspicuous Radical, and several members, like Congressman Oaks Ames, were quite moderate; only Senator Zachariah Chandler and Congressman William D. Kelley were considered advocates of a stern policy toward the South. According to Michael Les Benedict, the URCEC

---

6. Owens, "The Union League of America," 481–82; "Names of Speakers and Organizers Employed or Aided by the Union Republican Congressional Committee," September 12, 1867, in Robert C. Schenck Papers, Rutherford B. Hayes Memorial Library, Fremont, Ohio. In Alabama these included Peyton Finley, John C. Keffer, Holland Thompson, and B. W. Norris; in Mississippi they included E. J. Castello, Nelson Gill, G. S. C. Hussey, James Lynch, and Frederick Parsons.

7. Washington *Great Republic*, July 26, 1867.

8. Owens, "The Union League of America," 481; [?] to T. L. Tullock, August 2, 1867, in Schenck Papers, Hayes Library.

argued that Reconstruction entailed no "fundamental conflict" with southern whites, a position Benedict describes as "conciliatory."[9]

The League's National Council took its cue from such discretion and disavowed extremism of any sort. Edmunds and his cohorts even tried to convince planters that their long-term interests lay in joining the movement. The National Council's moderate posture was genuine, and the leadership consistently followed a cautious line. For example, the national organization kept close watch on political trends in nearby Virginia. President Edmunds forced the League there to downplay civil rights demands in the interests of Republican unity, and a northern League delegation actually was sent to lobby with the Radical faction for a moderate line. In another instance, the national office intervened against labor strikes near Lincolnsville, Virginia, refusing to charter any new councils in that rural locality.[10]

The National Council's restrained approach showed clearly in dealing with the volatile issue of land redistribution. The leadership distanced itself from the Stevens confiscation proposals of early 1867, arguing that such measures were only possible if southerners illegally hindered Reconstruction. Edmunds wrote that the public should "not be frightened by the senseless cry of a war of races, or led away by the supposed prospect of confiscation." This was the mainstream Republican response to the issue, as Eric Foner pointed out. The League's disavowal of confiscation, in the face of apparent black receptivity to the idea, illustrates the cautious tendency of Edmunds and his comrades. Since the organization was structured hierarchically, it was more responsive at the national level to the wishes of Congress than to those of the freedmen.[11]

The policy adopted by the National Council did become more Radical over time, but during the critical period of the League's

9. Abbott, *The Republican Party and the South*, 111; Michael Les Benedict, *A Compromise of Principle: Congressional Republicans and Reconstruction, 1863–1869* (New York, 1974), 260–61.

10. Washington *Great Republic*, June 20, 1867; George Parsons Lathrop, *History of the Union League of Philadelphia* (Philadelphia, 1884), 97–98; Owens, "The Union League of America," 165–68.

11. Washington *Great Republic*, June 20, 1867; Eric Foner, *Politics and Ideology in the Age of the Civil War* (New York, 1980), 142; Benedict, *A Compromise of Principle*, 260–61.

expansion, the organization maintained a moderate posture. The national leadership thus exercised a contradictory influence on political developments in the South. The resources the League provided encouraged political activity among the freedmen, thereby augmenting Radical tendencies among blacks. But the National Council's activities also restrained the freedmen, for the leadership hoped to channel the movement toward cautious demands. This outside intervention proved a critical factor in shaping black political activity. On confiscation and other issues, the wishes of the black community were subordinated to expediency as defined by the National Council of the League and by Republican leaders generally.

The initial successes of the League in Alabama, and to a lesser extent in Mississippi, occurred among the white yeomanry. During Presidential Reconstruction, many small farmers joined the League, especially in the Alabama hill country. Their Unionist tendencies, growing out of the war, constituted one of the major social forces creating the Republican coalition.[12] The poorer farmers' sympathies were significant in their own right, but they were of crucial importance in the politicization of the freedmen. Yeoman Leaguers provided many of the activists who expanded the movement into the black community. Their experienced leadership helped spread insurgency throughout the plantation region during the spring and summer of 1867.

League support in the hill region of northern Alabama, and to some degree in the wire-grass counties of the southeastern part of the state, developed from yeoman Unionism during the Civil War. One important source was farmers' traditional animosity toward their slaveholding social betters. Even in the antebellum period, Alabama politics reflected sharp regional and class conflict; shared hostility to wealthy planters underlay the Democratic party's long domination of state government. Northern Alabama resisted immediate secession, and many yeoman whites entertained antiwar feelings. One upland farmer expressed such sentiments, claiming that all the

12. For a more detailed discussion of this subject, see Michael W. Fitzgerald, "Radical Republicanism and the White Yeomanry During Alabama Reconstruction, 1865–1868," *Journal of Southern History,* LIV (1988), 565–96.

slaveholders wanted was "to git you pu[m]pt up and go to fight for there infurnal negroes and after you do there fighting you may kiss there hine parts for o they care."[13]

Disaffection increased as the costs of the conflict mounted. As described by Malcolm C. McMillan, the war's burdens fell on Alabama's small farmers with disproportionate severity. Yeomen were drafted en masse by the Confederacy; planters owning over twenty slaves were exempt. Soldiers were paid in almost worthless currency, but their struggling families paid taxes collected in kind on their crops. The geography of the conflict also contributed to anti-Confederate sentiment. Southern Alabama's plantations went almost untouched until the last months of war, while combat devastated the Tennessee Valley and the surrounding mountain areas. Huntsville, for example, raided twenty-one times before the close of 1863, became a center of dissatisfaction with the Confederate cause. The misery of those who lived in the war-torn region was intense, and marauding armies stripped the area of food. Small wonder that many farmers complained it was a "rich man's war and a poor man's fight."[14]

Massive suffering provoked resistance to the Confederate government. Desertion became epidemic as soldiers returned to aid their now destitute families. Many farmers also spent most of the Civil War hiding from conscription officers, and the forests and swamps swarmed with bands of armed "tories" and deserters. In September, 1862, Confederate General Gideon Pillow estimated that there were ten thousand Union sympathizers in the mountainous section of Alabama. One such individual, a future League leader, described his wartime exploits: "A few weeks befor the advance of Rosecra[n]s into North Ala., in 1863, I made it convenient to take a 'french furlough' and when I got home I wrote the boys that they had better come

13. James B. Bell to H. Bell, April 21, 1861, quoted in Hugh C. Bailey, "Disloyalty in Early Confederate Alabama," *Journal of Southern History*, XXIII (1957), 525. For prewar Alabama politics with its class and sectional tensions, see J. Mills Thornton III, *Politics and Power in a Slave Society: Alabama, 1800–1860* (Baton Rouge, 1978).

14. Malcolm C. McMillan, *The Disintegration of a Confederate State* (Macon, Ga., 1986); Armstead L. Robinson, *Bitter Fruits of Bondage: The Demise of Slavery and the Collapse of the Confederacy, 1861–1865* (forthcoming); Georgia Lee Tatum, *Disloyalty in the Confederacy* (Chapel Hill, 1934), 22–23; W. Lee to Jefferson Davis, May 4, 1861, in Berlin, Reidy, and Rowland (eds.), *The Black Military Experience*, 282.

home which many of them did." He and his fellow deserters actually formed themselves into a company and were mustered into Union service. Many postwar white Leaguers had such backgrounds. Over 2,600 white citizens of the state joined the 1st Alabama Cavalry and other Union regiments. The warfare that grew out of this situation of divided loyalties was extraordinarily bitter. In addition to both armies, irregular forces of "bushwackers" roved the countryside, committing depredations upon persons and property. General Pillow described the Unionists as "vicious as copperheads," but in reality violence was indiscriminate on both sides.[15]

Hostility continued unabated after the war. Unionists were angered as Presidential Reconstruction turned state and local government over to former Rebels, and they feared that their opponents would use the opportunity to even scores. Many former Federal soldiers continued to drill in self-defense. This proved fertile ground for the growth of the Union League. The National Council's efforts at expansion met an enthusiastic response, and the League absorbed existing Unionist organizations such as the wartime Peace Society. Local bodies maintained considerable autonomy, but they were at least brought into a working relationship with the Republican leadership in Washington. The League was popular, as one leader pointed out, because it was clandestine. After word of the New Orleans riot, Union men were afraid to meet publicly. The League was therefore ideally suited to become the institutional voice of the white Radical movement.[16]

Powerful economic forces fed dissatisfaction and thus insurgency among up-country Unionists. Crop failures in 1865 and thereafter threatened north Alabama residents with continuing hunger. As Northern Methodist missionary and future Leaguer Aram S. Lakin wrote from Huntsville, the people had reached a "state of starvation" by late 1866. Small farmers operated on a thin margin in the best of times, but now drought combined with wartime devastation to pro-

15. William Stanley Hoole, *Alabama Tories: The First Alabama Cavalry, U.S.A., 1862–1865* (Tuscaloosa, 1960), 6, 14; E. Latham to Figures, April 16, 1867, in [Military] Governor Wager Swayne Papers, Alabama Department of Archives and History, Montgomery, hereinafter cited as ADAH; Fleming, *Civil War and Reconstruction in Alabama*, 116.

16. Montgomery *Mail*, August 30, 1866.

duce large-scale want. Livestock was gone, fences ruined, and good seed difficult to procure. Only massive aid provided by the Freedmen's Bureau enabled the region to escape complete privation. Two and sometimes three times as many whites as blacks received Bureau rations each month, a striking statistic in view of the freedmen's poverty. Even this help did not entirely provide for the population, since thousands of destitute whites descended into the plantation area of the Tennessee Valley. The mountain region lost 10.2 percent of its white population between 1860 and 1866, and the neighboring Tennessee Valley gained some 8.4 percent. Yeoman Unionists were among those who suffered worst, since they were the poorest and "most ignorant portion of our people," in one observer's words.[17]

Political issues growing out of general destitution reinforced the importance of crop failures, and even relief became a subject of contention. The Bureau gave food to local authorities for distribution, leaving the Unionist poor at the mercy of generally hostile officeholders. "Those who now have control of the issue of supplies are eminently disloyal men," a Bureau official wrote. Charges of unfair treatment were commonplace. In Cherokee County, over a hundred Leaguers met to complain they were not receiving a proper allotment of corn. In their petition, they observed that the people who were suffering received little, because "the Rebels get control of all these things." The *Great Republic* noted similar reports of unfairness against Leaguers in other north Alabama localities. In Blount County, claims of Rebel discrimination against impoverished Unionists led to the appointment of League leader William C. Garrison as Bureau agent; he was given the responsibility of distributing relief. Soon Blount County Conservatives themselves complained of "a collusion, in regard to the distribution of supplies."[18]

17. A. S. Lakin to Chalfant, October 1, 1866, in Freedmen's Aid Society Correspondence, ITC Gammon Theological Seminary Archives, Woodruff Center Library, Atlanta University, Atlanta, hereinafter cited as ITC Archives; Elizabeth Bethel, "The Freedmen's Bureau in Alabama," *Journal of Southern History,* XVI (1948), 59; Robert Arthur Gilmour, "The Other Emancipation: Studies in the Society and the Economy of Alabama Whites During Reconstruction" (Ph.D. dissertation, Johns Hopkins University, 1972), 74–75; [?] to Patton, July 31, 1866, in Governor R. M. Patton Papers, ADAH.

18. J. B. Callis to Swayne, January 15, 1867, in Records of the Assistant Commissioner for Alabama, Microcopy Number 809, Record Group 105, Records of the Bureau of Refugees,

Political bitterness over the relief issue was extreme. A telling indication occurred when a delegation from St. Clair County, headed by League leader B. T. Pope, arrived in Memphis soliciting relief. The Memphis *Avalanche* condemned the effort, observing that the "people reported to be starving are the political brethren of these Radicals." All the "starvation and destitution" had been the fault of the Republican party, and so the "'Unionists' (so called) of North Alabama" should look to their political brethren for aid. Obviously, partisan differences grew still more heated when they determined who was fortunate enough to have food to eat.[19]

The Unionists' poverty also invested local judicial proceedings—especially for debt—with political significance. Demands for a "stay law" or other debt relief were common, among small farmers as well as planters. One spokesman for debtors noted that if court proceedings continued, people would be ruined by forced sale of property. Since yeoman Unionists were often the poorest property owners in the population, such sentiments were widespread among them. In piedmont Chambers County, destitution was rampant. A correspondent wrote the commanding general Wager T. Swayne about many "hard working men" discouraged because of large "confederate" claims hanging over them. Moreover, Unionists were convinced the legal system would not deal fairly with them, and this belief had some basis. In Cherokee County, the sheriff refused to accept white Leaguers for jury duty. Enforcement of tax laws reportedly was biased against Unionists, and the civil authorities met resistance. In Blount and St. Clair counties, for instance, they collectively refused to pay taxes to the "Rebel State." Local organizations "notified the Sheriff not to go among them to execute any process, and if he did go not to take any papers . . . or . . . be 'bushwacked.'" The attempted seizure of a mule for debt resulted in actual bloodshed. Several Unionists were wounded in a gunfight with a sheriff's posse

---

Freedmen and Abandoned Lands, National Archives, hereinafter cited as Records, M809; L. J. Stanford to John Pope, May 11, 1867, in Swayne Papers, ADAH; Washington *Great Republic*, June 26, 1867; W. C. Garrison to Callis, April 18, 1866, in Letters Received by the Sub-Assistant Commissioner [hereinafter cited as SAC] Huntsville, Vol. 58, RG 105; J. W. Moore to Patton, April 9, 1867, in Gov. Patton Papers, ADAH.

19. Huntsville *Advocate*, May 26 (quoting Memphis *Avalanche*), May 30, 1866.

in September, 1866. Hard-pressed Unionists were quite willing to resist the appropriation of their property by former Rebel civil officials.[20]

Unionist dissatisfaction gave rise to armed insurgency in several localities. Leaguers organized to defend themselves, and something close to warfare developed in the hill counties. In Randolph, for example, "the *Leaguers* have been banded to murder or drive out . . . every man who sympathised with the Confederate cause." No arrests could be made because of the League's influence in the countryside. Likewise in St. Clair, Leaguers reportedly beat people and set fire to buildings. After the killing of a Leaguer, one hundred of his comrades threatened to drive all former Rebels out of the county. One leader allegedly claimed that in the event of conflict "the negroes would fall on their side," and the two groups combined would destroy the county. Such accounts were perhaps exaggerated, but clearly the Unionists' mood was combative. A Blount County Leaguer wrote the Bureau in April, 1866, that "we can no longer do without troops unless you allow the loyal men to kill the traitors out." In De Kalb County a Unionist made an identical request for permission to "kill them out" in response to Rebel persecution. In both cases, strikingly enough, Sub-Assistant Commissioner John B. Callis of the Bureau endorsed the formation of militias. Beyond doubt, violence was common between Unionists and former Confederates in the up-country.[21]

Along with self-defense measures, electoral activities also developed before Military Reconstruction. During the war, the Peace Society contested Confederate elections; in August, 1863, it elected six Unionists to the Congress in Richmond, and it also sent several antiwar men to the state legislature. Once the war ended, the League or unconditional Unionists vied with the Conservatives for su-

20. Mobile *Advertiser and Register*, October 19, 1866; A. W. Dillard and W. V. Hare to Patton, March 20, 1867, in Gov. Patton Papers, ADAH; N. H. Rice *et al.* to Smith, September 16, 1868, in Governor William Hugh Smith Papers, ADAH; A. M. Gibson and J. W. Moore to Patton, August 16, 1866, in Gov. Patton Papers, ADAH; Mobile *Advertiser and Register*, September 4, 1866, quoting Huntsville *Independent*.

21. Dean and Mc Craw to Patton, December 27, 1866, [?] to Patton, July 21, 31, 1866, all in Gov. Patton Papers, ADAH; Garrison to Callis, April 18, 1866, J. T. Sparks to Callis, July 16, 1866, both in Letters Received SAC Huntsville, Vols. 58, 63, RG 105.

premacy in the mountain region. They met with mixed success. In Blount County, the head of the League ran for probate judge in May, 1866; he lost, but Unionists were successfully elected as magistrates in various neighborhoods. In Elmore County a League ticket was "signally rebuked" by the voters, but in Cleburne County the slate reportedly swept all the offices in early 1867. While the League's campaign demonstrated some achievements, clear limits to potential success existed. Without black suffrage, Unionists remained a permanent minority, and only in a few counties did they have a real chance to win elections.[22]

Just how large a minority they were in Alabama is difficult to determine. One activist saw the League as possessing a working majority in Fayette, Marion, Walker, and Winston counties. Fleming quoted sources that gave the League 40 percent of the vote in north Alabama. In June, 1866, the State Council claimed a membership of 18,000 whites, some two-thirds of whom had unsullied Unionist backgrounds. Estimates by State Secretary John C. Keffer went as high as 30,000 or even 40,000 in 1867. "The mountain men are not only loyal but very Radical," he wrote. Such assessments doubtless were inflated, but the Democratic press agreed the number was large. As the Montgomery *Mail* commented, "The Radicals and Loyal Leaguers in Alabama claim 30,000 white votes. Let us admit they have ten thousand." At the time of the enactment of Military Reconstruction, the number was probably between 10,000 and 15,000, or between one-fifth and one-seventh of the white electorate. Most of these Radical voters probably had some affiliation with the Loyal League.[23]

One final point should be made about yeoman Unionism that became significant after freedmen received the ballot. If Alabama's

22. Tatum, *Disloyalty*, 60–61; Fleming, *Civil War and Reconstruction in Alabama*, 358–59; Moore to Callis, May 11, 1866, in Letters Received SAC Huntsville, Vol. 58, RG 105; Montgomery *Mail*, January 16, February 22, 1867.

23. Washington *Great Republic*, January 3, 1867; Fleming, *Civil War and Reconstruction in Alabama*, 556; Athens *Post*, May 16, 1867; J. W. Forney to W. P. Fessenden, October 21, 1867, in John Wien Forney Papers, LC; Washington *Great Republic*, March 28, 1867, quoting Montgomery *Mail*. Total white registration in the summer of 1867 was 61,295 (Fleming, *Civil War and Reconstruction in Alabama*, 491). Fleming claimed that the League was strong in north Alabama in 1865, but he seems to have been mistaken. Organization officials in Washington reported only 3,000 Alabama members late in the year. Many Unionist local groups existed at that time, but most affiliated with the League early in 1866.

white Leaguers were Radical in 1867, they were not egalitarian on racial issues. Most saw the need for black votes and therefore endorsed Military Reconstruction, but the antebellum heritage of racism made coalition with the freedmen difficult. For example in Fayette County, a League stronghold, Unionists demanded the "colonization of the colored race when such a measure shall become practicable." Activists in Shelby County noted with evident discomfort that "the Negro question has come up befor this League . . . some of our neighboring Leggs have been initiating them but they have failed to explain to us by what authority they do it. If you will be so kind as to explain the matter." White Union Leaguers generally recognized that they must "meet fully the demands of the present hour," as the State Council put it, and endorse a limited commitment to black suffrage and civil rights. But this tactical measure was adopted to keep their adversaries out of power. In the words of League State Secretary Keffer, the Republican leaders of northern Alabama "have never been sound in their faith concerning equal rights. . . . [T]hey will use the negro to help them put down rebels, but wish to give him no further rights than will accomplish this, and none politically after it is accomplished." The issue would become a critical force that weakened the Republican coalition over time.[24]

In Mississippi the situation among whites was entirely different from that in Alabama. Partly for geographic reasons, the League never acquired much of a following among the yeomanry. Mississippi possessed no isolated cluster of poorer farmers that was comparable to north Alabama's mountain region. As a result, wartime Unionist activity remained at relatively modest levels. Bands of deserters and draft evaders existed in the northeast and southeast sections of the state, but these represented no real challenge to Confederate rule. The politically developed insurgency of the Alabama Peace Society had no counterpart here. Mississippi thus lacked the militant base upon which rested the League's expansion in Alabama.

24. Washington *Great Republic*, November 15, 1866; J. M. Hare and A. H. Merrell to Patton, May 29, 1867, in Gov. Patton Papers, ADAH; Mobile *Nationalist*, January 24, 1867; Keffer to Howard, June 6, 1868, in O. O. Howard Papers, Bowdoin College Library, New Brunswick, Maine.

Only a handful of leagues were present during Presidential Reconstruction, and few yeomen ever found the League a suitable expression of their Unionism.

Anti-Confederate sentiment in Mississippi among yeomen developed slowly during the Civil War. Some poorer regions had supported immediate secession, in contrast to the reluctance of north Alabama's upland farmers; this initial enthusiasm slowed the growth of antiwar feeling. As one historian observed, "The mass of yeoman farmers and poor whites would doubtless have opposed disunion if they had known that it would result in war, but they were under the mistaken impression that Southern independence could be achieved peaceably." By early 1863, however, dissatisfaction with the Rebel cause increased: here as elsewhere, conscription alienated small farmers. One Confederate document stated that the swamp regions of south Mississippi swarmed with deserters, and in Leake County, a future League stronghold, the "woods were full of them." Armed bands roamed across a wide region and in the aggregate numbered some few thousand Union sympathizers.[25]

In a few Mississippi localities, the existence of these groups gave rise to the partisan strife witnessed in northern Alabama. In Choctaw County, for instance, five hundred deserters were present by 1864, and fully half were in armed, organized bands. Soon after the war, these men formed a "Union League association." According to Unionist leader William M. Pollan, its goals were to "suppress crime and keep down rebelion and keep good order and discipline amongst the negro population." That last was significant in view of the League's eventual biracial character.[26] Hostility between the Leaguers and the former Confederates remained intense long after Appomattox. For example, one leader claimed that Unionists were "driven" from the town of Greensboro by "threats & frequent

25. Glover Moore, "Separation from the Union," in Richard A. McLemore (ed.), *A History of Mississippi* (Hattiesburg, 1973), I, 445; Tatum, *Disloyalty*, 100; James Wilford Garner, *Reconstruction in Mississippi* (1901; rpr. Baton Rouge, 1968), 25; Henry W. Warren, *Reminiscences of a Mississippi Carpetbagger* (Holden, Mass., 1914), 41.
26. William C. Harris, *Presidential Reconstruction in Mississippi* (Baton Rouge, 1967), 36; William T. Blain, "'Banner' Unionism in Mississippi: Choctaw County, 1861–1869," *Mississippi Quarterly*, XXIX (Spring, 1976), 213–20; William M. Pollan to Sharkey, July 20, 1865, in H. Clay Sharkey Papers, Mississippi Department of Archives and History, hereinafter cited as MDAH.

fisticuffs." A force of seventy young Unionists, resolved to resist such treatment, besieged the county seat and demanded an end to Rebel oppression. A truce was arranged, then violated when civil authorities reportedly started arresting the Unionists as insurrectionaries. Such social conflict had direct political implications, for the League became the center of a faction "opposed to the collection of debts." This group, known as the "Fejees," actually carried the Choctaw County elections of mid-1866 and remained electorally competitive throughout Presidential Reconstruction.[27]

While clusters of Unionist yeomen did exist in eastern Mississippi, most did not become affiliated with the League. One reason was the rudimentary level of Unionist organization, but responsibility also rested in Washington. The League's National Council apparently regarded Mississippi Radicals as too few to matter. For example, the Mississippi State Council was set up more than a year after the establishment of one for Alabama. The National Council did little in Mississippi until Thomas Conway arrived in June, 1867, several months after the enactment of Military Reconstruction. The result of this policy was that few leagues existed during the immediate postwar period. As the National Council put it, the scattered leagues set up behind Federal lines during the conflict were "suspended" when the war ended. Therefore, the League did not become the political vehicle for Unionist sentiment as it did in Alabama and most other southern states.[28]

Even after the establishment of the Mississippi State Council, the League recruited few yeoman whites. In Alabama the League spread among the whites first, but in Mississippi the appeal was to both races simultaneously. The difference proved decisive, for the admission of masses of freedmen seemed to deter Unionists. Leake County, one of the few areas where "large numbers of the 'poor whites' joined," suggests the critical pattern. In explaining his League's success, one organizer wrote, "Colored men were not admitted to the League in that vicinity," adding that "they may have

---

27. W. C. Bridges to "Commanding Officer," February 14, 1867, in Records of the Assistant Commissioner for Mississippi, Microcopy Number 826, RG 105, hereinafter cited as Records, M826; W. Brantly to B. G. Humphreys, August 22, 1866, in Governor Benjamin G. Humphreys Papers, MDAH; Huntsville *Advocate*, May 19, 1866, quoting Jackson *Clarion*.
28. ULA, *Proceedings, 1869*, p. 13; Washington *Chronicle*, July 17, 1867.

been in other parts of the State."[29] The League's problem in Mississippi was a combination of racism and poor timing that prevented the League from obtaining a white mass base, even among those few yeoman Unionists present. Thus, in both states, wartime social trends created a white Unionist movement, though these forces proved far more powerful in Alabama than they were in Mississippi. The initial divergence proved critical in the political development of these two states during Reconstruction.

In social terms, the main force behind the expansion of the League came from the black community. During the immediate postwar period, freedmen became increasingly restive. Once the euphoria of emancipation wore off, blacks became aware of legal and economic constraints on their liberty. They resented the resemblance their situation bore to servitude. The plantation system offered a graphic demonstration: landowners tried to conduct agriculture much as they had under slavery. Tension escalated in the cotton belt as planters sought control over their labor force in the face of black resistance. By the beginning of Military Reconstruction, an acute social crisis gripped the plantation regions of Alabama and Mississippi, and black dissatisfaction fed political insurgency even before the emergence of the League. Thus the Union League tapped an existing black political movement, rather than creating one, and this was a key to the organization's rapid growth.

The character of black political activity during Reconstruction derived from the experience of antebellum servitude. A strong sense of community grew out of shared racial oppression and contributed to the eventual politicization of the freedmen. But if this collective background was important in a general sense, it did not immediately spark organized political activity after the war. Emancipation occurred under confusing circumstances, and wartime disorder contributed to the uncertain situation. The result, as Leon Litwack noted in *Been in the Storm So Long*, was a "diverse and complex reaction" to liberation. Freedmen moved hesitantly to explore what the changes meant in concrete terms for their lives; they often looked

---

29. Warren, *Reminiscences*, 44–45.

toward individual measures to enhance their freedom and avoided organized political agitation.[30]

One of the freedmen's strongest desires was to shun conditions reminiscent of slavery. They wanted to differentiate their new status from the enforced labor they had known. What many blacks did first after becoming free, for example, was desert their old plantations. Some looked for family, and others headed for towns and cities, but most simply wanted to leave. "It did not really matter where they went; the act of departure itself proved symbolically they were no longer slaves," Peter Kolchin pointed out in *First Freedom*. A basic component of the response to emancipation was desire for autonomy, the wish that their former masters would no longer intrude upon their lives. Eric Foner noted that this characteristic explains a range of behavior: "Whether in withdrawing from churches dominated by whites, refusing to work under drivers and overseers, or in their ubiquitous desire for forty acres and a mule, blacks made it clear that, for them, freedom meant independence from white control." Even in matters seemingly tangential to slavery, this assertiveness was often present. Black enthusiasm for education represented more than a pragmatic response to their new freedom; it also possessed symbolic appeal. Freedmen saw ignorance as bearing the stigma of slavery and, conversely, perceived that increased knowledge implied greater equality with whites. In many such indirect ways, the black community rejected the heritage of servitude.[31]

Agriculture became a focal point for black dissatisfaction. The evolution of the postwar plantation system will be examined in detail in Chapter 5; here, a brief synopsis will suffice. After the war, planters tried to farm as much as possible in the antebellum manner. James L. Roark commented in *Masters Without Slaves*: "Rebuilding plantations along familiar lines required the continuation of work gangs, white supervision, task systems, clustered cabins, and minimal personal freedom for blacks. Subservience and regimentation were the planters' goals. Unable to accept the implications of emancipation, they sought to keep blacks as nearly slaves as possible."

30. Litwack, *Been in the Storm So Long*, 212.
31. Kolchin, *First Freedom*, 4; Foner, *Politics and Ideology*, 107.

Many planters even continued to rely upon whipping as an incentive for labor. The editors of the Columbus *Mississippi Index* knew of "several plantations where the overseers inflict corporal punishment on the negroes," and added that the blacks benefited by the practice. Not surprisingly, many freedmen grew restive, and the terrible postwar economic disruption augmented their anxiety. Heavy rainfall, insects, and a host of war-related problems produced catastrophic crop failures. Declining cotton prices and labor uncertainty pushed planters into debt. As a result, few freedmen made much beyond room and board in 1865, 1866, or 1867. The widespread belief that they were being swindled compounded the freedmen's dissatisfaction, and their solution was to opt out of the plantation system altogether. In Roark's words, "Freedmen sought independence, not gang labor. . . . If they could not own land, then they wanted to rent land, and if they could not rent, then they hoped to sharecrop."[32] Blacks' desire to establish themselves as independent farmers, however, faced a significant obstacle: landowners were flatly unwilling to give freedmen access to acreage.

At first the freedmen hoped their needs would be met by the federal government. Inspired by wartime confiscation of planters' land, and also by the promises of the Freedmen's Bureau as late as the summer of 1865, the former slaves anticipated "forty acres and a mule." Their eagerness represented something more than a rational expectation; such hopes also demonstrated exasperation with the plantation system. By all accounts, these rumors circulated widely in late 1865. One Federal officer reported from Mississippi that the freedmen were "ineradicably filled with the idea that the government is to divide the land among them about Christmas, and so will not make engagements to work beyond that time. Agents of the Freedmen's Bureau address them to disabuse them, but they will listen and then say 'This ain't no Yankee. He is a Southern man in disguise.'" But confiscation would not come to pass, and after Christmas came and went, this became increasingly obvious. The freedmen reluctantly contracted for another year's work, but as expectations of forty acres and a mule died away their anger grew. Most

32. Columbus *Mississippi Index*, April 22, 1866; Roark, *Masters Without Slaves*, 142.

freedmen had been content to wait while the hope of confiscation remained; now, however, they became increasingly intractable as workers and prone to militant protest. [33]

The policies of the postwar southern governments added to the disquiet in the black community. Freedmen perceived themselves to be victims of official abuse. During Presidential Reconstruction, planters regained control of state government, subject to some oversight by the Freedmen's Bureau. Through discriminatory legislation, known as the Black Codes, southern lawmakers remanded freedmen to a position of legal inferiority. As Litwack argued, "The Black Codes embodied in law the widely held assumption that he [the freedman] existed largely for the purpose of raising crops for a white employer." Mississippi's codes, for instance, required all blacks to be under labor contract or else receive permission for independent work from local authorities. The penalty for non-compliance was arrest as a vagrant. Blacks could not rent land outside of city limits, nor could they possess firearms without official permission. Limitations were even placed on their capacity to testify against whites. Alabama passed similar laws, as did the other southern states. The Bureau eventually voided the most offensive of these enactments, but the planters' repressive intentions were manifest to the freedmen. Small wonder that much of the earliest black political activity came in direct response to the codes. In Vicksburg, mass meetings began as early as June, 1865; the freedmen demanded universal suffrage and denounced the Black Codes as "practical re-enslavement." A statewide freedmen's convention also was held in the city, the leaders of which informed President Johnson of their opposition to anything resembling servitude. "To this [we] will not submit in any form, and you may know what that means," they wrote ominously. [34]

Had there been any possibility that the unlettered freedmen might

33. McFeely, *Yankee Stepfather*, 104–106; M. F. Force to W. T. Sherman, December 2, 1865, in William T. Sherman Papers, LC.

34. Litwack, *Been in the Storm So Long*, 367; Donald G. Nieman, *To Set the Law in Motion: The Freedmen's Bureau and the Legal Rights of Blacks, 1865–1868* (Millwood, N.Y., 1979), 73–76, 78, 92; Vernon Lane Wharton, *The Negro in Mississippi, 1865–1890* (Chapel Hill, 1947), 86–89; New York *Tribune*, July 11, 1865; Colored Men's Convention of the State of Mississippi to Johnson, November 24, 1865, in Andrew Johnson Papers, LC.

miss the significance of the Black Codes, local authorities quickly demonstrated the social uses of political power. Various communities restricted blacks' access to employment, for fear they would compete with white workers. In Mobile and Vicksburg, for instance, draymen had to pay high license fees, the intention being to drive blacks out of that lucrative occupation. Vagrants received particularly harsh punishment, and blacks without jobs were generally sentenced to long periods on the chain gang. In Mobile, sentences during a typical week averaged just under six months. As one Montgomery paper noted of the chain gang: "This is an institution introduced since the negroes became free; and a good substitute for imprisonment in the guard house. It cuts the pride of the freedmen." Beyond official hostility, freedmen also resented the degree to which whites could abuse them with impunity. Actual violence toward freedmen was common during the postwar period, with few white perpetrators ever brought to justice. In the words of a Mobile resident, "The negroes generaly are insolent But offenders generally get knocked over. One got killed yesterday for insolence to a white man."[35]

The frustration of raised expectations encouraged the politicization of the freedmen. The agricultural crisis in particular bred discontent, but if the potential for an insurgent movement existed, it only gradually became reality. Initially most black public activity was conciliatory, especially in rural areas, and revolved around religious, educational, fraternal, or relief purposes. Often having political undertones, these efforts did not directly challenge Conservative rule. Despite the limitations, such activities helped to lay the basis for the later growth of the League. In addition to these moderate endeavors, a more Radical political movement took shape during Presidential Reconstruction. Protest meetings were held in large towns, and, more important, a black-owned press network spread

---

35. Magdol, *A Right to the Land*, 66; Montgomery *Mail*, January 30, 1866; Mobile *Nationalist*, January 18, 1866; "Twelve 12 Men" to General Sheridan, January 30, 1867, in Berlin, Reidy, and Rowland (eds.), *The Black Military Experience*, 821; Montgomery *Daily Ledger*, December 6, 1865, quoted in Howard N. Rabinowitz, "The Search for Social Control: Race Relations in the Urban South, 1865–1890" (Ph.D. dissertation, University of Chicago, 1973), II, 575; Mobile *Advertiser and Register*, July 9–14, 1866; T. Benningham to W. P. Browne, July 12, 1865, in William Phineas Browne Papers, ADAH.

through both states. Thus the Union League did not arise in a vacuum among the freedmen; there existed a structure of black organizations upon which to build. The League brought to culmination the black community's earlier attempts to secure greater autonomy, efforts that grew more political and sophisticated over time.

Black religious activity illustrated this tendency. The postwar years were a time of religious ferment, as vast numbers of freedmen withdrew from denominations they saw as tainted with racism. In Kolchin's words, "They saw little reason to remain in a subservient position in the churches of their ex-masters. Leaving the white churches and establishing their own black ones was as much a part of the new freedom as leaving the old plantations." Hostility to racism motivated the establishment of black churches, and these new congregations proved sympathetic to later civil rights agitation. Religion represented an important means for the spread of the League, as indicated by the fact that the ministry formed the largest single occupational category among black activists. Moreover, church leadership and the League's hierarchy overlapped to a striking extent. In Mississippi, two prominent black Leaguers, James Lynch and Thomas W. Stringer, were leading ministers in the Northern Methodist and African Methodist Episcopal churches, respectively. Lynch actually organized League councils as well as Methodist congregations as part of his missionary tours. In Alabama, Holland Thompson was a leading lay Baptist and an important black Leaguer. While not all church spokesmen supported the League, most did, and their aid encouraged the growth of the Republican party.[36]

A similar pattern developed in secular organizations. Just after the war, a large array of black fraternal and social groups formed, commonly articulating some kind of "self-help" philosophy. A Bureau official in Natchez observed that "the colored people (the leaders) are making commendable progress in organizations for their improvement. . . . There is more method & organization among them than with any other class here." These bodies were diverse, ranging from

36. Kolchin, *First Freedom*, 110; Ralph E. Morrow, "The Methodist Episcopal Church, the South, and Reconstruction" (Ph.D. dissertation, Indiana University, 1954), 319, 322; Howard N. Rabinowitz, "Holland Thompson and Black Political Participation in Reconstruction Alabama," in Rabinowitz (ed.), *Southern Black Leaders of the Reconstruction Era* (Urbana, 1982), 252–53.

volunteer fire companies to the educational societies scattered widely through both states. In Mobile, a colored benevolent association collected money for the poor every week. Jackson's freedmen established a benevolent society that included a group insurance system, with some funds earmarked for relief of the indigent. In another Mississippi town, blacks formed a society to read newspapers aloud for purposes of self-improvement. Such groups often blurred the distinction between political and nonpolitical activities. In Montgomery, for instance, freedmen called a public meeting on educational matters that actually wound up nominating delegates to a forthcoming Radical convention. A striking example of such interconnection appears in the activities of the Reverend T. W. Stringer. Besides being a leader in the Vicksburg League and the African Methodist Episcopal church, he also founded Negro Masonry in Mississippi, Louisiana, and Pennsylvania. Clearly his political function overlapped other forms of community leadership.[37]

Once Military Reconstruction occurred, a close relationship developed between existing community organizations and the burgeoning League. Fearing violence, League activists cloaked their political work in religious and fraternal guise; they operated through such groups both to legitimize and to camouflage Republican gatherings. One black activist even claimed that the League itself was a relief organization. A Mississippi Conservative testified that the leagues in his neighborhood "were organized as benevolent societies, under the name of freedmen's aid societies. That was the first organization that came here. We had no intimation of the political character of the organization until we came to vote upon the Constitution in June, 1868." The interaction between Leaguers and other community leaders was not entirely without friction, however. In Tuscumbia, Alabama, League activists and the leaders of a local benevolent society quarreled, largely because the locals claimed the Leaguers

37. E. E. Platt to E. W. Preston, July, 1867, in Records, M826, RG 105; Armstead L. Robinson, "'Plans Dat Comed from God': Institution Building and the Emergence of Black Leadership in Reconstruction Memphis, 1865–1880," in Burton and McMath (eds.), *Toward a New South?*, 71–102; Mobile *Advertiser and Register*, November 2, 1866; Mentzer[?] to Preston, April 6, 1867, in Records, M826, RG 105; E. C. Gilbrath to H. W. Smith, August 31, 1867, in Letters Sent SAC Brookhaven, Vol. 98, RG 105; *Prince Hall Masonic Digest*, VII, No. 4 (1957–58), 21.

were too Radical and also were taking over meetings held in common. But such instances appear to have been rare. The evidence suggests that the churches and other black organizations had an important partisan role, just as the Democrats claimed. The Macon *Beacon* commented on one Freedmen's Aid Society, "It is a glaring lie to say it is not a political organization." The League, the newspaper argued, was simply being hidden under another name.[38]

In addition to the various community organizations, black political entities formed during Presidential Reconstruction, and these helped lay the groundwork for the later League. Some of the initial efforts were moderate or even conservative, being designed to reassure whites that the freedmen were not a threat. In Tuskegee, for example, black leaders publicly decried idleness and loafing among members of their race. Still more forthrightly, a body of "old Mobile negroes" called upon city authorities, offering to put down "any riots that may be caused" by Yankee agitators, the blacks apparently frightened by the recent bloodshed in New Orleans. Despite the conciliatory nature of many of the early activities, any overt intervention by blacks in the political system represented a huge change. Moreover, several of the blacks who became prominent through this civic activity later became League leaders.[39]

Radical activities were also under way, especially in the urban centers. Freedmen repeatedly met in Vicksburg to protest Mississippi's Black Code. In Mobile, an Alabama freedmen's convention gathered during late 1865, and it called for equal suffrage and for blacks' right to farm land on their own. Public meetings of a Radical tenor were also held in Montgomery. In rural areas, on the other hand, it is difficult to tell what specific measures freedmen were taking; their activities were necessarily secret and subject as well to distortion in the Conservative press. There were reports of militias drilling in several localities, and of Radical societies spreading, long before Military Reconstruction. For example, in November, 1865, a

---

38. Union Springs *Times*, August 14, 1867; *Testimony Taken by the Joint Select Committee to Inquire into the Condition of Affairs of the Late Insurrectionary States* (Washington, D.C., 1872), *House Reports*, 42nd Cong., 2nd Sess., No. 22, XI, 569, hereinafter cited as KKK Report; William Cooper Diary, July 4, 1867 (MS in ADAH); Canton *Mail*, February 12, 1870, quoting Macon (Miss.) *Beacon*.

39. Tuskegee *News*, November 8, 1866; Mobile *Times*, August 18, 1866.

Bureau agent reported on meetings in Noxubee County, Mississippi, that had an "insurrectionary character." The freedmen did not believe that they would "receive justice at the hands of their late masters," and in response they were gathering arms. In Montgomery a "Freedmen's League" allegedly regulated wages among farm workers in 1865, and Georgia's Equal Rights Association crossed the border into Alabama at one town and possibly others. There is even evidence of an isolated black League council in Alabama as early as April, 1866. The "Uion Leauge" in Eufaula requested a school in their area. The leaders also wanted advice from the military, asking one officer to "please frame us a Constitution how to conduct [ourselves]." Clearly, freedmen were mobilizing politically in several areas before the League became widespread.[40]

An important aspect of this early political organizing was the creation of a black newspaper, the Mobile *Nationalist*, in late 1865. The freedmen commenced the enterprise themselves, and raised the capital among Mobile's blacks and Creoles through the sale of small-denomination stock and various contests and benefits. Although the paper had two successive carpetbagger editors, most of the staff and correspondents were black. The *Nationalist* was one of the most influential Radical newspapers in the South, employing a network of promotional agents throughout Alabama and Mississippi. These men acted as political propagandists; they called meetings in isolated communities and talked about civil rights while urging freedmen to subscribe. In one Conservative's words, a "speech-making mania" seized the freedmen as an outgrowth of these activities. This was the

40. L. H. Gest to E. Bamberger, November 15, 1865, quoted in William Leon Woods, "The Travail of Freedom: Mississippi Blacks, 1862–1870" (Ph.D. dissertation, Princeton University, 1979), 125; Mobile *Nationalist*, December 23, 1865; G. W. Bardwell to Johnson, November 24, 1865, in Johnson Papers, LC; Mobile *Advertiser and Register*, January 4, 1866; Montgomery *Mail*, January 4, 1867; Columbus *Mississippi Index*, May 15, 1866; Whitelaw Reid, *After the War: A Tour of the Southern States, 1865–1866* (1866; rpr. New York, 1965), 373; W. E. Connally to Smith, August 8, 1867, H. M. Turner to Sen. Henry Wilson, February 25, 1867, R. Graves *et al.* to Swayne, April 11, 1866, all in Records, M809, RG 105. The Eufaula petition does not explicitly identify the council as composed of freedmen. But since the petition came from a plantation region, and dealt with education, a favored topic of the freedmen, it seems very likely that this was indeed a black council. In addition, an examination of the population schedules of the 1870 census reveals that several names on the petition belonged to local freedmen, but none to whites.

first contact many rural freedmen had with protest politics. It made them aware that a larger movement was under way, and the paper itself put them in touch with regional developments. In particular, it counteracted the Conservative press embargo on news important to Radicals—a fact candidly admitted by at least one Democratic paper.[41]

A measure of the importance of the *Nationalist*'s role was the degree of white hostility. An agent in Wetumpka, Alabama, discovered this anger when he gave a public address and the local justice of the peace threatened him with arrest. Later, the magistrate assaulted the freedman "in a furious way," first breaking a cane over his head and then drawing a knife on him. (For this crime, a ten-dollar fine was levied.) In Selma, leading blacks were reluctant to have a *Nationalist* representative speak, for fear "the whites would become excited." In Mobile, Conservatives boycotted the Republican paper's advertisers. The Democratic press frequently accused the *Nationalist* and its agents of demoralizing the freedmen. There seems little doubt that the newspaper fostered political agitation in many areas.[42]

The existence of the *Nationalist* directly influenced the growth of the Union League. Agents were natural political leaders for the freedmen, and they were in a position to bring numbers of rural blacks into the movement in 1867. When the paper's staff entered the League, they provided the nucleus for the organization's growth in several localities. Both white editors of the *Nationalist*, John Silsby and Albert Griffin, became prominent League activists and Republican officeholders. The paper's black traveling agent, Lawrence S. Berry, helped found the League in Mobile. In the Alabama hinterland, agents Holland Thompson of Montgomery, William V. Turner of Wetumpka, and Shandy W. Jones of Tuscaloosa became League leaders. All three went on to serve as Republican legislators, as did Robert Gleed of Columbus, Mississippi. Other prominent

41. Mobile *Nationalist*, January 25, March 22, June 7, 28, 1866, April 16, 1868; Allen Woodrow Jones, "Alabama," in Henry Lewis Suggs (ed.), *The Black Press in the South, 1865–1979* (Westport, Conn., 1983), 23–27; A. Griffin to M. E. Strieby, March 29, 1866, J. Silsby to G. Whipple, November 2, 1865, both in American Missionary Association Papers, Fisk University, Nashville; Marion *Commonwealth*, April 4, 1867.

42. J. D. Williams to Patton, September 11, 1866, in Gov. Patton Papers, ADAH.

black Radicals, such as Alex Webb of Greensboro and Congressman Ben Turner of Selma, began their public careers as local agents. These men were a large portion of the paper's entire staff.[43]

Thus it appears that the League built upon an existing network of politically interested and literate freedmen scattered throughout the region. The League absorbed the *Nationalist*'s activist base, as it did the leadership of other black institutions, in the mass upheaval following Congressional Reconstruction. The growth of the *Nationalist* network itself was one indication of the black population's restiveness, of the widespread inclination toward social protest. Across the plantations, throughout the entire region, the freedmen were aware that they remained in semi-slavery. Their increasing disaffection provided the impetus for political agitation, which was given a focus once freedmen received the vote. Combined with the efforts of the League's National Council, and also with the emergence of white yeoman Radicalism, this set the stage for the Union League's expansion into a mass movement.

43, See Mobile *Nationalist*, June 7, 1866, for a list of the paper's employees.

TWO

The Process of League Organizing Among Freedmen

In addition to the divergent roles of the white yeomanry in Alabama and Mississippi, other important differences existed between the League movements in the two states. In Alabama, the League, with aid from sympathetic military officials, was well organized and centrally directed. Mississippi's League, on the other hand, had a structure that was virtually anarchic, largely because of army hostility. This contrast meant that the League developed differently in each state, as did the process of Reconstruction as a whole.

Although these structural differences were politically significant, their relevance to individual League councils was limited. The larger contrasts dissolved at the local level, where neighborhood concerns supplanted strictly partisan ones. The average League in both states evolved in roughly similar ways. At first, freedmen's inexperience and League secrecy enabled organizers to exert a powerful influence over their councils. These mostly white activists dominated their leagues and directed them as exclusively toward politics as circumstances would permit. Over time, however, leagues became more responsive to wider black concerns as freedmen became more familiar with politics, and aggressive black leaders arose who prodded the leagues toward greater militancy.

As the leagues became increasingly democratic they took on a less narrowly partisan character and incorporated other local concerns of the black community. Freedmen reoriented their councils away from

the national focus stressed by the League's white leaders. For example, widespread informal militias arose at the freedmen's initiative.
White organizers generally deprecated such activities, but freedmen
persisted nonetheless. Martial drilling, and the mass actions that
grew out of it, demonstrated blacks' grasp of the need for self-
defense. Such activity also reflected the freedmen's unhappiness
with the plantation system, for drilling deprived employers of their
labor at a time of acute agricultural conflict. The democratic character of local leagues thus transformed them into a vehicle for black
aspirations for autonomy. Freedmen soon gained control of the
leagues and increasingly turned them toward the critical issues for
the black community: the agricultural labor system and self-defense.

Soon after the enactment of Congressional Reconstruction in early
March, 1867, League agitation spread among newly enfranchised
blacks in the South, but the institutional character of this activity
varied. In Alabama the League maintained a relatively centralized
structure and quickly reached the entire state. In Mississippi, by
contrast, it grew slowly and imperfectly, and League officials possessed little control over what occurred in the hinterland. These
patterns did not arise primarily from the actions of the National
Council or Republican party leaders. Instead, most of the reason lay
within the states themselves. Alabama's General Wager Swayne
sympathized with Reconstruction, whereas Mississippi's military
officials were hostile.

Under General Swayne's command, both federal troops and the
Freedmen's Bureau encouraged League expansion in Alabama.
Swayne's attitude was odd in one sense, for as military commander
and assistant commissioner, he had been conciliatory toward planters. His moderation even won praise from Fleming and other Dunning school historians. Personal ambition may have played a role in
this—Swayne hoped to become a United States senator—but in
addition, southern intransigence had led to his disillusionment with
compromise. Alabama, in his estimate, was not yet "fit for a free
government." Continuing violence against freedmen troubled
Swayne, but the real catalyst for his shift to Radical views was the

state's rejection of the Fourteenth Amendment. Swayne had lobbied the legislature hard for ratification, and this defeat convinced him that sterner measures were necessary. "Immediately after the passage of the Reconstruction Bills," Swayne noted, "I set to work to increase the efficiency of the Bureau, employing new agents, sending inspectors to the jails of various counties to release persons imprisoned for vagrancy & c., abolishing the chain gangs, and providing a method of release for persons improperly apprenticed, and in other ways." This burst of activity spilled into the political sphere as Swayne turned toward bringing the freedmen into the Republican party.[1]

General Swayne occupied a strong position from which to take up a partisan role. He had influential connections in the national capital: his father was Associate Justice Noah Swayne of the U.S. Supreme Court, and General O. O. Howard of the Freedmen's Bureau was a personal friend. Furthermore, his immediate superior, General John Pope in Atlanta, strongly supported Congressional Reconstruction. Pope observed of affairs in his military district, "The white [voter] Registers are all or nearly all members of the Loyal League & out & out Republicans who will not fail to use their opportunity properly."[2] Pope emphatically believed that Reconstruction would be a failure unless it secured victory for the Republican party.

Pope's partisanship certainly encouraged similar efforts by his subordinates, and Swayne took an active stand, appearing at many Republican gatherings in 1867. His political exertions actually earned him a reprimand for neglecting Bureau affairs. While Swayne knew political participation to be outside his "strict official duty," he thought himself obliged because he contributed to the "right direction of the movement." Swayne joined the Union League in mid-1866, and he assisted the organization whenever possible. In one instance, he prevailed upon Federal Judge Richard Busteed to

1. Fleming, *Civil War and Reconstruction in Alabama*, 492–93; McFeely, *Yankee Stepfather*, 77–78; Hilary A. Herbert, *Why the Solid South? Or, Reconstruction and Its Results* (1890; rpr. New York, 1969), 41; Wager Swayne to O. O. Howard, January 28, 1867, in Howard Papers, Bowdoin College; Swayne to Salmon P. Chase, June 8, 1867, Salmon P. Chase Papers, LC; Swayne to Howard, June 8, 1867, in Howard Papers, Bowdoin College.
2. J. Pope to Schenck, May 20, 1867, in Schenck Papers, Hayes Library.

allow the Mobile Council to meet in his courtroom. Swayne publicly stated that the League was "saving Alabama," adding that the freedmen were "well trained in its councils."[3]

Perhaps the clearest indication of Swayne's support for the League was his choice of John C. Keffer as chief clerk. Keffer at the time was secretary of the Alabama State Council of the League and also chairman of the Republican State Executive Committee. He once stated that he had "perhaps organized more Union Leagues South of the Ohio than any other person in the United States." Keffer was closely aligned with Pennsylvania Radicals such as John W. Forney of the Philadelphia *Press* and the Washington *Chronicle*, as well as Congressman William D. Kelley. From the time of his arrival in Alabama in May, 1866, he functioned as political specialist for the Bureau. Swayne commonly endorsed to Keffer the political correspondence he received, and Keffer exerted substantial influence over Swayne's choice of appointments. Keffer basically ran the League's business out of the Montgomery Bureau office, and his duties also permitted him frequent travel about the countryside.[4]

Besides Keffer, several other employees at headquarters were League leaders, notably Robert Barber, Mark Brainard, and Charles A. Miller—all future Republican officeholders. The situation developed similarly elsewhere in the state. "It is simply impossible," commented one officer, "to keep out of the councils and caucuses of the Union men and blacks, who, as if by instinct, turn to the Bureau." W. E. Connelly of Eufaula wrote Swayne, apologizing for his delayed speaking tour among the freedmen, and pointing out that he had organized a "Col[ored]. U.L.A. at this place which will spread rapidly, throughout the District." He also planned the creation of a white council. Sometimes the extent of the Bureau's partisan activity appeared to be almost comic. For example, one agent reported that, though ill, he spent days writing out Republican tickets for the

3. Swayne to Howard, June 8, 1867, in Howard Papers, Bowdoin College; Washington *Great Republic*, July 26, 1867; Herbert, *Why the Solid South?*, 41–42.
4. L. B. Osborne *et al.* to W. H. Smith, September 12, 1868, in Gov. Smith Papers, ADAH; Horace Mann Bond, *Negro Education in Alabama: A Study in Cotton and Steel* (Washington, D.C., 1939), 33–34; C. A. R. Dimon to Swayne, April 18, 1867, Albert Griffin to Swayne, April 22, 1867, J. H. Davis to Swayne, July 18, 1867, all in Swayne Papers, ADAH. The letters to Swayne are endorsed to Keffer.

freedmen to vote in an upcoming election. This officer almost provoked a riot by substituting Republican tickets for the Democratic ones that whites had deceived freedmen into taking.[5]

Political involvement for Bureau employees was common at all levels. In Swayne's own words, he used agents "pretty freely" to instruct freedmen in their political rights. The general's immediate underlings, the various sub-assistant commissioners, were especially active. For instance, a hostile observer noted that at Demopolis, "Maj [Charles W.] Pierce has helped to organize all the Loyal Leagues in this District, & has controlled all the nominations for the [constitutional] Convention—which he had no right to do." The Bureau's political ties were manifested in the composition of the congressional delegation elected in February, 1868, when four of the six representatives chosen were high Bureau officials, all prominent in the League. Small wonder that visiting organizer Thomas Conway could write, "The officers of the Bureau are mostly devoted to the great work . . . of our League. . . . [T]here will be a day when these Leagues will speak with a power."[6]

General Swayne's implementation of voter registration demonstrated the Bureau's partisan activity well. Swayne's choice to head the registration bureau, Colonel William Hugh Smith, was a "prominent member" of the Union League who would soon be elected the first Reconstruction governor of the state. John Keffer himself selected a number of the registrars. All the registration officials were at least nominal Republicans, and several seem to have signed up voters by day and initiated freedmen into the League by night. One registrar noted that he had "forty L.L.L.L. in this place now . . . [and] hope to have five hundred." He noted that these Leaguers would "wish to organize in their own places on their return home," and he asked Bureau officials to send him more copies of the League ritual. A Bureau agent in Talladega found that the registrars were "energetic and spare no paines to instruct and enlighten the freedmen in

5. James J. Gillette to Mrs. Gillette, January 8, 1868 [misdated 1867], in Gillette Family Papers, LC; Connelly to Swayne, June 25, 1867, in Swayne Papers, ADAH; R. W. Healy to Kinsman, October 31, 1867, in Records, M809, RG 105.

6. Swayne to Howard, July 11, 1867, in Howard Papers, Bowdoin College; A. W. Dillard to Johnson, October 5, 1867, in Johnson Papers, LC; Thomas Conway to Howard, May 1, 1867, in Howard Papers, Bowdoin College.

view of securing to them any advantage which may be realized by their being franchised. There is also a Union League which controles every loyal man white & black." A third of the registrars selected by Smith and Swayne were black, and these men seem to have been especially active; several had been associated with the Mobile *Nationalist*, and some were already emerging as League leaders. For example, George Washington Cox, the registrar sent to Tuscaloosa, wrote Keffer that he would set up a new council in his locality as soon as he found a place to meet.[7]

Beyond the evident partisan role of Swayne and the Bureau, other factors encouraged League growth among Alabama's freedmen. For one, a relatively large and well-organized white Unionist base existed in the up-country. Building upon yeoman farmers' wide disaffection with the Confederate war effort, the League became strong in north Alabama by 1866. After Military Reconstruction passed, these white leagues often took steps to propagandize among the freedmen. Some began to admit blacks into their leagues; others were willing to participate in racially mixed Republican activities. For example, a League rally on the Fourth of July attracted "country people and negroes" in Bibb County. The country people were those "who skulked during the War, and are now rampant for the Union."[8]

Most Unionists heeded the logic of the Alabama Grand Council of the League: "In the nature of things the black man is your friend. . . . Shall we have him for our ally, or the rebel for our master?" White Unionist leaders, in particular, found such reasoning persuasive. Prominent Unionists, aware that without black votes their constituency would remain a permanent minority, began to initiate freedmen into the League. Thus motivated by both personal and political objectives, these individuals descended from their mountain homes to the plantation regions to engage in political organizing. Standing out among them were future congressmen Thomas Haughey of Morgan County—who organized eleven leagues while registering voters—and Robert S. Heflin of Randolph

7. John Keffer to Smith, April 13, 1867, in Swayne Papers, ADAH; Montgomery *State Sentinel*, June 28, 1867; Augustus C. Rose to C. A. Miller, September 19, 1867, G. W. Cox to Keffer, June 29, 1867, both in Swayne Papers, ADAH; Montgomery *Advertiser*, May 22, 1867.
8. Josiah Gorgas Journal, July 4, 1867, ADAH.

County. Both had fled the Confederacy during the war, Heflin escaping charges of treason. Such backgrounds were common among scalawag League organizers. Some of these men would prove opportunistic in their appeal for black votes. Others were more sincere, like Daniel H. Bingham of Limestone County. He saw both blacks and Unionists as common victims of Rebel persecution. But regardless of the motives of specific individuals, freedmen were initially so enthusiastic about suffrage that almost any League organizer received a warm welcome. One scalawag wrote from Talladega that he was "doing very well about making voters of the Blacks[.] I have taken about five hundred in the *League* and am taking them in about one hundred a week." The upshot was that the Unionist Leaguers met with great success in organizing freedmen.[9]

Between the yeoman Unionists and the Bureau, political agitation spread swiftly among the freedmen. According to Lawrence N. Powell's calculations, an impressive 96.3 percent of the black potential electorate was, by October, 1867, registered to vote.[10] Although the membership claimed for the Alabama League is problematic, the general upward trend is clear enough. By April, the Grand Council estimated 30,000 League members total, organized in two hundred subordinate councils throughout the state. Soon Keffer stopped citing specific figures for the freedmen and spoke instead of numbering them "by the acre." This image of explosive growth was confirmed by one organizer who reported that 2,398 members joined in his county in a single week. A Republican editor described the significance of these numbers. "There are forty thousand white men enrolled in the Leagues," he wrote, "and these, with the blacks, will give us the state in perpetuity if we are only wise."[11]

9. Mobile *Nationalist*, January 24, 1867; Thomas Haughey to Swayne, April 15, 1867, Haughey to Keffer, July 12, 1867, both in Swayne Papers, ADAH; Tatum, *Disloyalty*, 67; Montgomery *Mail*, January 14, May 17, 1868; Sarah Woolfolk Wiggins, *The Scalawag in Alabama Politics, 1865–1881* (University, Ala., 1977), 26–27; C. A. Bingham to Smith, April 11, 1867, in Swayne Papers, ADAH.

10. Powell developed this estimate for a forthcoming article on black political participation during the period. He kindly made available the results of his research (Powell to the author, July 14, 1987).

11. Mobile *Nationalist*, January 24, 1867; New York *Tribune*, April 10, 1867, quoting Montgomery *Advertiser*; Athens *Post*, May 16, 1867; Union Springs *Times*, January 18, 1868; Washington *Chronicle*, September 26, 1867; Forney to Fessenden, October 21, 1867, in Forney Papers, LC.

Such figures only tell part of the story. As important as its numerical growth was the centralized structure of the Alabama League. The Grand Council in Montgomery, through its titular president Thomas O. Glascock—but actually through Keffer—maintained its influence over League activities in the hinterland. Keffer's standing with General Swayne was important, but so was his perceived power in Washington. Activists used Keffer to communicate with the national leadership, as one Radical indicated in concluding a description of opposition violence. "Remember me kindly to Barber and Keffer & all the friends about HDQR's," he wrote. "Tell Keffer to write to the Great Republic about this affair." Keffer used his reputation as a significant person to gain an informal influence over local leaders.[12]

Control over the granting of League charters to subordinate councils strengthened the hand of the Alabama State Council. Freedmen perceived that such documents conferred legitimacy upon organizers. Black legislator James H. Alston of Tuskegee testified in reference to his lodge charter:

Q. Did you have a good deal of influence with the colored people?
A. I had them every one, just from my authority; that is true . . . from my assurance to them that I had acted for them where they placed me as my constituents, I had them right with me to do whatever I wanted done in the county. I had that commission from the grand lodge, and I took a vote to that thing. I worked altogether by that, and I never varied from it a letter up to the time I was shot.

Possessing a charter was a political asset, especially at first, when lack of official sanction could undermine an organizer's influence. In one activist's words, the absence of charters and League rituals was "embarrassing" his operations, and Keffer received many such requests for aid. While the Grand Council did not handpick local leaders, its members could exercise some control over individual League organizers and their methods.[13]

John Keffer, in particular, functioned as a League "troubleshooter" throughout the state. In one case he revoked the charter of a white League for opposing ratification of the new Radical constitution. On

12. Charles Pelham to W. H. Smith, September 19, 1867, in Swayne Papers, ADAH.
13. KKK Report, IX, 1019; Griffin to Keffer, April 11, 1867, in Swayne Papers, ADAH.

several other occasions he rebuked local spokesmen for adopting too cautious a position on civil rights. In Bullock County, for example, he praised a Radical black speaker, to the detriment of a more conciliatory Leaguer who was placating planters. Keffer also assessed the character of local activists, and he turned on those who displeased him. Of one voter registrar and League organizer he wrote: "Dr. Rose acted disgracefully here at Elba. He was all the time in fear of his life. . . . He ought to be instantly replaced. . . . The whole people white and black are laughing over his manifest cowardice." Rose soon complained to the Bureau about his difficulty procuring League documents, a problem that likely grew out of Keffer's distrust of his leadership. State Secretary Keffer also upbraided some Leaguers for too confrontational a speaking style. In one case he mounted the rostrum of a Democratic rally and—no coward, he—offered to mediate the differences between whites and a local Leaguer who infuriated them. He informed those freedmen present that parading under arms, however understandable, was unsanctioned by the League and dangerous. Keffer clearly tried to hold local activities within a certain range he thought appropriate.[14]

The most conspicuous of Keffer's local interventions occurred in Mobile. Days after the first Reconstruction Act passed, two white carpetbaggers, George F. Harrington and W. W. D. Turner, seized the initiative and organized a council. This League immediately adopted a militant line, urging direct action to integrate the streetcar system, and it also became involved in a major strike spreading from the docks. More cautious white Radicals, like Albert Griffin of the *Nationalist*, grew frightened at the possibility of confrontation. In response, General Swayne sent Keffer and John Silsby, a fellow Leaguer, to take stock of the situation. Having investigated, Silsby wrote Swayne that inflammatory addresses had been made by Harrington, who had influence only on the "less stable" portion of the black community. Silsby observed: "Our efforts . . . were directed towards correcting, as best we might, these evils. By remonstrances

---

14. Mobile *Times*, December 13, 1867; Union Springs *Times*, September 25, 1867; Livingston *Journal*, January 25, 1868; Montgomery *State Sentinel*, December 14, 24, 1867; Livingston *Journal*, August 17, 1867; Keffer to Smith, September 10, 1867, Osborne *et al.* to Smith, September 12, 1868, both in Smith Papers, ADAH.

with Mr Harrington etc Mr Keffer succeeded in obtaining a pledge from him that he would no longer talk as he had done. And in the organization of a Union Leauge over which Mr Horton was made President. An organization of the Colored people was commenced in which Mr Harrington could no longer take the lead." Although the effects of this mission proved temporary—Harrington would eventually recover influence—moderate Leaguers professed satisfaction with these results. As Griffin observed in the *Nationalist*, Keffer's "business in relation to the Union League" had produced much good.[15]

The League in Alabama was centrally directed to a significant extent, especially while Swayne maintained his position as military commander, and this was the critical period when the League spread across the state. Through close ties with the Freedmen's Bureau, and other means at its disposal, the State Council in Montgomery orchestrated League activity. A strong, well-organized, and politically powerful statewide structure resulted that lasted through 1867. Through his personal influence, State Secretary Keffer was instrumental in the rapid growth of the League. Keffer's power was reflected in the circumstances surrounding the League's eventual demise. In mid-1869, Keffer concluded that the League had served its function, for it was already in decline and its secrecy served as pretext for Klan terror. Keffer sent word for the leagues to either disband or restructure themselves as open Republican clubs, and most Leaguers followed this advice. Thus was demonstrated at the League's death, as at its birth, Republican party officials' considerable influence over what transpired in the hinterland.[16]

In Mississippi, the head of the League's State Council, Alston Mygatt of Vicksburg, presided over a poorly organized and thoroughly decentralized political entity. Mygatt and his cohorts had only limited control over events in the state's interior, and entire plantation counties experienced no effective Republican activity before

---

15. Silsby to Swayne, April 1, 1867, in Swayne Papers, ADAH; Mobile *Nationalist*, April 4, 1867.

16. Montgomery *State Sentinel*, September 16, 1870; KKK Report, X, 1017.

mid-1869. The paucity of native white Leaguers slowed organizing among freedmen, but the main reason for this weakness lay in the Mississippi League's lack of support from military officials. In marked contrast to the situation in Alabama, Mississippi's military and Bureau personnel tended toward conservative politics. League activity appeared suspect and inflammatory to such officers, who discouraged Republicans themselves and ignored local authorities' efforts to intimidate League organizers. Individual activists had to depend on outside protection. The result was that the Republican party was relatively weak in Mississippi during the first years of Military Reconstruction, despite blacks' clear majority among the state's voters.

General E. O. C. Ord, Mississippi's military commander during 1867, and his successor Alvan C. Gillem had similar political views. Ord distrusted black suffrage, at first believing that the planters would control their employees' votes. He expressed his views frankly in the draft of a letter to U. S. Grant's confidant Adam Badeau: "Tell Gen'l Grant I am getting along here all right. If Mississippi dont vote for a Convention and give a chance to a handful of Republicans to try and govern it—it will be much for the best. There are not intelligent republicans enough in Miss. to give me registrars. And the state offices would require ten times that no. to fill them. I dont know how they would govern the state if they had it." On another occasion, Ord privately denounced the "ill bred" and "knavish" demagogues who were organizing the freedmen. Given this outlook, it is not surprising that his official acts reflected hostility to League activities. Ord's General Order Number 5, issued soon after Military Reconstruction passed, urged freedmen to work instead of wasting time at political meetings. In September he forbade "assembling of *armed* organizations under any pretense whatever" and ordered the army to enforce the ban. Since freedmen often carried arms to League meetings, for obvious reasons, this policy pitted the military against party activities. In December, Ord even telegraphed Grant that a "war of races" was about to break out, apparently because of the actions of League organizers. He thereupon issued an order that seemed to call upon the leagues to disband. Grant found this such an overreaction that he rebuked the general, who soon resigned his command in favor of General Gillem, assistant commissioner of the Freedmen's Bureau.[17]

Ord's attitude had a noticeable effect on registering the freedmen to vote. He appointed as registrars mostly individuals who lacked strong political opinions, and he forbade their running for office or even engaging in partisan activity. Ord also appointed some Conservatives, and their motive for searching out black voters was probably not compelling. Ord so construed the Reconstruction Acts as to allow many apparently disfranchised former Confederates to vote, and for this, his military superiors reprimanded him. The contrast with the situation in Alabama is stark. Planter-scalawag R. W. Flournoy of Pontotoc County described the result of Ord's policies: "It is not only dangerous but impossible to form a Republican Party here, unless we are assured of the protection of the government, to prevent our being molested and murdered." The question, to Flournoy, was whether the freedmen's right to hold political meetings would be respected at all.[18]

If Ord felt unsympathetic to the Republican party, Gillem was doubly so. Gillem, a Tennessean, enjoyed the personal favor of President Johnson, and his politics were decidedly Democratic. At one point he wrote that the "people of Miss. will never support any party that harmonizes with [League president] Mygatt." Congressional leaders were displeased from the beginning with his appointment as head of the state's Bureau, and Mississippi Leaguers lobbied hard to have him replaced. One Republican leader claimed that "Gillem deliberately designs the destruction of the party in this state. He cannot be trusted even with the selection of a constable.

17. Draft of E. O. C. Ord to Badeau, July 21, 1867, in Edward Otho Cresap Ord Papers (C-B 479), The Bancroft Library, University of California at Berkeley, text crossed out on original copy; Ord to W. T. Sherman, November 6, 1867, in W. T. Sherman Papers, LC; General Order Number 5, from Headquarters 4th Military District, April 15, 1867, General Order Number 28, from Headquarters 4th Military District, September 9, 1867, both in Ord Papers, UC Berkeley; Mobile *Nationalist*, August 29, 1867; Ord to U. S. Grant, December 7, 1867, Ord to Grant, n.d., both in Ord Papers, UC Berkeley; Natchez *Democrat*, November 23, 1867; *The Diary of Orville Hickman Browning* (Springfield, Ill., 1933), II, 171.

18. William C. Harris, *The Day of the Carpetbagger: Republican Reconstruction in Mississippi* (Baton Rouge, 1979), 70–72; Natchez *Democrat*, August 10, 1867; R. W. Flournoy to Grant, May 7, 1867, in B. F. Butler Papers, LC.

The Freedmen's Bureau is made a nullity by him & he has been trying to divide & distract Republicans. We look to Congress for relief & protection." Under General Gillem, members of the Bureau hierarchy took a dim view of Radical political activity. In one instance, Gillem determined that a planter could dismiss a laborer for attending a rally during working hours, and that the freedman fired for that reason would forfeit the crop if the contract so provided. It is scarcely surprising that many freedmen thought that the Bureau "might as well be in the Mississippi River." Most Republicans agreed that Gillem had little interest in defending their political rights.[19]

Gillem encouraged Bureau agents to be conciliatory to the native white population, and they pursued this policy with such zeal that co-optation sometimes resulted. In Natchez, for instance, Colonel James Biddle got along famously with the planters. On one occasion he upheld the decision of a local justice of the peace, despite the protests of the town's Radicals. Afterward, the whites "could not do enough for us," as Biddle's wife put it. The magistrate offered Biddle use of an unoccupied plantation, which the colonel saw fit to accept. Biddle and family moved in, and their retinue included coachmen, nurses, a cook, horses, dogs, and fighting cocks. The Bureau agent evinced an impressive capacity for accommodating himself to the way of life in Natchez. Mrs. Biddle commented in her memoirs that her husband "had become a great favorite in the town with the men, and the women were coming to see me. We were invited to luncheons, dinners, and receptions, all of which pleased me very much; I had not gone into society before my marriage (being considered too young) and I thought it delightful." The city's Union Leaguers found the colonel's social life less appealing. They declared him biased against the freedmen, and after two years of complaints they succeeded in having him reassigned. In Natchez, as in other

19. A. C. Gillem to Fowler, April 1, 1869, in Joseph S. Fowler Papers, Southern Historical Collection, Library of the University of North Carolina at Chapel Hill (hereinafter cited as UNC); Gillem to Howard, July 27, 1867, A. Mygatt to Howard, July 18, 1867, Stringer to Howard, July 18, 1867, all in Registers and Letters Received by the Commissioner, Microcopy Number 752, hereinafter cited as Registers and Letters, M752, RG 105; J. Tarbell to Butler, December 2, 1868, in Butler Papers, LC; S. D. Lee to G. S. Smith, October 25, 1867, in Letters Received SAC Macon, Box 45, RG 105; H. R. Pease to J. W. Alvord, June 15, 1867, in Letters Received Education Division, Microcopy Number 803, RG 105.

localities throughout Mississippi, the Bureau represented a hindrance, rather than an aid, to freedmen's political activity through the League.[20]

While the Bureau in Mississippi generally demonstrated hostility to Reconstruction, the point should not be pressed too far, because some Bureau officials sympathized with the Republican party. Several agents in isolated areas, free from effective oversight, indicated to the freedmen that it would be in their own best interest to vote Radical. Some of the voter registrars surreptitiously organized leagues, and a few of these men later emerged as Republican leaders, but only those officials less subject to Gillem's control overtly aided the movement. For instance, Henry R. Pease, state superintendent of education and future U.S. senator, had influential political connections. Pease could act somewhat more freely, as he informed a Bureau superior in Washington: "I have taken what might be construed an active part in reconstructing this state on the Congressional basis. . . . I have organized over one hundred Leagues and Republican Clubs in the state. I have done it 'on the sly.' I am the President of a council of the *U. L. A.* numbering over a thousand members. I am also Grand Dpty for the state[,] am also a member of the state executive Committee [of the Republican party]." National Bureau officials, such as school inspector John Mercer Langston, also organized leagues as they traveled about the South. Because General O. O. Howard of the Bureau in Washington strongly supported the Radicals, those individuals accountable directly to him could take a forthright political role.[21]

Despite these exceptions, the Bureau and the military as a whole opposed the Radicals, and Gillem himself admitted that "a majority of the troops in Mississippi are opposed to this [the Radical] constitution, and . . . in that majority are many of those appointed by General Ord and myself." This fact had a variety of implications, direct and indirect, for League operations at the local level. Gillem and Ord certainly gave little encouragement to Union League activity and often impeded it. Their behavior caused one Leaguer to complain

20. Ellen McGowan Biddle, *Reminiscences of a Soldier's Wife* (Philadelphia, 1907), 30, 31, 34, 40; Natchez *Democrat*, June 15, 1867.
21. H. R. Pease to Alvord, October 22, 1867, in Letters Received Education Division.

that officers who professed to be "neutral in politics" invariably supported the "democratic or slavery side of the question." This pattern presented itself clearly in these officers' laissez-faire attitude toward civil government. Many local officials devised quasi-legal means to interdict League activity, and the military normally did not intervene unless the violation of law was grave. Conservative authorities—those still holding office—were thus emboldened to harass Union Leaguers.[22]

Local officeholders often tried to stop the leagues because they were sincerely frightened. One sheriff wrote Gillem that "there are some evil disposed white persons as well as ignorant and illy advised Colored people who may at any moment involve our whole community in riot and bloodshed." The resulting official intimidation took a variety of forms. In several areas, leagues were broken up as unlawful assemblies, and the Democratic press praised such actions. In one neighborhood a justice of the peace fired upon what was apparently a League gathering. In Scott County, official persecution was particularly virulent. A freedman named Berry Harper began distributing Republican tickets prior to the June, 1868, elections, and immediately the Democratic candidate for the state senate assaulted him on the street. Worse was in store for Harper: he had been arrested some months before on a wife-beating charge. Now, however, the white neighbor who had posted bail withdrew his bond. Harper was re-arrested and held in an iron cell for nine days in the middle of summer. The local Bureau agent only intervened after he became convinced that the man's life was in danger, but even so, Gillem ordered the agent only to secure Harper's satisfactory treatment. The general directed that Harper not be freed by military authority, insisting that he must stand trial on the original charge. Gillem's reluctance to interfere with civil law clearly meant tolerance for political harassment by local officials.[23]

22. *House Miscellaneous Documents*, 40th Cong., 3rd Sess., No. 53, p. 61; Pease to Alvord, October 22, 1867, in Letters Received Education Division.

23. M. M. Phares to Gillem, November 18, 1867, in Records, M826, RG 105; Washington *Chronicle*, October 29, 1867; Montgomery *Mail*, July 16, 1868; McKnight to Montague, October 21, 1867, in Letters Received SAC Natchez, Box 51, RG 105; G. W. Corliss to Greene, July 5, 1868, in Letters Sent SAC Forrest, Vol. 185, RG 105; A. Y. Harper to I. McDowell, June 30, 1868, in Letters Received SAC Forrest, Vol. 184, RG 105.

Such proceedings, though politically motivated, at least possessed the virtue of being arguably legal. Rather different were such cases as the one reported in the Enterprise *Star*: "A Loyal League swindler was captured last Thursday at Shubuta, in the act of making loyal speeches and collecting one dollar a head off the negroes at that place. We think the name of this loyal vagabond is Alex Rogers, and we hope Mr. Rogers is making himself very comfortable in the Quitman Jail. . . . Judge Norris has the thanks of all good people." The judge, however, seems to have lacked charges on which he could incarcerate Rogers. This fact did not unduly trouble local officials. In Yalobusha, Ben MacKey complained to the Bureau of his arrest for having "spoken to freedmen about voting the Radical ticket." The jailers offered to release him if he would endorse the opposition; when he refused, they held the freedman for over a month, and the Bureau took no action. Such reports were frequent, especially from isolated communities in the interior of the state. In Vaiden, no Republican could speak without grave danger, and the leading Radical actually left prior to election day in order to urge the military to void the results. R. W. Flournoy observed, with pardonable exaggeration, that there was "not a foot square in this state where a meeting of white and black persons would be permitted to organize a republican party. Mobs and murder would certainly be the result. . . . [W]e must be protected or we can do nothing."[24]

Due largely to this harassment, as well as the military's conduct, the League spread only slowly into the interior. As of May, 1867, according to the Jackson *Clarion*, "the contaminating influence of mischievous counselors" was felt "only in the cities and villages, along the main thoroughfares." Black voter registration in Mississippi seems to have lagged behind that in Alabama, and Lawrence N. Powell estimates that certain areas in the interior of the state accounted for most of the difference.[25] The League did expand gradually, but whole counties were barely touched until mid-1869. The

24. Vicksburg *Times*, February 19, 1868, quoting Enterprise *Star*; Complaint Book, July 24, 1868, SAC Grenada, Vol. 144, RG 105; Jackson *Clarion*, July 8, 1868; Flournoy to Butler, May 23, 1867, in Butler Papers, LC.

25. Jackson *Clarion*, May 9, 1867. Powell calculates that only 82.9 percent of the potential black electorate was registered to vote by the time of the first elections. This contrasts rather starkly with the 96.3 percent reported for Alabama, and the figure for Mississippi is the lowest

Democrats took advantage of this, and in areas where Republican activists were kept out, planters sometimes persuaded freedmen not to vote or even to vote Conservative. Rural freedmen were often perplexed by their new status, and the appropriate political course baffled many. A Bureau agent in Grenada commented that "the freed people are registering generally and take much interest, but are very anxious to have some one to tell them just what the Govt. expects or wants them to do. They are a unit in their feelings and anxious to be instructed how they should vote to further their interest and they will not believe what the citizens here tell them unless it is endorsed by some Govt. officer." In the absence of a strong Republican organization, intimidation or persuasion caused numbers of isolated freedmen to vote Democratic.[26]

Conservatives exerted that power during the June, 1868, elections to approve the new Radical state constitution. In one small town, Klansmen herded the freedmen to the polls with the collusion of the local army garrison. In another community, a squad of Leaguers from Jackson encouraged the freedmen to vote Radical, but could not sway some of those who opposed the constitution. In backwoods Winston County, several leading blacks talked freedmen into voting Conservative in exchange for individual promises of land, and the Democrats allegedly also tried to have the freedmen lynch the only black Radical in the area. In all, the League's restricted growth represented a major factor in the Republicans' sweeping defeat in the 1868 elections. In areas of the state insulated from Radical contact and outside scrutiny, it proved possible to overawe a significant number of freedmen.[27]

One reason for the League's ineffectiveness during the 1868 can-

---

in any of the Reconstructed states (Powell to the author, July 14, 1987). Powell finds that in most Mississippi counties, black registration averaged 95 percent by 1868, but that in certain other counties, it hovered at about 75 percent. These exceptional counties often had white majorities and were generally isolated areas in the interior (Lawrence N. Powell, "The Mississippi Ratification Election of 1868: A 'Fair and Free Election'?" *Journal of Southern History*, forthcoming).

26. A. Murdock to B. G. Humphreys, April 2, 1867, in Gov. Humphreys Papers, MDAH; J. Shipley to A. W. Preston, June 30, 1867, in Records, M826, RG 105.

27. S. A. Bunton to L. Clark, June 28, 1868, in Juanita Brown Collection, University of Mississippi, Oxford; Jackson *Clarion*, June 23, 1868; J. Williams to M. Barber, December 19, 1867, in Letters Sent SAC Louisville, Vol. 189, RG 105.

vass was the character of the League's leadership. William C. Harris in *The Day of the Carpetbagger* argued that the State Council was weak and its activities shadowy, and, as a result, local councils "lacked effective central direction." He described the president of the Mississippi Council, Alston Mygatt, as "particularly ill prepared for the difficult task of managing the state organization." It is not clear, however, how much of the League's trouble grew out of Mygatt's shortcomings and how much resulted from the limited means at his disposal. Certainly the idealistic Mygatt was well intentioned. A storekeeper originally from New York, and a college classmate of the abolitionist Gerrit Smith, Mygatt apparently had harbored doubts about slavery, despite his long residence in Vicksburg. During the war he remained an outspoken Unionist, at considerable personal risk, and he participated in the founding of the first white Union League in the state in 1863. Mygatt saw Radical Republicanism as a means for spreading education and for gradually breaking up the plantations into small farms, thereby giving Mississippi a more democratic social structure. His long tenure as League president, lasting the life of the organization, at least gave it stable leadership, and his position as chair of the Republican State Executive Committee carried League influence into party councils.[28]

Whatever Mygatt's abilities, absence of Bureau patronage and an increasing lack of funds crippled statewide operations. The Mississippi League started recruiting freedmen later than the leagues in other states did, for the State Council was established months after leagues elsewhere were in full swing. Moreover, Mygatt did not journey about, observing the conduct of local leagues, as Keffer did in Alabama. Nor did Mygatt seem to keep close control over distribution of charters and rituals. If the State Council paid any attention to such matters, no evidence of it exists. The League president did oversee activities in Natchez and other towns on the Mississippi River near his home, but his range was limited. As James Lynch observed, apparently of Mygatt and his colleagues, "the Vicksburg Republicans have wrought well for their county, but outside of it

28. Harris, *The Day of the Carpetbagger*, 100–102; Vicksburg Union League to Lincoln, February 15, 1864, in Abraham Lincoln Papers, LC; Washington *New National Era*, February 13, 1873; Natchez *Democrat*, August 10, 1867.

they have done nothing."²⁹ Mygatt's most important duty seems to have been corresponding with Washington politicians to complain about the military.

A. C. Fisk, a member of the Republican State Executive Committee, described the imperfect organizational network resulting from Mygatt's activities: "In many of the interior Counties there is not a single white Republican, hence it has been impossible to effect thorough organizations. . . . Every white Republican who had means spent in his own way, but if a few thousand doll[ar]s could have been expended in sending intelligent Colored men throughout the entire state, organizations could have been effected through the Union League, and the freedmen instructed in their rights." These difficulties were compounded by the belated organizing campaign. By the time of the June, 1868, election, the national party's funds for the South had dried up, probably because of the approaching presidential contest. The results were drastic in Mississippi. In one Leaguer's words, "We were all poor and [had] no money to spend in the election and none to be had of the National Executive Committee. Ten thousand, or even five thousand, one month prior to the election would have given us a victory." Other Republican leaders agreed that the shortage of funds was crucial.³⁰

In the aftermath of this defeat, the League's structure deteriorated further. The Democratic press widely reported the disbanding of many local bodies. Although that was typical after elections, more was involved. League leader Jonathan Tarbell pointed out: "It is a fact, as alarming as it is serious, that we are losing control of the colored vote in large numbers of the interior counties." Another Leaguer observed that the freedmen had no organization at all, now that the Klan had terrorized them. This resulted partly from unfortunate timing: the congressionally mandated dissolution of the Bureau followed hard upon Grant's election. According to Tarbell, the freedmen did not "understand it" and its effects were "fearfully

29. Washington *Chronicle*, July 17, 1867; ULA, *Proceedings, 1869*, pp. 12–13; F. Parsons to Mygatt, July 17, 1867, in Letters Received SAC Natchez, Box 50, RG 105; E. A. Peyton to Mygatt, August 2, 1867, in Records, M826, RG 105; J. Lynch to [Schenck], July 9, 1867, in Schenck Papers, Hayes Library.

30. A. C. Fisk to W. E. Chandler, July 4, 1868, in W. E. Chandler Papers, LC; J. Tarbell to Butler, July 15, 1868, in Butler Papers, LC.

depressing." During these months, League leaders lobbied Congress to void the previous election as fraudulent and declare the Republicans victorious. They were not successful.[31]

In August, 1869, League officials in Washington revoked Mississippi's charter and appointed Mygatt special commissioner to reorganize the order there. His efforts, better coordinated and funded this time, proved more successful. Black organizers such as William T. Combash were sent into the Delta region and other areas previously ignored. President Grant's replacing General Gillem as military commander with General Adelbert Ames also helped immensely. Future U.S. senator Ames was much more sympathetic to the Republican party than either Ord or Gillem had been. In November, 1869, the amended constitution was resubmitted and passed, and the Republicans swept the elections by an impressive two-to-one margin. Despite this belated victory, the League's weakness had helped delay, by well over a year, the Radicals' accession to power.[32]

In essence, the Mississippi League possessed structural deficiencies even at the height of its expansion. Lacking Bureau aid and military protection, the League spread only imperfectly through the state, and hostile civil officials often drove out or silenced activists. The State Council, under Alston Mygatt, was unable to maintain close control of the chartering and the functioning of local leagues. The network of organizers so prominent in Alabama had only a weak counterpart in Mississippi. The circumstances of the League's eventual decline reinforce the contrast. In Alabama the League disbanded at State Secretary Keffer's orders; in Mississippi it would be dismembered by the Klan piecemeal. By 1870, many leagues in Mississippi ceased to function because of escalating terror, though some survived well into the decade. Individual activists abolished or altered their councils, and the League as a statewide organization gradually expired. This pattern of dissolution demonstrated the de-

31. Jackson *Clarion*, June 19, 1868; *Hinds County Gazette* (Raymond, Miss.), July 24, 1868; *House Miscellaneous Documents*, 40th Cong., 3rd Sess., No. 53, p. 277; U. Ozanne to T. D. Eliot, January 1, 1869, in file HR 40A-F10.4, Record Group 233, Records of the U.S. House of Representatives, NA.

32. Washington *Chronicle*, August 12, 1869; Vicksburg *Herald*, September 21, October 7, 1869; Jackson *Pilot*, January 8, 1870.

centralized character the League had exhibited throughout its entire existence.

Despite the contrasting developments in Alabama and Mississippi, local activists often behaved similarly in both states. They responded more to immediate circumstances than to central directives, and the League councils they created had certain characteristics in common. Secrecy not only provided security from hostile whites but also allowed members to speak freely. Councils were initially dominated by those activists—often white—who had organized them, and the local leagues generally stressed a teaching effort directed toward the members. Over time this changed. Freedmen grew more familiar with politics and began to use the local leagues' democratic structure for their own ends. Leagues became forums for collective decision-making in black communities. The original organizers either followed the wishes of their constituents or lost their positions as leaders. Freedmen gradually took over direction of their councils, often propelling them toward a more militant stance.

League leaders initially tried a variety of techniques for spreading the organization among freedmen. The most straightforward was calling public meetings. Activists did so in larger towns when safety seemed assured or if they were unusually audacious. John C. Keffer of Alabama, for instance, followed a set procedure on his speaking tours. He would unfold a flag, call the freedmen together in the center of town, and give a two-hour talk on the League's goals. Interested listeners would then adjourn to a secluded location, where Keffer initiated new members and established a council. This technique had the virtue of speed—Keffer once created twenty-two leagues during a two-week trip through the black belt. It was also hazardous. During the same tour, hostile whites assaulted him three times, shooting him once. Even in the cities, occasional bloodshed punctuated public gatherings, for Radical rhetoric infuriated Democratic onlookers. Congressman William D. Kelley of Pennsylvania encountered a heckler during a speech in Mobile in May, 1867. Gunfire broke out, and there were several casualties. Despite these dangers, some Leaguers found that a high profile was productive. Thomas Haughey of Decatur, for example, made a practice of attending Democratic functions directed at the freedmen. He would invite them to the League, boldly assuming that Democrats on their best behavior would be reluctant to interfere. Haughey had success with this technique, though he was run out of town on one occasion for using it.[33]

Public meetings had the advantage of allowing interested freedmen to make contact with the League. Rural freedmen desired information on how best to proceed, and large gatherings provided a focus for their curiosity about what the Reconstruction Acts meant. Traveling organizer Thomas W. Conway described this process after talking to a freedmen's convention in Mobile: "The hands employed on plantations hearing that there is to be a meeting 'in town,' each contribute something toward defraying the expenses of their best man, who is . . . sent off. . . . This person, after learning all he can, returns to the plantation. Soon a meeting is called and the messenger makes his report, which is usually very correct." Conway met with such leaders at the gathering and initiated them into the League; the freedmen were then able to establish councils in their own homes. In this manner, he "insured the organization of at least twenty more counties in this State." Once Leagues were founded in the cities and towns, the freedmen themselves spread the organization into the countryside, at least to some extent.[34]

In rural areas, such public gatherings occurred less frequently, and secrecy was an abiding feature of operations in the hinterland. Leaguers relied on word of mouth to spread news of meetings, which were loosely described as intended to benefit the colored race. This general statement piqued the freedmen's interest enough to ensure large crowds. Numbers involved in each council differed greatly, but in the cotton regions generally, there were between fifty and five hundred adult males; in such areas, most of the men present were black. Councils met weekly, primarily on Saturday nights. The members gathered in secluded places, using schoolhouses, private homes, stores, and even the outdoors. Churches became a favored location, since freedmen's comings and goings would attract little

---

33. Washington *Chronicle*, September 26, 1867; Athens *Post*, January 23, February 20, 1868.

34. Washington *Great Republic*, July 26, May 16, 1867.

attention, and since League leaders were often ministers. As the Jackson *Clarion* complained, "certain colored clergymen" brought freedmen together, ostensibly for religious services, and then administered the "irreligious and blasphemous oaths of the Loyal League."[35]

Secrecy assured that councils could meet in safety. Leaguers took pains to protect their gatherings; armed sentries were posted, and members had to give passwords to be admitted to council meetings. Leaguers often challenged whites who wandered too close, and sentries occasionally escorted such intruders on their way. Also, the freedmen themselves were heavily armed. These precautions made it difficult for the Conservatives to stop leagues from meeting. The meetings, according to a Mississippi historian summarizing white oral testimony, "were a subject of great vexation to the Democrats, who sought in vain to locate them. . . . The Democrats often rode all night hunting for the gatherings." In one instance, they located a meeting, only to have it become an animated religious service just before the nightriders arrived. Once the freedmen were organized into the leagues, however, secrecy became less critical. Freedmen normally began drilling soon after meetings began, and they became increasingly capable of defending their councils.[36]

The League's secrecy removed the freedmen from the watchful eyes of their former masters, and a requirement that members not divulge proceedings served a similar function. These measures undercut the planters' power to intimidate their former slaves. The future scalawag-politician James Lusk Alcorn warned his fellow planters that "the Loyal League is upon you. Even a brief experience of the workings of that voting machine would satisfy you, as it has me, that all which our people claim for the influence of the 'old master' on the freedmen is neither more or less than *nonsense*. The terrible necessities of our position demand blunt speaking. The general fact . . . ought to satisfy the dullest intelligence as to the power of the 'old master' in the presence of the Loyal League. . . . The 'old

35. Florence *Journal*, May 23, 1867; H. H. Russell to Pope, April 12, 1867, in Swayne Papers, ADAH; Jackson *Clarion*, June 6, 1868.

36. J. J. Bailey to Patton, September 16, 1867, in Gov. Patton Papers, ADAH; Fred M. Witty, "Reconstruction in Carroll and Montgomery Counties," *Publications of the Mississippi Historical Society*, X (1909), 123.

master,' gentlemen, has passed from fact to poetry." Gathering large numbers of freedmen together gave them a sense of power, and the Leaguers' vow of secrecy reinforced the sense that they could talk freely. Republican rhetoric proved persuasive in these congenial surroundings. Once convinced they could speak their minds, freedmen needed little urging to denounce the memory of slavery and those who continued to oppress them. In the words of one rank-and-file Leaguer, freedmen "talked pretty big" at meetings, and they took pride in rejecting even the symbols of white supremacy. The League's organizing technique encouraged a militant approach to political issues, and this tendency became more pronounced over time.[37]

The League did not meet with universal success among freedmen, and some blacks resisted the organization. In Columbus, Mississippi, for example, prosperous freedmen reportedly refused to have anything to do with it. Freedmen who depended on white patronage—barbers, for example—commonly avoided the League. In one north Alabama town, the leaders of a benevolent society were affronted by Leaguers who seemed unduly Radical and refused to cooperate with them. Black leaders of cautious inclination were often lukewarm to the group. For instance, James Lynch publicly denounced the League in order to conciliate Conservative whites, despite his having formed "Union Leagues twice at Vicksburg and one at this place [Jackson]" not long before. Other blacks had different motives for opposing the organization. Future congressman James T. Rapier started Radical activity in Florence, Alabama, on his own initiative. When carpetbagger-organizers appeared in his vicinity, the college-educated Rapier pronounced himself appalled at the order's superstitious trappings, though perhaps jealousy of potential competitors played a part. At all events, Rapier turned up at the first meeting and denounced the organizers as frauds, with devastating effect on their efforts. Some white Radicals also objected to the League's secretiveness. R. W. Flournoy of Mississippi thought the League smacked of the Know-Nothings and refused to participate. It needlessly alarmed whites, he believed, and would only cause trou-

37. James Lusk Alcorn, *Views of the Honorable J. L. Alcorn on the Political Situation of Mississippi* (N.p., [1867]), 3; KKK Report, IX, 685.

ble. Despite such instances, the League on the whole spread quickly among freedmen.[38]

The earliest function of the League was to disseminate information, because the organizers had political experience that freedmen realized they themselves lacked. At the first meetings, white and black leaders gave long speeches on the meaning of the Reconstruction Acts, the various elections, and politics generally. "At each meeting of the local councils," wrote League president James M. Edmunds, "after initiation of members, there should be a lecture or discussion, on some current question of interest, in which the members should be induced to take part." The leagues were thus conducted hierarchically, as a sort of political school. In the words of one black activist, the organization was intended "to teach our ignorant colored men."[39]

This educational function appeared clearly in another important League activity. A major function of meetings was reading aloud such newspapers and pamphlets as would "instruct and interest the Council," and Radical publications, like the *Great Republic*, were favored texts. The former slaves' desire for information was so intense that they would listen for hours to a reader; their interest paralleled blacks' often noted enthusiasm for education after emancipation. In councils that had no literate members, freedmen would send individuals to other leagues who would report back on the contents of the newspapers. A similar practice occurred in a South Carolina League: "Radicals found that many Negroes had photographic memories, for one reading would enable many of the unlettered Negroes to become so familiar with the material that they were able to explain it to other Negroes. In a few cases such Negroes followed the printed pages going through all the motions of a reader." The retentive memory commonly associated with preliterate peoples was put to similar use in Alabama and Mississippi. Several League documents even urged overt encouragement of education. For example, Edmunds told Thomas Conway that if there were any

38. Jackson *Clarion*, September 28, 1867; Panola *Star*, October 5, 1867; Lynch to [?], July 9, 1867, in Schenck Papers, Hayes Library; Florence *Journal*, May 23, 1867; Loren Schweninger, *James T. Rapier and Reconstruction* (Chicago, 1978), 47; KKK Report, XI, 86.

39. Edmunds to Conway, April 9, 1867, in Loring Moody Papers, Boston Public Library; KKK Report, IX, 1001.

illiterate members of a council, the most feasible measures should be taken to correct the problem. Clearly, politically minded teaching was a major concern.[40]

This catechistic function suited the nature of the early League leadership. The organizers and activists who created councils maintained a strong influence over them, at least initially. One League leader mused on his interaction with the freedmen, "How many of them have seen you and yet they all believe in you." Arthur Bingham of Talladega, for example, organized and led the leagues in his area and became their perennial candidate for office. Bingham drafted the local freedmen's first political manifesto, and in one instance, he and a white comrade were granted the power to *appoint* delegates to the first statewide Republican convention. Bingham's personal role remained significant throughout Reconstruction. Activists often became political tutors. A leader in Linden, Alabama, commended the organization precisely because it gave him the power to direct political gatherings: "We had a meeting of the Council at night, and all was quiet and harmonious and that is I think the proper place for discussion and instruction, when we can command attention, keep order and give instruction. We now have 525 members here and I made a short address to the members, which was well received and I hope was useful." Traveling League organizers such as Keffer also maintained a good deal of power through choice of leaders for councils. Freedmen commonly deferred to such guidance in electing officers for their leagues.[41]

Organizers' influence in general eroded quickly. As freedmen grew more familiar with politics they became more assertive. The leagues' democratic structure encouraged this process. Issues were debated and resolved through majority vote, and officers were subject to periodic reelection. Thus, little prevented freedmen from seizing control of local councils, save deference to the mostly white leadership.

40. Edmunds to Conway, April 9, 1867, in Moody Papers, Boston Public Library; Owens, "The Union League of America," 136; Montgomery *Mail*, May 2, 1867.

41. J. R. Fairbanks to Swayne, March 29, 1867, in Records, M809, RG 105; Washington *Great Republic*, May 27, 1867; Talladega *Alabama Reporter*, May 23, 1867; Thomas Woolf to Pierce, September 24, 1867, in Letters Received SAC Demopolis, Box 27, RG 105.

The deference proved initially powerful, perhaps due to the lingering legacy of slavery. In Vicksburg, "white people were the leaders," according to one freedman, and the evidence suggests that this was common.[42] An examination of 362 identified League leaders in the two states reveals that 234, or 65 percent, were white.[43] Whites often dominated the leadership in the larger towns and cities, though blacks often led the smaller councils in the countryside. Likewise, according to a white organizer, the freedmen at first acted "sensibly" in their demands for public office. They had "no candidate" and did not expect to have any "for some time to come."[44]

Despite this pattern, overtly racist or opportunistic activists soon found themselves in trouble. For example, R. C. Merryman of Meridian, Mississippi, led local leagues and was elected to the state constitutional convention. Once there, however, he cooperated with the Conservatives and spread false rumors about the character of League activities. Black leaders deposed Merryman in absentia, and they allegedly wrote him not to return to town because they did not want to have to hang a candidate. Less treacherous leaders also came under scrutiny. Carpetbagger Albert Griffin of the *Nationalist* had a consistent record in support of civil rights before Military Reconstruction, yet even he complained of "colored people, with strong, positive minds who are either suspicious of all white men, or wish their people to put them into offices which they know some white man is better qualified to fill. Controlled by suspicion or ambition, they are constantly appealing to their colored friends to demand this, that, and the other, and if their wishes are not immediately complied with, denunciation follows." Increasing skepticism toward these allies was related to the emergence of a more militant stance on civil rights. Insurgent blacks found that such an approach effectively isolated leaders who were inclined toward moderation. But even when no substantive issue emerged, the desire for blacks in leadership roles became powerful. It seemed to follow logically from

42. *House Reports*, 43rd Cong., 2nd Sess., No. 265, p. 123.
43. This calculation includes 227 individuals identified as "confirmed" League leaders, and the rest are identified as "probable." The proportions remain about the same if confirmed activists only are considered.
44. Fairbanks to Swayne, March 29, 1867, in Records, M809, RG 105.

League rhetoric and from freedmen's own perceptions of their needs.[45]

Insistent demands for positions of leadership reflected blacks' growing assertiveness as well as their increasing influence over local leagues. In part, they had become disaffected with their white allies. Freedmen soon realized that activists were not motivated solely by disinterested benevolence. Ambitious individuals asked why white Republicans received the lion's share of the offices if freedmen provided most of the votes. A Conservative correspondent in Montgomery believed that "for a time, what with the formation of leagues . . . everything went on swimmingly the freedmen being as tractable as the most ardent aspirant to office would desire. Getting at last some smattering of political machinery into his head, the first use made of it has been to insist that he and his race are to have an equal division of offices." The potency of this impulse was demonstrated graphically in Vicksburg. Carpetbagger Charles E. Furlong, the Warren County sheriff, seized control of the powerful League machine in 1869 through aggressive espousal of black officeholding. He thereby supplanted state League president Mygatt as leader of the local League, a position he retained until his eventual defeat by Thomas W. Cordozo, an educated black South Carolinian. Freedmen's wishes to have more of their race represented in leadership roles grew stronger over time, and the issue became a major point of factionalism in the Republican party as a whole.[46]

Another factor strengthening the freedmen's influence over their councils was black leaders' growing political sophistication. The cogent observations of George Houston, a League activist in Alabama's Sumter County, illustrate this trend. Not a learned man, he exhibited sensible caution toward his white Republican allies, coming to have "mighty little" confidence in them. Many politicians claimed to be Radicals to get positions, he found. Houston said that if a leader did "what he promises to do, I am his man," but anyone who tried "to get me to be used as a tool, why, he will find my edge is

45. Jackson *Clarion*, February 8, 1868, quoting Meridian *Mercury*; John Richard Dennett, *The South as It Is, 1865–1866* (1866; rpr. New York, 1965), 300–304; Mobile *Nationalist*, May 30, 1867.

46. New York *World*, October 11, 1867, quoting Montgomery *Mail*; Harris, *The Day of the Carpetbagger*, 99.

going to break off; and if it breaks off once, he never can grind it any more." Houston praised one scalawag, Daniel Price, as the only local white who acted appropriately once in office, and there is evidence that Price was indeed diligent in furthering the freedmen's interests. The point is that George Houston was not alone in his conclusion that he would "stick to the man" who "proves himself."[47]

Leagues taught freedmen about political operations, and as blacks gained knowledge councils grew more responsive to their concerns. Blacks gradually took over their leagues, both in policy and in positions as individual leaders. These tendencies were augmented by the segregation that frequently characterized League councils. Many leagues, especially in large towns, were de facto segregated, due primarily to whites' sense of racial propriety. Some leagues excluded blacks altogether; others permitted a favored few to join or participate in League activities. Blacks were therefore predominant in their own "Lincoln" councils. Indeed, members of one black League regarded its white allies as guest lecturers rather than full-fledged members. Obviously such a structure would strengthen racial nationalist sentiment in black-dominated leagues, especially since some freedmen resented the whole notion of segregated councils. The Mobile Freedmen's Convention, meeting just after the creation of a white League in that city, considered resolutions urging that both races hold their meetings together. Freedmen asked their allies "not to discriminate against us because we are black" and in exchange promised not "to discriminate against them because they are white." The convention decided that approving such a resolution was not expedient, but resentment over separate leagues lingered. One black, for example, complained that of the seventy or so in the white League, not more than a dozen were "straight-out" Republicans. Some freedmen clearly regarded the existence of segregated councils as an insult.[48]

The result was that freedmen increasingly dominated their local councils. Those white activists who retained influence espoused an

47. KKK Report, IX, 998, 1003.
48. Herbert, *Why the Solid South?*, 41; Montgomery *State Sentinel*, July 2, 1867; Hattie Magee, "Reconstruction in Lawrence and Jeff Davis Counties," *Publications of the Mississippi Historical Society*, XI (1910), 191; Warren, *Reminiscences*, 44; Mobile *Nationalist*, May 9, 1867.

increasingly Radical line, at least in public. Quite a few actually maintained positions of leadership, but their independent power diminished nevertheless. They became dependent spokesmen for the aspirations of the black community. Although secrecy and other aspects of the leagues let organizers break the planters' hold over the freedmen's politics, their own power proved transient, and freedmen increasingly controlled the leagues. The democratic structure of the local bodies, and the increasing self-confidence of freedmen and their leaders, made black determination of policy inevitable. In particular, leagues became involved in the struggle in the countryside over agricultural labor. As black domination of the leagues grew, these bodies more and more reflected blacks' hope for freedom from planters' economic and social control.

The spontaneous creation of militia companies illustrated blacks' increasing influence on League policy. Although not part of the organization's institutional structure, these groups frequently grew out of League activities. This "spin-off" occurred at the initiative of the freedmen themselves, for the League leadership generally discouraged formation of these bodies. Freedmen thus demonstrated their control of League policy at the local level. Blacks' resolve to defend themselves would eventually emerge as a major factional issue within the Republican party, dividing moderate leaders from the militant local leagues. Freedmen's martial drilling, and the mass actions that resulted, show their capacity for independent activity based on their own ideas of security and self-interest.

As the League and Radical agitation spread, reports of drilling by freedmen became prevalent. Some were doubtless exaggerated, occasioned by armed Leaguers going to and from meetings. Other tales arose from the League practice of attending the polls in large groups, to lessen fraud and intimidation. This technique was common. A Mississippi historian observed, "The negroes . . . under the organization of the Loyal Leagues were accustomed to form in a solid phalanx in front of the polls, so that no white influence could reach them." Nonetheless, it is clear that actual military preparations occurred among freedmen. General Gillem observed that he "almost daily" received petitions asserting "the existence of organized companies of freedmen and asking the presence and protection of troops." Gillem felt certain that such organizations operated in several areas of Mississippi.[49]

League officials were ambivalent about this activity, especially prior to the Klan's arrival in early 1868. They looked upon military display as provocative and therefore counterproductive. John Keffer, acting for the Alabama State Council, urged freedmen to attend League gatherings unarmed. At one rally he had them stack their guns on the podium before he would speak; at another he persuaded a local League to stop drilling, telling them that the organization did not countenance such behavior. Most local activists also discouraged martial display. For example, one prominent white Leaguer thought the freedmen could easily end up in serious trouble, and he wrote the Bureau that "it would be well to order a disbanding of all military organizations in this county." Black Leaguer Holland Thompson likewise urged Tuskegee freedmen to forget about drilling. In Wilcox County, Alabama, local blacks asked two northern planters for "the privilege of forming a Military Company," from which the two—both League activists—managed to dissuade them. White organizers commonly described themselves as thus restraining the freedmen, especially in time of crisis.[50]

The initiative for drilling came from the freedmen themselves. It is difficult to say much about this activity that is specific: most of the time, Leaguers met unofficially and marched about on Saturday afternoons. Sometimes, however, the local leagues conducted exercises. The Jackson *Clarion* stated of one group on their way to a council meeting, "The squad marched with such regularity that we know it could have only been acquired by constant drilling. . . . This is no hearsay but we saw it." The blacks were obviously serious about self-defense, and these militias sprang into action when conflict threatened. Armed freedmen would descend upon the scene of trouble and act as circumstances dictated. They might form a posse

49. W. H. Braden, "Reconstruction in Lee County," *Publications of the Mississippi Historical Society*, X (1909), 141; Jackson *Clarion*, December 29, 1867.

50. Union Springs *Times*, September 25, 1867; Osborne *et al.* to Smith, September 12, 1868, in Gov. Smith Papers, ADAH; Charles Hays to Pierce, September 18, 1867, in Letters Received SAC Demopolis, Box 27, RG 105; Fleming, *Civil War and Reconstruction in Alabama*, 512; M. Y. Candee and Colton to Adams, [July, 1867], in Swayne Papers, ADAH.

to apprehend wrongdoers or even to threaten retaliation. Despite the militant nature of this conduct, and the often inflammatory talk, freedmen rarely initiated bloodshed. The pervasive rumors that blacks were seizing land or preparing to slay large numbers of planters were mythical. Even Walter L. Fleming conceded that "on the whole, there was very little actual violence done the whites,—much less than might have been expected" as a result of League mobilizations. Freedmen wanted to defend themselves and their rights, not start general conflict.[51]

Two examples will illustrate this pattern. In Eutaw, Alabama, black Leaguer James K. Green made a stop on his speaking tour. While on the platform he was threatened and nearly assaulted by the local sheriff. As Green left the area, his armed escorts fired their weapons in salute, and the gunshots were mistaken for sounds of battle. The rumor spread among the already angry freedmen that he had been attacked. "Semi-military or militia organizations" from the countryside marched on Eutaw, with some freedmen supposedly threatening to burn the town. The situation was tense until local officials convinced the blacks that it was all a mistake. A Bureau report on the incident found that the freedmen acted on their own and were not following orders from League leaders; in fact, the white activists in the area were disconcerted by these events. An affray in West Point, Mississippi, ended less peacefully than did the trouble in Eutaw. A quarrel at a local ferry ended with a white "accidentally" shooting a freedman. The next day, a group of blacks conducted an extralegal arrest of the perpetrator, whereupon they themselves were captured and fourteen of them placed in jail. Freedmen in the region then became "much excited" and threatened to "forcibly return their brethren." An actual armed clash took place before the affair was finally settled.[52]

The freedmen's determination to defend themselves took on a new political dimension after the rise of the Ku Klux Klan. Freedmen insisted on firm action against terrorists, and League leaders began to

---

51. Jackson *Clarion*, May 28, 1868; Fleming, *Civil War and Reconstruction in Alabama*, 562.
52. H. G. Claus to C. W. Pierce, September 20, 1867, C. Hays to Pierce, September 18, 1867, both in Letters Received SAC Demopolis, Box 27, RG 105; Samuel Andrew Agnew Diary, December 11, 13, 1869 (MS in UNC); Mobile *Tribune*, December 20, 1869, quoting Troy *Messenger and Advertiser*.

call for the induction of blacks into the official state militias. They wanted freedmen to be issued arms and to be paid for fighting the nightriders. This important issue came to divide moderates from Radicals within the party, once Republicans gained power. Governors William Hugh Smith of Alabama and James Lusk Alcorn of Mississippi responded similarly to these demands. Both tried to conciliate Conservative opinion and avoided stern measures. In *Negro Militia and Reconstruction*, Otis Singletary pointed out that Smith had "elaborate paper plans" for a militia but took no action. Likewise, Alcorn organized militias in a desultory manner after his inauguration in 1870, but he did not arm any black troops. Such moderation hardly recommended itself to freedmen susceptible to Klan violence in the countryside.[53]

Black dissatisfaction with this policy was voiced well by the nearly illiterate leaders of a Republican club. Writing Governor Alcorn from embattled West Point, these men complained that blacks had been killed "so Miney ways . . . they Dont under stand nothing." These freedmen asked the right to arm as a militia. They had long expected that Alcorn's permission would be forthcoming, and they expressed disappointment at his delay: "We has got a Constitution to Raise a body of men of merlish [militia] & Was to be organized by the Military Department & it has gon Down by not Reciving the organization[.] if We are intitel to the organization We hope We Can get it short[ly.] That was great Consolation to our Pepol but we never Could get organize & the[y] became disharted." Certainly freedmen wanted to defend themselves, and they turned their desire into a concrete demand, demonstrating the blacks' growing militancy and their increasing ability to establish their own political objectives. Local leagues clearly followed the freedmen's dictates on the whole issue of self-defense and ignored the contrary wishes of the white Republican leadership.[54]

League-sponsored drilling may also have served the freedmen's interest in another way. Beyond intimidating planters, it deprived employers of freedmen's labor. The evidence is tentative, but blacks'

---

53. Otis A. Singletary, *Negro Militia and Reconstruction* (1957; rpr. Austin 1963), 12, 14; *Montgomery Mail*, June 23, 1870.
54. Petty *et al.* to Alcorn, March 17, 1871, in Governor J. L. Alcorn Papers, MDAH.

rampant disaffection with the centralized plantation system renders the interpretation plausible. Conservative sources widely reported that freedmen used militia activity and political meetings to avoid work. "Our crops are poor enough," complained the Holly Springs *Reporter*, and the "indolence and worthlessness of the negro are making them fivefold worse. We learn that in our neighborhood they leave their work for whole days together to attend militia meetings." Many planters made similar comments, and they often seemed more upset about the lost time than any threatened violence. An Alabama Bureau agent agreed, noting that one day a week devoted to politics would "seriously jeopardize the whole planting interest and result in general bankruptcy." Even Republican papers warned blacks against neglecting the cotton for militia exercises. It is not evident that freedmen deliberately used this means to pressure planters to rent them land or to make other concessions, but certainly their willingness to drop work manifested dissatisfaction with the labor system. Suggestive in this regard is the fact that the drills commonly occurred on Saturdays. Planters' insistence on Saturday-afternoon work had been a grievance since the war, and drilling allowed blacks to escape the labor they had long thought exploitative. Freedmen's enthusiasm for martial activities reflected hostility to the whole coercive regime derived from slavery, and in practice it proved one more force tearing apart the centralized plantation.[55]

The whole issue of blacks' drilling illustrates the local councils' independence. Whether or not they intended to pressure planters, freedmen certainly acted of their own volition. Disregarding the League leadership and often local activists as well, freedmen took defensive measures. In time of crisis they mobilized, forcing planters to face the possibility of resistance. Eventually the Leaguers' tendency toward direct action brought them into conflict with Republican leaders, because in neither Alabama nor Mississippi would Republican governors incorporate freedmen into the state militias. In short, the Leaguers' receptivity to martial actions demonstrated the democratic character of the local councils. The freed-

55. Panola *Star*, October 15, 1870, quoting Holly Springs *Reporter*; Christian to Swayne, May 15, 1867, in Records, M809, RG 105; Montgomery *State Sentinel*, May 22, 1867; Jackson *Pilot*, October 29, 1870.

men's militant desires took precedence over the contrary wishes of the League hierarchy.

Early in this century, followers of the Dunning school depicted the League as allowing white agitators to dominate the freedmen. In Fleming's words, the organization "made it possible for a few outsiders to control the negro by alienating the races politically." This portrayal bears some resemblance to reality as regards the League's leadership, especially at first. In Alabama the state structure was strong because of Bureau aid; in Mississippi, there was no such help and the leagues were weak. In both, however, white activists dominated the state leagues. At the local level, such leaders initially played a crucial role as political tutors.[56]

This situation quickly changed. As freedmen learned more about politics and became more skeptical about their allies, they grew more aggressive. Blacks began forwarding more radical demands and promoting their own leaders. This assertiveness was readily apparent in freedmen's self-defense measures, since they clearly followed their own counsel in their drilling and in the mass actions that often resulted. The leagues gradually became political institutions directly responsible to the freedmen as blacks' deference to white organizers wore away. The democratic nature of the local movement was thus more pronounced over time.

One aspect of this transformation is of larger significance. Local councils became enmeshed in the agricultural strife rocking the countryside. The League's explosive spread contributed to the disruption of the old-style plantation. Freedmen tended to involve the leagues in their attempt to force planters to grant them greater autonomy. The responsiveness of local councils to freedmen's desires is important, because the leagues became a major force in the conflict over the agricultural system.

56. Fleming, *Civil War and Reconstruction in Alabama*, 568.

THREE

Statewide Factionalism and Local
Leadership

The character of League leadership reflected the organization's
structural deficiencies. Activists operated with relative autonomy,
and over time the League's ideological unity disintegrated. In both
Alabama and Mississippi, the League acted initially as a Radical
caucus within the Republican party, but political reverses eroded
that unanimity of purpose. Struggles over patronage rapidly became
divisive, and various factions began developing. Individuals chose
sides, deciding on the basis of their own ambitions rather than ideology, and the resulting organizational disarray encouraged opportunism and self-aggrandizement among the leaders.

In spite of the confused pattern of factional division, certain kinds
of behavior were typical among activists. League organizers provided social services that the former slaves needed to ease the transition to freedom. In agricultural matters especially, their role was
crucial, far more important immediately than were larger political
concerns. League leaders counseled blacks in their dealings with
planters and mediated the freedmen's demand for autonomy with
the power structure. White organizers, in particular, provided legal
and other professional services for the former slaves. Mere literacy
qualified them to look over contracts, correspond with Bureau officials, and generally help the freedmen deal with employers. If the
carpetbaggers and scalawags often seemed opportunistic in their
political behavior, they nonetheless helped blacks free themselves

from dependency on their former masters. The black leaders' role was somewhat different, for they were community spokesmen rather than providers of services. But all League activists assisted freedmen in their difficult transition from servitude on the plantation.

Despite the major differences in the League's development in Alabama and Mississippi, important similarities existed in its political role. Factional alignments were complicated, but a pattern emerged in both states: the League began as a cohesive force, acting as a Radical caucus within the Republican party. Unity eroded swiftly, however, as Klan violence and political reverses demolished the League's central structure. Intraparty struggles followed as individual ambitions and patronage became more pressing concerns. At the local level, the League retained some significance, but in both states its decline as a statewide Radical organization was relatively quick.

In Alabama, the League started as a Radical bloc. For various reasons, both the leaders of the Unionist element and those engaged in organizing the freedmen endorsed similar policies. Thus the League was unified during the critical period of its expansion. During 1867, Keffer's State Council presided over an ideologically Radical organization, despite the racial diversity of the League's composition.

The Radicalism of many Unionist yeomen developed from a combination of political forces; though transient, their militancy at first was strong. During 1866, thousands of Unionists in the Alabama up-country flocked to the Union League. Once Military Reconstruction passed, the leaders of this element were hostile to former Confederates who now proclaimed their loyalty. These League spokesmen adopted strong rhetoric to stress their Unionism. Two important meetings in Decatur in April, 1867, illustrated the dynamics of this rivalry. At the first "Union" meeting, moderates dominated the proceedings. They favored setting up a state government under the Reconstruction Acts, but refused to adopt the Republican label. The moderates simply passed resolutions declaring their acceptance of Reconstruction. The next day, delegates of the Loyal Leagues met and repudiated the previous gathering. These Unionists stated that "no man can be a true friend to liberty and free Republicanism who 'accepts the situation' as an ill to be endured." The Leaguers welcomed Reconstruction as the only means by which loyal men could rule Alabama.[1]

This forthright support was typical of the leaders of the yeomen-based leagues. They saw themselves as aggressively Radical, and they favored stern measures to maintain unconditional Unionists in power—wholesale removal of former Rebel civil officeholders, widespread disfranchisement, and possibly confiscation. One organizer actually recommended banishment. Leaguers also endorsed such civil rights as were necessary to secure black support for Unionist candidates. In the first months of Military Reconstruction, white Leaguers were actually considered more Radical than were the blacks. One planter wrote a Republican politician about an approaching convention: "I hope you will be able to influence the North Ala. delegates to adopt a mild and temperate course. Inflamatory speeches will do much harm. The colored delegates will return home excited, call public meetings—address their people—poison the minds of the ignorant, & evil disposed, & perhaps produce a conflict of races very soon." In the spring of 1867, white Unionists were arguably the most violent opponents of continued planter rule.[2]

An analogous process transpired in the cotton belt, where League activists faced competition from displaced politicians and Reconstructionist planters who hoped to control the black vote.[3] Conservatives divided on the wisdom of appealing to freedmen, but in most areas a serious attempt was made. Wealthy landowners held large barbecues for freedmen and tried in many other ways to influence them. Many Democrats professed certainty that "old master" could influence his former slaves' votes, a boast that even some Republicans

1. Montgomery *Mail*, April 17, 1867.
2. W. T. Stubblefield to W. H. Smith, June 20, 1867, in Swayne Papers, ADAH; A. B. Moore to R. M. Patton, June 1, 1867, in Gov. Patton Papers, ADAH.
3. The term *Reconstructionist planter* or *Reconstructionist conservative* denotes those who believed that their states should organize under the provisions of Military Reconstruction, but that enough black votes could be secured to defeat the Republican party. This position initially had some support, until the overwhelming black majorities the Republicans received in the fall of 1867 undermined its plausibility (Perman, *Reunion Without Compromise*, 285–93).

feared was accurate. In response, League organizers strongly endorsed equal rights. They thereby distinguished themselves from the opposition. The strategy of being wholeheartedly on the freedmen's side proved successful.

Conservative arguments fared poorly before League rhetoric, as events in Selma demonstrated. Here planters tried to appeal to the freedmen "without any commitment which might injure their social standing." Immediately after enactment of Military Reconstruction, several Conservatives tried to preempt the Radicals by holding a meeting to inform the freedmen of their new rights. A number of prominent speakers addressed a vast crowd of freedmen, calling for education for all and interracial good will, but little else of substance. Their efforts fell flat when white Leaguer J. R. Fairbanks offered resolutions supporting the "Union party known as the Republican Congress." While these were voted down after protracted debate, the polarization over the issue alerted freedmen to the planters' politics. Over the next weeks, the Selma *Messenger* reported the spread of Loyal Leagues among the freedmen. Reconstructionist planters could denounce the organizers as carpetbaggers, but they could not match the appeal that civil rights rhetoric had for the freedmen. So Fairbanks could "out-general" the Conservatives by declaring boldly for the Republican party and full rights for the former slaves.[4]

Between the militancy of white Unionists and the egalitarian speeches of organizers in the cotton belt, the Alabama League became thoroughly identified with Radicalism. Largely accurate through 1867, this reputation stayed with the League throughout its existence. Keffer and his comrades espoused a forthright line during this early period. With the power of the military behind them, these leaders prodded the Republicans toward support of equal rights. The organization's legitimate political role always remained unclear, largely because of the League's secrecy, but in practice it functioned as a Radical bloc within the Republican party. Moderate Republicans often looked upon the League with suspicion, and they frequently declared the League an inappropriate means of influencing the freedmen's vote. These moderates instead endorsed public clubs, often in

4. J. Fairbanks to Swayne, March 29, 1867, in Records, M809, RG 105; Selma *Messenger*, March 16, April 11, 27, 1867.

order to oppose the League's power. In Mobile, for example, a scalawag wrote that "Grant Clubs are being formed in this city with a view of [countering] . . . this carpetbag influence, so prevalent in some quarters." Moderate Republicans often maneuvered to restrict the League's influence.[5]

Republican infighting in Huntsville illustrated the depth of this enmity; after initial attempts to cooperate, the Republicans divided into ideologically distinct factions. Moderates complained bitterly of Leaguers stirring up the blacks against the whites. In the words of Joseph P. Bradley, a leader of this faction, "It is our duty to try & convince the Negroes . . . to support Union men & the Republican party,—but go no further." Bradley and his allies continually battled League activists. Nicholas Davis, another moderate, testified that black Leaguers "forbade me to speak here on this street. That would provoke it [the League]. They forbid me to speak right in front of this court house." The freedmen accused Davis of being a Rebel and a closet Democrat, and they declared they wanted no part of such traitors. In response, Davis had one of the hecklers arrested, claiming that no law permitted freedmen "to come up and speak against a white man." The real issue in Huntsville, according to one Leaguer, was that the Radicals were not willing to take a back seat to Davis, Bradley, and their allies.[6]

The League functioned as a Radical caucus in several ways, perhaps the most important of which was selecting potential Republican officeholders. Leagues frequently petitioned military officials to appoint individuals to civil office, and councils lavished considerable energy on such efforts. Some leagues nominated party tickets directly, dispensing with the traditional public conventions. More commonly, the leagues would agree upon a slate and then ratify the selections in a public forum. One Republican described the general pattern: the leagues "as such" did not pick candidates, but they dominated many nominally open gatherings. In Montgomery, for

5. W. G. Johnson to Smith, June 26, 1868, in Gov. Smith Papers, ADAH.

6. J. Bradley to Smith, May 1, 1867, in Gov. Smith Papers, ADAH; KKK Report, IX, 783; Callis to Kinsman, August 10, 1867, in Records, M809, RG 105; *House Reports*, 43rd Cong., 2nd Sess., No. 262, p. 965; A. Lakin to J. F. Chalfant, May 28, 1867, in Freedmen's Aid Society Correspondence, ITC Archives.

example, a candidate for minor office publicly refused a place on the Republican slate. He was "supposed to have been nominated by a County Convention," but in actuality had been "NOMINATED DAYS BEFORE BY A COLORED LEAGUE." Another reluctant candidate wrote, "The freedmen of this *county* under instruction from *their leaders* (the *leagues* I suppose), are holding meetings all over the county."[7] Obviously, this manner of selecting nominees minimized the power of those Republicans who were not League members.

Even if moderate elements sometimes packed conventions successfully, they accomplished little if they alienated freedmen in the process. For example, moderate Joseph W. Burke—a Bradley ally—won nomination as congressman in a northern Alabama district after a bitter struggle. His main opponent, Sub-Assistant Commissioner John B. Callis of the Bureau, bolted the party and ran as an "Independent Republican." Callis was an outspoken Radical and a League organizer, and he secured the nearly united black vote over the official Republican nominee. Aided by a substantial white boycott of the election, Callis crushed Burke in the February, 1868, canvass. Clearly the League exercised substantial influence over the selection of candidates and thus strengthened the Radical wing of the party.[8]

The League affected policy decisions as well, acting as a caucus at Republican gatherings. During the Mobile Freedmen's Convention in May, 1867, for example, League members dominated the proceedings and drafted the strong resolutions finally adopted. Likewise, at the first Republican meeting in Montgomery, with Keffer, Glascock, and Swayne in attendance, Leaguers took a leading role in pushing a Radical line. According to the Mobile *Advertiser and Register*, "no opposition was made by those present who dissented from the action of this meeting, their alleged reason for so doing was that everything was cut and dried beforehand, and that it was understood the meeting was to be controlled by Federal officers and officeholders and Loyal Leaguers." The organization thus dominated many meetings

7. Mobile *Times*, January 10, 1868, quoting Montgomery *State Sentinel*; Montgomery *Mail*, January 4, 1868; Z. Alexander to G. Meade, January 15, 186[8], in Records of the Third Military District, Office of Civil Affairs, Box 5, Pt. 1, RG 393, Records of the United States Army, Continental Command, NA.

8. J. W. Burke to J. A. Garfield, January 9, 1868, in Howard Papers, Bowdoin College.

during the early months of Military Reconstruction. A Republican paper actually stated in May that members of the League would surely control the Republican party for the next year or two.[9]

The statewide convention summoned to found the party demonstrated this tendency well. Delegates from across Alabama convened at the capitol in early June, 1867. Some Alabama Leaguers met at the same time, and most of them were convention delegates. The press claimed that Leaguers actually drew up the Republican convention agenda, and it is evident that the League met privately before and after each day's open sessions. Some party members complained that the Leaguers monopolized leadership roles and were unwilling to allow "outside *Union men*" any prominence at the public gathering. Clearly the League had a major role behind the scenes, working out difficult political issues. At one point, Mobile delegates objected to the seating of Federal Judge Richard Busteed. The judge had antagonized Radicals by opposing black suffrage some weeks previously. Albert Griffin of the *Nationalist* and black delegates Ovid Gregory and John Carroway demanded that Busteed be excluded. Several white delegates disagreed, and the ensuing discussion created "the utmost confusion and disorder" on the floor. A hurried motion to adjourn was pushed through, whereupon a reporter present wrote that "the difficulty will doubtless be adjusted and the dangers of a split avoided at the League meeting to-night."[10]

Some settlement occurred, and the delegates barred Busteed from participating. The League functioned here as a Radical bloc; in the words of one observer, freedmen and untainted loyalists combined against former Rebels to exclude the judge. League meetings continued in Montgomery even after the Republican gathering had ended. According to a correspondent for the Mobile *Times*, several "white and colored delegates still linger in the city which is probably due to the fact that the League had not yet finished its business. I learn that a meeting was held this morning, and another will be held tonight. It has not yet transpired whether the work of the Conven-

9. Mobile *Advertiser and Register*, March 29, 1867; Washington *Great Republic*, May 16, 1867.

10. Montgomery *Mail*, June 4, 1867; Mobile *Times*, June 6, 1867; Montgomery *Advertiser*, quoting Huntsville *Democrat*; Montgomery *State Sentinel*, June 5, 1867; Lakin to Chalfant, May 28, 1867, in FASC, ITC Archives; Mobile *Times*, June 8, 1867.

tion is approved or condemned by that 'wheel within the wheel.'"
The League's prominence at the Republican convention indicated its
power within the party as a whole.[11]

The League attained the height of its Radical influence at the
Alabama Constitutional Convention in November, 1867. Since Conservatives had boycotted elections for the convention, the League
was well represented among the delegates. White organizers included John Keffer, Albert Griffin, Arthur Bingham, and Daniel H.
Bingham, and the black Leaguers James K. Green and Ben Royal
also attended. Of the one hundred delegates, thirty-six can be identified as League activists or nominees, and the evidence suggests that
another ten may have been associated with the movement. The Alabama Grand Council met in Montgomery at the same time the convention delegates gathered, and rumors circulated that the League
would nominate candidates for the various state offices. Obviously,
Radical tendencies would be strong, given the circumstances.
Unionist Daniel H. Bingham illustrated the uncompromising state
of mind of many convention members. He sent Thaddeus Stevens
his draft of a constitution that provided for broad revisions of state
law. Bingham wanted to void all civil litigation for debt during the
war and looked to shelter the poor from their creditors. Presumably
he hoped to assist the hard-pressed yeomanry of northern Alabama.
Another proposal involved canceling the charters of all the "blood-
sucking" railroad companies in the state that had aided rebellion.
Bingham also desired stringent measures against former Rebels,
intending to "restrict the elective franchise and the right to hold
office in the state a little beyond the military [Reconstruction] bill."
Not all Leaguers wanted such sweeping changes, but Bingham was
an influential delegate, and the prevailing mood as the convention
gathered was Radical.[12]

11. Montgomery *Advertiser*, June 18, 1867, quoting Huntsville *Democrat*; Mobile *Times*, June 8, 1867.

12. Mobile *Advertiser and Register*, November 10, 1867; Montgomery *Mail*, October 30, 1867; D. H. Bingham to Thaddeus Stevens, October 23, 1867, in Thaddeus Stevens Papers, LC. The identified League activists and nominees were: A. Bingham, D. H. Bingham, W. T. Blackford, M. Brainard, C. W. Buckley, J. H. Burdick, D. Coon, J. H. Davis, W. T. Ewing, P. Finley, S. S. Gardner, W. C. Garrison, J. K. Green, A. Griffin, T. Haughey, C. Hays, G. Horton, B. Inge, R. M. Johnson, J. C. Keffer, S. F. Kennemer, H. McGowan, J. W. Mahan, J. J. Martin, B. O. Masterson, C. A. Miller, A. L. Morgan, B. W. Norris, T. M. Peters, R.

Once the convention sessions began, however, League unity eroded, and national party leaders were partly responsible. In the fall of 1867, Republicans lost ground in northern local elections, and influential party figures now backtracked on their controversial southern program. They counseled moderation, fearing that drastic measures would damage Republican chances in the upcoming presidential canvass. Alabama bore the brunt of this pressure, since it was the first state to undergo the Reconstruction process. The delegates gathered in Montgomery knew that they needed their allies in Congress, and therefore many took such advice seriously. In the words of the New York *Times*, "The desire uppermost in the Alabama Convention evidently is, so to act that Congress shall offer no obstacle to the completion of the work." John Keffer, in particular, now urged his fellow delegates to avoid stringent voting qualifications. He had just returned from Washington, where he had become aware of changing congressional sentiment. In these efforts, Keffer initially met opposition from the majority of the delegates who favored "sweeping provisions of disfranchisement." Dissension broke out among the delegates, who were indeed in an impossible situation. Continued support from Republicans in Congress was indispensable, but breaking the power of the planter oligarchy—and putting Radicals in office—seemed to necessitate proscriptive measures. Only direct lobbying by Republican leaders, such as Horace Greeley and Senator Henry Wilson, along with Generals Pope and Swayne, induced the delegates to make concessions on the important issue of disfranchisement. More extreme measures, such as land redistribution and debt relief, received quiet burials.[13]

This turn of events damaged Radical unity, and rivalries for state

---

Reynolds, B. Rolfe, B. Royal, J. Silsby, H. Springfield, J. R. Walker, and J. A. Yordy. Richard L. Hume, "The 'Black and Tan' Constitutional Conventions of 1867–1869 in Ten Former Confederate States: A Study of Their Membership" (Ph.D. dissertation, University of Washington, 1969), 45–50, examines these delegates' voting patterns. He finds that of the thirty-six individuals listed, thirty-one (86.1 percent) voted with the "Radical" faction, four (11.1 percent) were "Non-Aligned," and one (2.8 percent) voted as a "Conservative." These findings support the identification of the League with the Radical faction.

13. New York *World*, November 20, December 6, 14, 1867; New York *Times*, November 18, 1867; Natchez *Democrat*, December 7, 1867; Washington *Chronicle*, November 12, 1867, February 20, 1868; Montgomery *Mail*, November 12, 1867.

offices made the divisions worse. Native white delegates, who were in the majority, resented newcomers receiving lucrative positions. The issue was brought to a head by the disclosure of an alleged League ticket, which gave Keffer the nomination for governor and other Leaguers prominent positions. Turmoil resulted, and the Selma *Messenger* boasted that "our publication of the names agreed upon by the 'Loyal League' managers at Montgomery for the various high offices . . . stirred up something of a muss among the faithful. A multitude of native 'loilists' who had been left out in the cold, and another multitude of lesser lights from the distant north, who had not been provided for, rebelled against the nice little arrangement of Keffer & Co., and plainly told the managers that unless the programme fixed up was modified they would bolt the ticket and defeat the ratification of the proposed Constitution." Whether or not this description is accurate, the delegates did demonstrate some resentment toward the League leadership. According to one observer, Keffer and D. H. Bingham attempted to adjourn the convention without selecting Republican party candidates, because Keffer recognized that he could "get no nomination from this convention for any office that is worth having." The outcome of this confusion was a compromise; the new constitution contained concessions to the freedmen on several civil rights issues, but moderates, such as future governor William H. Smith, dominated the state ticket.[14]

Before the constitutional convention, the League had been relatively unified, but now there were divisive struggles over policy and personal rivalries. A series of blows in early 1868, the culmination of this process, demolished the League as a centralized organization. At the beginning of the year, President Johnson ordered that Wager Swayne be removed from command, along with his superior, John Pope in Atlanta. Swayne's successor, General Julius Hayden, decided on the Bureau's "immediate purification" because agents had placed themselves "among the propagandists of the Union Leagues." Hayden began removing active Radicals from Bureau posts, at the

14. Selma *Messenger*, November 26, December 5, 1867; Mobile *Advertiser and Register*, November 8, 10, 1867; D. L. Dalton to Patton, December 1, 1867, in Gov. Patton Papers, ADAH.

height of the campaign to ratify the new constitution.[15] For his actions, Hayden was himself relieved by General Howard in Washington, but his removal came too late. Hayden had devastated the infrastructure of the League at a critical time.

Beyond this purge, a further difficulty gradually emerged. The provisions of the new constitution troubled white Unionists, particularly the abandonment of disfranchisement and the absence of any clear appeal to their economic needs. Given this situation, many yeomen proved susceptible to Democratic race-baiting. A constitutional requirement that voters swear to uphold the civil and political equality of all men offended racist sensitivities. In addition, several Unionist leaders who had not been nominated sat out the canvass, and some of them even urged defeat of the constitution. The vote totals reflected this disaffection. In September, 1867, some 18,500 whites had cast ballots to call the constitutional convention; by February, 1868, only about 7,500 voted in favor of ratifying the constitution. The effect on white League membership was still more drastic, for the press identified the League with blacks and with civil rights generally. While the Republican party maintained a significant following among the yeomanry, the League was fatally compromised in their eyes.[16]

Along with up-country whites, some freedmen also grew restive about the League leadership, though for different reasons. Although the evidence comes primarily from hostile sources and is thus suspect, it seems that some blacks resented the choice of Republican nominees. According to one account, leagues in eight cotton belt counties denounced gubernatorial candidate Smith as too conservative. Moreover, the lily-white party candidates for higher office also troubled freedmen. The Mobile *Advertiser and Register* noted that

15. J. Hayden to Howard, January 27, 1868, in John Carpenter, "Agents of the Freedmen's Bureau" (MS in John Carpenter Papers, Schomburg Center for Research in Black Culture, New York Public Library), 279; Washington *Chronicle*, February 20, 1868; New York *Tribune*, March 30, 1868; G. A. Farrand to Pierce, December 2, 1867, in Records, M809, RG 105; Hayden to Meade, March 18, 1868, in Records of the Third Military District, Office of Civil Affairs, Box 5, Pt. 1, RG 393.

16. On the interplay of race and class in the motivations of the yeomen, see Armstead L. Robinson, "Beyond the Realm of Social Consensus: New Meanings of Reconstruction for American History," *Journal of American History*, LXVIII (1981), 276–97; and Fitzgerald, "Radical Republicanism and the White Yeomanry."

"these nominations have caused an immense buzzing in the black Leagues at Montgomery. The colored men begin to smell a rat." In Tuscaloosa, according to a Republican source, "the colored League of this county, rightly concluding that the late Demopolis [District] Convention which nominated C. W. Pierce for Congress . . . was a partial and unfair assembly . . . have repudiated its nominations, and brought out S. W. Jones (Colored) . . . for Congress." Shandy Jones eventually withdrew from the race in the interest of Republican unity, but his candidacy revealed some displeasure among freedmen with the party's nominees.[17]

Both white disaffection and black resentment contributed to a decisive defeat for the League: the apparent rejection of the constitution in February, 1868. Democrats boycotted the election, thus preventing the constitution from meeting the congressional requirement that half the registered vote be cast. Although Congress eventually waived this obligation and declared the constitution enacted in June, the seeming repudiation hurt the League. Since Keffer and his cohorts had helped draft the document, the popular backlash reflected on them. In addition, the four-month delay in readmission bewildered Republicans. The League leaders' failure to win the February election outright diminished their influence in Washington, and their inability to persuade Congress immediately to readmit Alabama hurt them at home.

Then there was the Klan. Just before the election, and in the months that followed, terrorist activity escalated. League organizers represented a major target. D. H. Bingham died in January after a savage beating by nightriders. Because of such violence, many Republicans dropped out of the League as a tactical measure; others withdrew from politics altogether. The perception spread among sober Republicans that secret meetings only drew fire. Radical W. T. Blackford announced his "withdrawal from the Loyal League, fully satisfied that whatever may have been its original design, its tendency is to produce estrangement between the races and to result in

17. Loren Schweninger, "Black Citizenship and the Republican Party in Reconstruction Alabama," *Alabama Review*, XXIX (1976), 88; Mobile *Advertiser and Register*, December 5, 1867; Montgomery *Mail*, January 16, 1868, quoting Tuscaloosa *Reconstructionist*; Mobile *Times*, December 13, 1867.

evil." Public recanting of this sort became common in the press, and many activists concluded that the organization had served its purpose. Some disbanded their councils, or had them meet less frequently, or even converted them into less threatening public clubs. Leaguers tried almost everything they could devise in hopes of placating the terrorists. The effect was clear: the Klan demolished the League as a centralized political entity during early 1868.[18]

John Keffer's troubles illustrated the larger difficulties besetting the League leadership. At the constitutional convention, Keffer received the lowest position on the state ticket, commissioner of industrial resources. After this blow to his ambitions, it became certain that his mentor, General Swayne, would be relieved as military commander. The white Montgomery Council, which Keffer founded, split over disagreements about the constitution he helped draft; one faction denounced Keffer publicly, accusing him of misappropriating League funds. At the same time, Keffer lost his lucrative federal position as register of bankruptcy when the wealthy Republicans who had endorsed his bonds withdrew financial support; soon he filed for bankruptcy himself. He even spent a night in jail on a fraudulent charge of evading a hotel bill. In response to these difficulties, Keffer's politics grew more parochial. He turned his attention to maintaining his base among Montgomery's black population. He also became more of a centrist, apparently in hopes of patronage, and he eventually joined the Smith-Warner faction of the party. Thus Keffer found his way into the "moderate" group, despite having been Alabama's leading carpetbag Radical in the early stages of Reconstruction. His move mirrored the decline of the League as a Radical caucus within the Republican party.[19]

Between Swayne's removal, Klan violence, and the defeat of the constitution, little remained of the influence of the League leadership. Once it became clear that Keffer no longer had any real

18. Athens *Post*, January 9, 1868; Montgomery *Mail*, February 19, 1868, quoting Greensboro *Alabama Beacon*; Keffer to O. O. Howard, June 26, 1868, in Howard Papers, Bowdoin College.

19. New York *Times*, December 29, 1867; Montgomery *Advertiser*, December 12, 14, 24, 30, 1867, February 27, 1868; Montgomery *Mail*, December 22, 1867, January 12, 15, 1868, July 3, September 3, 1870, quoting Haynesville *Examiner*; Keffer to Howard, June 26, 1868, in Howard Papers, Bowdoin College.

power, League activists went their separate ways. The organization began to dissolve into a series of rival political machines. Many leagues continued to function, but the Union League ceased to act as a unified force within the party. Only on a few issues, such as supporting a strong militia, did local leagues find common ground. Patronage, railroad schemes, and other narrow interests became central. Such concerns had always been important to League activists, but now they became all-consuming. The Democratic boycott of the elections gave Republicans total control of the state, once readmission occurred; this encouraged factional bickering, and Leaguers joined in with as much enthusiasm as any.

Thus League leaders turned up on both sides of the emerging rift in the party in 1868. When Governor Smith moved to the center to conciliate Democratic opposition, his course received the support of several prominent white Leaguers or former Leaguers. This Smith-Warner or scalawag faction included Keffer, Swayne, and Congressmen C. W. Buckley, B. W. Norris, and Thomas Haughey. The other clique, led by U.S. Senator George Spencer, contained a number of League activists, though they seemed less prominent than were those in the other group. Spencer's carpetbag or Radical faction included John Hardy of Selma and others. Black leaders also were in both groups, though most apparently supported Spencer. The alignment seems to have revolved around patronage—and Smith's railroad projects—more than ideology.[20]

It is difficult to say what the average League member thought of this conflict. Spencer's Radicals had a strong black following in Mobile and Montgomery, but elsewhere this pattern did not hold. One historian observed that "blacks were by no means united in their views. . . . Although Senator Spencer maintained a substantial bloc of black support, many black people followed the leadership of Jere Haralson in supporting only candidates who had lived in Alabama before the war." Most freedmen seem to have disregarded the whole dispute; concerns closer to home—the Klan, for instance—absorbed their attention. Factionalism concerned activists who had personal interests at stake, but such issues normally did not

20. Montgomery *Mail*, August 30, September 3, July 3, September 9, 1870, quoting Haynesville *Examiner*.

evoke a deep mass response. The disruption of the League's central Radical tendency led many to focus on local affairs, rather than on the confusing and distant struggle for supremacy at the state level.[21]

The League in Alabama, then, took no consistent line in the divisions that erupted, once the party attained power. Both white and black leaders followed their individual and local interests, and the League's black membership grew apathetic. Most of the white Unionists dropped out of the League altogether. The League had functioned as a Radical organization during 1867, but not after the removal of Swayne and the rise of the Klan. Leagues often maintained an important local role but ceased to act as part of a statewide organization. Although Keffer would not formally disband the League until 1869, the leadership lost much of its influence well before that time.

In Mississippi, the Union League's factional role developed in much the same fashion. The initial Radical tendency eroded by late 1868 in response to the Klan and electoral reverses. Although local leagues often survived and remained militant, the organization no longer functioned as a statewide entity. Individual leaders' ambitions became crucial in determining political alignments after the League's demise, and former activists did not line up consistently in later partisan struggles.

Although the Mississippi League lacked a centralized hierarchy, largely because of the military's hostility, Alston Mygatt and the State Council presided over an organization with some ideological unity in 1867 and early 1868. League activists advocated civil rights in response to the competition of Reconstructionist planters for black votes, for the same dynamic that applied in Alabama was at work here. The League could even take a clearer line in Mississippi, partially because blacks represented a majority of the electorate, but also because the organization lacked much of a following among the yeomanry. Only in a few areas were white leagues in existence, so the State Council could espouse civil rights without provoking dissension. Moreover, the League's Radical tendencies were enhanced by

21. William McKinley Cash, "Alabama Republicans During Reconstruction: Personal Characteristics, Motivations, and Political Activity of Party Activists, 1867–1880" (Ph.D. dissertation, University of Alabama, 1973), 254.

the circumstances of its creation. The National Council sent travel-ing organizer Thomas W. Conway to set up a provisional state coun-cil in June of 1867. Conway and other outside speakers took a posi-tion that was, by Mississippi standards, Radical, and this had an impact on the local movement. The Natchez *Democrat* commented on speeches by Conway and others: "Even the arch Rad. [Thaddeus] Stevens would have blushed to have heard them and known how far he was out-Radicaled by these men."[22]

The Mississippi League exercised influence through many of the same means used in Alabama. Leagues nominated candidates for office and also packed Republican conventions. In Rankin County, for instance, one black candidate at a nominating convention obliged the delegates to uphold their League oaths and vote for him. Promi-nent League activists certainly proved to be Radical in sentiment. These individuals included League president Mygatt, Henry R. Pease, A. T. Morgan, E. J. Castello, and black leader Thomas W. Stringer. Even men who later emerged as moderates, such as black organizer James Lynch and Jonathan Tarbell, stood close to the prevailing Radicalism at this point. Tarbell, for example, demanded federal help in terms militant enough for any Radical: "The Presi-dent must not only be Impeached, but the Southern traitors must be disfranchised in a body—we can never control this state without— & they deserve it." These views were common among Leaguers at the first party gathering in September, 1867. The meeting founded the Republican party, urging civil rights for blacks and wide dis-franchisement for traitors. One historian wrote that the platform underscored the belief that Radicalism had "gained control of the Republican organization." The influence of Leaguers at this and other gatherings clearly strengthened militant tendencies within the Republican party.[23]

The Mississippi Constitutional Convention of January through May, 1868, manifested strong Radical influence, and a National Council report boasted that League members had carried the con-

---

22. ULA, *Proceedings, 1869,* p. 13; Natchez *Democrat,* June 10, 1867.

23. Jackson *Clarion,* June 3, 1868; Tarbell to Butler, March 15, 1868, in Butler Papers, LC; *House Miscellaneous Documents,* 40th Cong., 3rd Sess., No. 53, p. 63; Harris, *The Day of the Carpetbagger,* 106.

vention. It seems probable that the League acted as a caucus. In Mygatt's words, "We have [the] State League Convention and Union Republican Convention on the 4th and 5th Inst. On the 5th we will make our nominations for State and Congressional offices." Certainly the organization was well represented among the delegates who assembled in Jackson. As in Alabama, a Democratic boycott aided in the election of many Leaguers, and at least twenty-three of the delegates were affiliated with the League. Present were most of the leading organizers in the state, and these men generally took a militant approach. Leaguer A. T. Morgan of Yazoo, for example, wrote that he felt it his duty to "treat the 'disarmed' rebels as unworthy to lead in the work of laying the foundations of a free government. . . . Nine of every ten of that class were still determined to win . . . what they had failed to accomplish upon the field of battle. We knew what we were doing [in disfranchising former Confederate leaders]." The constitution disfranchised about 2,500 whites, and it required of voters an oath to uphold civil equality for all. An amendment providing for segregated schools was voted down. By these acts and others, Radicals demonstrated their dominant role in drafting the constitution. In the words of the Jackson *Clarion*, the Leaguers "elected the members of the Convention [and] the proposed Constitution is their legitimate offspring."[24]

That role became a liability when voters rejected the constitution outright. Several factors contributed to its defeat: the hostility of the military, poor League organization, and an effective Klan mobilization in the interior. This outcome damaged the League. In

24. ULA, *Proceedings, 1869*, p. 13; Mygatt to C. Sumner, February 3, 1868, in Beverly Wilson Palmer (ed.), *Papers of Charles Sumner*, Microfilm (London, 1987), reel 40, frame 682, by permission of the Houghton Library, Harvard University; New York *Herald*, January 13, 1868; Albert T. Morgan, *Yazoo; or, on the Picket Line of Freedom in the South* (Washington, D.C., 1884), 277–78; Jackson *Clarion*, June 3, 1868. The identified League activists and nominees at the convention were: H. N. Ballard, P. Bonney, J. C. Brinson, E. J. Castello, N. J. Chappell, C. W. Clarke, W. T. Combash, A. R. Howe, H. P. Jacobs, G. C. McGee, W. V. McKnight, H. Mayson, R. C. Merryman, J. A. Moore, A. T. Morgan, C. Myers, A. Mygatt, U. Ozanne, F. Parsons, J. R. Parsons, E. A. Peyton, T. W. Stringer, and H. W. Warren. Hume, "The 'Black and Tan' Constitutional Conventions," 361–67, performs a roll-call analysis of the votes of the constitutional convention. Hume finds that of the twenty-three delegates listed, nineteen (82.6 percent) voted as "Radicals," two (8.7 percent) were "Non-Aligned," and two (8.7 percent) were "Conservatives." As in Alabama, the League was strongly identified with the Radical faction at the convention.

Vicksburg, for example, a handbill summoned Leaguers to take part in the "obsequies of their late (so-called) friend. Punctuality is requested as the advanced state of decomposition renders the remains obnoxious." In the aftermath of this defeat, Mygatt and his allies urged Congress to declare the constitution enacted, but to no avail. Neither Congress nor President Grant desired to reverse an actual defeat at the polls. The state League structure deteriorated to the point that the National Council declared it was "not now active" in early 1869. Freedmen, their confidence in League leadership diminishing, reportedly dropped out of the organization in large numbers.[25]

In factional terms, this crushing defeat took the political initiative from League Radicals and placed it in the hands of moderate Republicans. Important Leaguers vanished from sight, and others less identified with the repudiated constitution stepped forward. According to William C. Harris, "Soon after . . . April [1869], a group of moderate regulars and formerly unobtrusive Radicals quietly began the task of unseating the Party leadership of stalwart Radicals or 'bitter-enders' like Eggleston, Gibbs, Castello, Mygatt and Flournoy and moving the party toward a moderate platform." Under new leaders, such as scalawag James Lusk Alcorn, Republicans resubmitted the constitution to the voters. Without the disfranchisement provisions, it passed overwhelmingly in November, 1869, and Alcorn became the first Republican governor of Mississippi. League Radicals had clearly been pushed aside.[26]

The League did play a role in the ratification of the constitution. Under orders from the National Council, Mygatt completely reorganized the state body in mid-1869, and it participated in the fall campaign. Even moderates recognized the League's success in recruiting first-time voters, and so the party sent organizers into areas previously untouched. Elsewhere, "Alcorn Clubs" or Freedmen's Aid Societies spread, and they often resembled leagues. Despite this limited resurgence, the League had ceased to be effective as a statewide body. Its leaders stood in disrepute, their policies abandoned

25. Handbill, dated July 11, 1868, on display at Old Court House Museum, Vicksburg; ULA, *Proceedings, 1869*, p. 13; *Hinds County Gazette* (Raymond, Miss.), August 14, 1868.
26. Harris, *The Day of the Carpetbagger*, 228, 262, 231.

by the party. Mygatt's fate in Vicksburg illustrated the State Council's eclipse. He gradually lost control of the local League to carpetbagger Charles E. Furlong. Sheriff Furlong outmaneuvered him by simultaneously supporting Alcorn's moderates in state politics and taking a Radical position on local issues—especially black demands for office. Mygatt later helped found an open Republican club, in hopes of competing with Furlong's League machine for black votes, but he had little success.[27]

Leagues or similar groups existed for years, operating locally, though not as part of any larger statewide political organization. In Meridian, Leaguers re-created their council in 1871, advocating armed struggle against the Klan, to the dismay of more cautious Republicans. Colonel Furlong's machine in Warren County survived until December, 1874, when scores of its members were slaughtered in the infamous Vicksburg riot—with Furlong, now on the other side, leading the whites. The survival of often militant local organizations, however, did not translate into consistent Radicalism at the state level. In later struggles between moderates and Radicals, Leaguers turned up in both camps. On the whole, the League's Radical tendency expired with the defeat of the constitution in June, 1868.[28]

In both Mississippi and Alabama, the same overall progression occurred. The League initially exercised a powerful influence, and it bore considerable responsibility for the drafting of Radical constitutions in both states. This militant unity was brief. Political reverses and Klan repression demolished the League as a Radical bloc. By early 1868 in Alabama, and later in the year in Mississippi, it dissolved into rival factions. The League had only a limited impact on later factional struggles, since patronage rather than ideology increasingly became the critical factor. Despite the League's short-lived existence as a Radical caucus, however, it often endured locally. Here the League still met the needs of the black community.

27. Washington *Chronicle*, August 12, 1869; Natchez *Democrat*, June 11, 1868, quoting Vicksburg *Herald*; Harris, *The Day of the Carpetbagger*, 98–99; Vicksburg *Times and Republican*, September 13, 1871.
28. KKK Report, XI, 48, 77, 136–37, 157; *House Reports*, 43rd Cong., 2nd Sess., No. 265, pp. 467–68.

In an influential article, Lawrence N. Powell described southern Republican leaders as "inordinately addicted to factional quarrels." The cause, he said, was that they were "unusually wedded to political patronage for economic sustenance and well-being."[29] Indeed, League organizers seized upon politics as means for upward economic mobility, and most of them proved overtly ambitious. Reconstruction promised that offices would soon be vacated, and they looked inviting to politically sympathetic individuals seeking advancement. Many leaders fit the description "young men in a hurry," and their desires became crucially important, once it appeared that there were not jobs enough to go around. Social cleavages ran so deep among Republicans that normal patronage struggles were devastating, fraught as they were with racial and class significance. During the period of the League's greatest cohesiveness, it contained such divisions, but when the organization's central Radical tendency broke down, factionalism increased. Leaguers' self-aggrandizement thus contributed to the infighting that plagued the party.

Some organizers fit the stereotypes portrayed by the Dunning school, behaving as opportunists who cynically manipulated black aspirations. For example, Leaguers elected R. C. Merryman of Meridian to the Mississippi Constitutional Convention; once there, he decided that he was a white supremacist. Merryman managed to get himself expelled after a midnight drunken brawl in the capitol chambers. His fellow delegate William T. Combash, a black lawyer from Sunflower County, also voted as a Conservative—until, that is, he was arrested for theft of convention warrants from another delegate. Other organizers were not content with political opportunism, preferring instead to fleece their followers. A black Leaguer reportedly solicited funds to set up a cooperative store and then ran off with the contributions he received. Bureau agent G. W. Hayes of Sumter County, Alabama, allegedly stated that he "did not care a damn about the nigger; that there was going to be money made out of them, and he was going to have his share." This League organizer absconded to Texas with $1,000 that freedmen had placed in his hands

29. Lawrence N. Powell, "The Politics of Livelihood: Carpetbaggers in the Deep South," in J. Morgan Kousser and James M. McPherson (eds.), *Region, Race, and Reconstruction: Essays in Honor of C. Vann Woodward* (New York, 1982), 315, 332.

for safekeeping. In Athens, Alabama, activist and Bureau agent James Danforth distributed relief supplies, which he reportedly used to accumulate a "harem" of destitute white women. Beyond such extreme behavior, some activists had less than sound reputations. A few had criminal records or drank too much; many of the scalawags were deserters from the Confederate army. Rumors circulated that organizers consorted with black women. Political liabilities of another kind were shown by a "chief in the organization of Union Leagueism" named Collins who killed Congressman Thomas Haughey—a fellow Leaguer—over a factional dispute. [30]

League leaders in Natchez demonstrated many of these shortcomings, for several were "dependent upon the negroes for a livelihood." Activists E. J. Castello and George St. Clair Hussey were financially "leagued" with a claims agent, S. M. Preston, who was recovering black veterans' military bounties from the government. The local Bureau agent reported that Preston was defrauding the freedmen, and a subsequent Bureau investigation backed the agent's story. Although the Leaguers may not have been guilty of improper behavior, the widespread abuse of the bounty system reported across the South makes such actions altogether plausible—as does the Leaguers' attempt to have the Bureau agent removed from his post. Even H. R. Pease, a Leaguer sent to look into the situation, found the activists to be "mere adventurers playing a shrewd game to make material and political capital out of the negro. They have since the passage of the Reconstruction Act become enthusiastically for the negro." [31]

Other Natchez Radicals had their weaknesses as well. After a split

---

30. Harris, *The Day of the Carpetbagger*, 647–48; *House Reports*, 43rd Cong., 2nd Sess., No. 265, pp. 467–68; State of Mississippi, *Journal of the Proceedings in the Constitutional Convention of the State of Mississippi, 1868* (Jackson, 1871), 240–41, 250–53, 309–15; Washington *Chronicle*, July 1, 1868, quoting Vicksburg *Republican*; KKK Report, X, 1663; *Wilcox County News* (Camden), August 30, 1867, quoting Tuskegee *News;* J. A. Powell to Bennett, April 7, 1868, in Register of Letters Received and Endorsements Sent, SAC Demopolis, Vol. 137, RG 105; A. Bennett to G. W. Hayes, March 31, 1868, in Letters Sent SAC Demopolis, Vol. 140, RG 105; W. P. Tanner to Woodard, August 20, 1867, in Records, M809, RG 105; KKK Report, VIII, 172–73. W. T. Combash returned to the League after his dalliance with the Democrats. He eventually died in a gun battle with hostile whites.

31. Report of H. R. Williams, June, 1867, E. E. Platt to H. R. Williams, June 17, 1867, both in M752, RG 105; G. Hussey to L. Edwards, May 7, 1867, in Registers and Letters, M752, RG 105; Clifton L. Ganus, Jr., "The Freedmen's Bureau in Mississippi" (Ph.D. disser-

in the local League, a member of one faction offered the following description of his opponents: "He spoke of one as having stolen silver from a wooden legged negro. Of another as having stolen chickens from negroes and of another (a colored Rev—& who came from Wisconsin & now a candidate for the Convention in this County.) as having supplied the female portion of his flock with a generous quantity of syphilis and that he and they had been treated by the notorious Dr. Geo. St. Clair Hussey. The accused were challenged to deny the charges." The allegations may have been exaggerated, but there is reason to doubt the disinterestedness of several of the Natchez activists. The freedmen had their reasons for supporting such men. Local Bureau agents were conservative and close to the gentry; any source of advice and Radical political leadership must have seemed welcome. But some of their leaders were in fact profiteers or created difficulties in other respects.[32]

Such conduct may not have been typical, for one can as readily cite instances of model leadership, but these manipulators illustrate the potential for abuse the situation held. Many activists seem to have been well motivated, yet they also wanted office, and over time these concerns conflicted. Nineteenth-century Americans commonly viewed politics as a vehicle for social mobility, and League activists were no exception. The hostility against them was so intense that only the strongly motivated persisted, and personal ambition proved a potent lure. Careerism among the Leaguers was enhanced by their relative youth. Alabama white activists for whom age can be determined had a median age of thirty-six years, with over a fourth of the total clustered in the group from thirty to thirty-four years old. A number of the younger leaders lacked established occupations, and several of the northern newcomers, like the Morgan brothers of Mississippi, had failed as planters after the war. Activists, especially whites, generally participated in the League expecting to gain office soon. The problem, in Joseph Bradley's words, was that there were too many "Pigs for the Tits." Patronage drew am-

---

tation, Tulane University, 1953), 153–58; H. R. Pease to J. W. Alvord, June 10, 1867, in Records of the Education Division, RG 105; Natchez *Democrat,* June 11, 1867, quoting Keokuk (Iowa) *Constitution.*

32. Leach to McKee, October 29, 1867, in Robert McKee Papers, ADAH.

bitious individuals to the League, but as time passed it also encouraged factionalism and opportunism.[33]

Future U.S. senator George E. Spencer exemplified this sort of political leadership. At the end of the war, Spencer wanted to "go somewhere and have a pleasant home and make money." Settling in Alabama in hopes of a patronage appointment, he invested heavily in southern cotton and served as an agent for northern purchasers. In addition, Spencer considered a "big speculation" in railroads, writing his friend Grenville Dodge of the Union Pacific about a line that could be bought for "five cents on the dollar." Meeting with financial reverses, Spencer left for California, but he returned after the enactment of Military Reconstruction and became active in politics; he reportedly led the Union League in Tuscaloosa. When Alabama was readmitted to the Union in 1868, Spencer asked Dodge to help him campaign for the Senate. Spencer promised that if elected, Dodge could rely upon him to "do anything for either yourself, your interests or your friends that you may desire." Once in Washington, Spencer became the sole dispenser of Grant administration patronage in the state, apparently by securing the defeat of his Republican colleague, Willard Warner, in the 1870 election. Spencer thus proved himself skilled at factional infighting, but he damaged the party in the process.[34]

Patronage matters were a critical issue for League activists, and yeoman Unionists showed the centrality of such concerns immediately after passage of the Reconstruction Acts. Believing that the military would soon vacate all civil positions held by former Rebels, white Leaguers bombarded General Swayne with petitions for appointment to office. For example, in Blount County, Alabama, the Grand Council sent a list of twenty-eight local offices occupied by disloyal men. The council unanimously recommended Unionist replacements, a vote that somehow does not seem surprising. The

33. Bradley to Smith, May 1, 1867, in Swayne Papers, ADAH. In the "Young Man" category, the figure is 1; ages twenty-five to twenty-nine, 4; thirty to thirty-four, 11; thirty-five to thirty-nine, 5; forty to forty-four, 6; forty-five to forty-nine, 4; fifty to fifty-four, 4; fifty-five to fifty-nine, 3; sixty to sixty-four, 1; and in the "Old Man" category, 2.

34. Spencer to Dodge, April 16, October 14, 1865, August 3, 13, 1867, July 2, 1868, all in Grenville Dodge Papers, State Historical Society of Iowa, Des Moines; Tuscaloosa *Monitor*, March 18, April 7, 1868; Wiggins, *The Scalawag in Alabama Politics*, 66.

Alabama League's John Keffer encouraged these expectations, sending out one thousand circulars asking that recommendations be forwarded "to head off rebel applicants." If he had his way, he wrote, every disloyal judge and sheriff would be removed instantly.[35]

Difficulties with this approach presented themselves swiftly, as Leaguers squabbled among themselves over these places. Infighting became so intense by May, 1867, that D. H. Bingham and other Leaguers denounced the "wild hunt of office-seekers before the State has any office to give, as we think there will be time enough to canvass the claims and merits of men to fill the permanent State and Federal offices after state and civil Government is organized by the people and approved by Congress." Soon Swayne became "much annoyed with complaints of Party factions," and he determined to ignore them, since the object was "to make removals of those holding office to make place for others." Once Swayne announced this policy—probably because of pressure from General Pope—League activities among whites seem to have declined. Keffer thought it devastated Republican prospects. Clearly, yeoman Leaguers were, from the beginning of Military Reconstruction, acutely interested in patronage and position.[36]

League leaders' political behavior presents another indication of this tendency. Many eventually became Democrats, often out of pique that they did not secure office. For instance, Dr. Joseph H. Davis organized councils in his section of Alabama, but when he lost a coveted congressional nomination, he deserted the Republicans. Soon he was chairing Conservative meetings. Congressman Robert S. Heflin of Alabama did the same thing after not being renominated, despite having once been Radical enough to espouse confiscation. Perhaps such conversions were sincere, for scalawags could easily turn racist after being defeated by black votes, but other recantations were clearly cynical. One Radical carpetbagger wrote Senator Spencer demanding federal office and, upon being rebuffed, ran

35. W. C. Garrison *et al.* to Pope, August 3, 1867, in Swayne Papers, ADAH; Keffer to S. Hale, July 26, 1867, in Howard Papers, Bowdoin College.

36. Washington *Great Republic*, May 30, 1867; Keffer to S. Hale, July 26, 1867, in Howard Papers, Bowdoin College; Patton to [?], May 7, 1867, in Governor Patton Letterbooks, ADAH; Pope to Grant, April 24, 1867, in Letters Sent, Records of the Third Military District, Office of Civil Affairs, Pt. 1, RG 393.

for Congress with Democratic support. Such opportunism under-scores the importance of patronage in many activists' minds.[37]

This picture is overdrawn in that it does not describe the attitude of black leaders. White activists were generally ambitious from the beginning, but blacks only gradually became interested in seeking office. Their organizing activity grew out of being community spokesmen such as ministers or teachers, and their prominence made them natural political leaders. It was difficult for such men to take Radical ideals lightly—though some did—and social ties to the freedmen exerted a powerful political discipline. Even so, most Union League organizers were white, and their political activities possessed a healthy dose of self-interest. Organizers' characteristic ambition not only encouraged the disruption of the League in both states but also enhanced the importance of the League's demise when it did occur.

During 1867, while the state leagues still exercised some central oversight, individual ambitions could be subordinated to the good of the cause. Factional strife developed within the party, especially between Leaguers and non-League moderates, but seldom did councils themselves split. Open feuds, such as the one in Natchez, were rare. Organizers would go to great lengths to maintain League affiliation. For example, in Tuscaloosa, a militant black named G. W. Cox gained appointment as registrar of voters through Keffer's influence. Cox disparaged the work of local activists, writing Keffer that the "U. L. is at very low *ebb* here." He soon set to work creating a black council under his personal direction. The local leaders were furious, decrying the choice of Cox as an "unnecessary insult," but they accepted him as registrar without leaving the League. Clearly, the Alabama Council maintained significant influence over local developments. An activist in Talladega testified to this power in seeking outside help: "Sims and Ballou are dissatisfied with the nomination [to the constitutional convention] and I verily believe that he Sims is going to run on a ticket . . . against the nominees. . . . [T]hey are both loyal & have been very efficient in organizing leagues and if they run against the nominees I fear the Conservatives will elect their

37. Montgomery *Mail*, January 14, May 17, 1868; Wiggins, *The Scalawag in Alabama Politics*, 64; G. E. Spencer to Dustan, January 9, 1869, in C. W. Dustan Papers, ADAH.

men." The author urged W. H. Smith to write Sims and tell him that "if he ever intends to have any sense," this was the time to exercise it. Likewise at the Alabama Constitutional Convention, the League heard a dispute between two Republicans who claimed election as delegates. With the eventual demise of the League as a Radical caucus, it lost the capacity to mediate such conflicts and factional strife intensified.[38]

The character of the leadership proved of special importance when the Republicans took power. Once an individual was elected to office, opportunities for personal gain beckoned, as Charles Furlong demonstrated in Vicksburg. His "Courthouse Ring" apparently plundered the Warren County treasury for years, and the city and county debt rose steeply under League control. According to Harris, "Manipulation of the local warrant market was developed to a fine art in Vicksburg, where . . . Furlong began defrauding the taxpayers soon after the military commander appointed him sheriff." Moses Kellaby, a local freedman, described how Furlong maintained his popularity. At one mass meeting in the countryside, Furlong "treated out nearly $25 or $30. . . . They all had whiskey and something to eat." Furlong dispensed these favors "to get big money," according to Kellaby.[39]

Eventually, equally venal black leaders deposed Furlong, but not before he amassed a fortune. He then assisted in the overthrow of Reconstruction, and he was elected to several terms in the legislature as a Democrat. Finally losing influence, Furlong spent the remainder of his life at posh New York hotels, and he took annual vacations from Borneo to Greenland, reportedly visiting "every city in the world of over 100,000 inhabitants." When Furlong died in 1907, he left an estate worth perhaps half a million dollars, and he was remembered primarily for carrying a huge roll of bills with which he tipped servants lavishly. While this former storekeeper obviously prospered

38. G. Cox to Keffer, June 29, 1867, R. Blair to Smith, June 25, 1867, both in Swayne Papers, ADAH; W. Miller to Kinsman, June 27, 1867, in Gov. Patton Papers, ADAH; Charles Pelham to Smith, September 19, 1867, in Swayne Papers, ADAH; Mobile *Advertiser and Register*, November 8, 10, 1867.

39. Harris, *The Day of the Carpetbagger*, 37; William L. Royall, *A Reply to "A Fool's Errand, by One of the Fools"* (New York, 1881), 15–16; *House Reports*, 43rd Cong., 2nd Sess., No. 265, p. 205.

from his activities as a Leaguer, there is reason to doubt that freedmen benefited much from his leadership.[40]

Corruption seemed especially prevalent at the state level. Furlong's conduct was by no means typical of Leaguers in municipal or county government, for freedmen could keep close watch on their behavior. Former slaves tolerated corrupt leaders, but only when these individuals acted in their interest overall. This restraint disappeared in Jackson and Montgomery, where the voters' rural isolation and illiteracy shielded legislators. They could quietly seek private gain, as long as they did nothing to damage their Radical credentials with their constituents. Bribery was common, as was furthering private interests through favorable enactments.

Railroad legislation in Alabama illustrated these tendencies. Government financing of transportation projects furnished a rich field for corruption, and Alabama suffered badly. Mark W. Summers' study, *Railroads, Reconstruction, and the Gospel of Prosperity,* cites Alabama's Governor William H. Smith as among the "fools" on aid measures. Smith seems to have helped the Alabama & Chattanooga in exchange for financing for his own railroad company. He and State Treasurer Arthur Bingham, another former Leaguer, issued hundreds of thousands in unauthorized railroad bonds. John Hardy of Selma, one of the men "controlling the League," reportedly received a $150,000 payment from the Alabama & Chattanooga. Rumor had it that with this sum he persuaded fellow lawmakers to grant the company a $2-million loan. According to one black representative, bribes of $50 to $500 were doled out wholesale, and Leaguers indeed voted heavily for the loan. Many of these legislators would probably have supported the bill anyway, seeing it as a public works project benefiting the freedmen, but such graft brought bad publicity to the Republican party. Alabama Leaguers may not have been the principal figures in this corruption, but some former League activists profited from it to the detriment of the organization's reputation.[41]

The situation in Mississippi developed somewhat differently,

40. New York *Times*, September 26, 1907.

41. Mark W. Summers, *Railroads, Reconstruction, and the Gospel of Prosperity: Aid Under the Radical Republicans, 1865–1877* (Princeton, 1984), 246, 213–36 and *passim*; Selma *Times and Messenger*, April 18, 1868; A. B. Moore, "Railroad Building in Alabama During the Recon-

since the Radical constitution of 1869 prohibited state aid to private corporations. The result was that the state "suffered no great railroad swindles during the period." Even so, Leaguers helped set up railroad companies and thus used their influence to advantage. Railroads offered Republicans positions with their companies, hoping thereby to induce freedmen to support municipal and county subsidies, which were permitted under state law. For instance, T. W. Stringer, a black organizer, served on the board of directors of the Memphis & Vicksburg along with white activist C. W. Clarke and Governor Alcorn. Robert Gleed, a black organizer from Columbus, gave speeches and lobbied for the Selma & Memphis. Many Leaguers had this kind of corporate connection, and their influence aided passage of a number of local bond measures. By the political standards of the time, this activity was legal and acceptable, but the question of conflict of interest arises. While Leaguers padded their fortunes, they acted upon motives distinct from, and perhaps in conflict with, those of the Republican party and of the freedmen themselves.[42]

On the whole, League organizers were an ambitious group. Most hoped to gain office, and eventually wealth, through their activities. They may not have been more mercenary than contemporary politicians were, but by modern standards they were unabashed in their moneymaking, and the leaders' ambition had important implications. At first, it helped the League by encouraging individuals to undertake unpaid and dangerous organizing work. The hope of office also inclined them to subordinate themselves to the state League in anticipation of future favor. But when it became evident that there were not positions enough to satisfy everyone, the League's central power dwindled, and factions formed around various individuals. This process contributed to the disruption of the League as a Radical caucus in both Alabama and Mississippi. Many organizers actually

struction Period," *Journal of Southern History*, I (1935), 428–30; KKK Report, VIII, 232; John Ralph Scudder, Jr., "The Alabama and Chattanooga Railroad Company, 1868–1871" (M.A. thesis, University of Alabama, 1951), 51; Fleming, *Civil War and Reconstruction in Alabama*, 593–94.

42. John F. Stover, *The Railroads of the South, 1865–1900* (Chapel Hill, 1955), 95; Harris, *The Day of the Carpetbagger*, 549; KKK Report, XII, 718–28; Summers, *Railroads, Reconstruction, and the Gospel of Prosperity*, 122.

left the party after not receiving offices they thought they deserved. Beyond encouraging factionalism, the self-interest of League activists hurt in quite another manner. Once elected, Leaguers were tempted to enrich themselves through taking bribes and using their positions to financial advantage. Away from the pressure of their constituents, Leaguers succumbed to corruption in the state capitals. They thereby weakened the prospects for the Republican party's continued rule and did their constituents a disservice in the process.

Despite the limitations of the League's activists, freedmen responded enthusiastically to their leadership. The reason was not the freedmen's ignorance, as the Dunning school argued, but it was instead their desire for greater autonomy. Beyond simply agreeing with what Radicals said, former slaves needed the skills that organizers possessed. Emancipation exposed freedmen to increased interaction with white officialdom; they now also dealt with contracts and other written documents with which they were unfamiliar. If freedmen did not want to rely upon their former masters, then they required advice from some other source. League organizers, especially whites, met this need: they gave legal and financial counsel in exchange for the freedmen's votes. They provided a range of social services as part of their political role, particularly on work-related issues. Activists thus encouraged the disruption of the centralized plantation, assisting freedmen in their efforts to escape the gang system and other coercive relics of slavery. This constituted a crucial feature of their leadership.

A vast number of petitions document the scope of this intervention, for Leaguers constantly lobbied on behalf of the freedmen. Most demanded removal of hostile civil officers, but the range of topics was broad. For example, in Columbus, Mississippi, Leaguers circulated a call for replacing the local Bureau agent. In nearby Aberdeen, freedmen requested appointment of a League organizer to the Bureau and also asked assistance in building a schoolhouse. Appeals for official pardon were also common; in Natchez, "Radicals and freedmen" circulated a petition to release some men accused of horse theft. In Mobile such a document was "signed by a secret body styling themselves a Loyal League." In the "Dog River" rape case, the Mobile leagues sent numerous requests for clemency; all the city's major activists signed these petitions; and one also served as lawyer for the defendants. Leaguers even journeyed to the capital to plead with the governor for the lives of the accused freedmen.[43]

Activities of this sort occurred at the highest levels of League leadership. Radicals in Montgomery launched an effort to secure freedmen an expanded role in the federal courts. The Austrian-born carpetbagger Paul Strobach stated that "as the Secretary of the Union League of Alabama, Committee on the State of the Union, I was elected chairman of a committee, to wait on [Federal] Judge Busteed and ascertain his view on *Equal* Rights, and especially in reference to the empanelling of *colored* men as jurors in his court." Strobach had "three very important interviews" with Busteed on the topic, and his exertions eventually paid off: the judge soon admitted blacks to jury duty, despite being conservative on most civil rights issues.[44]

Mississippi's Leaguers demonstrated similar zeal. Alston Mygatt asked O. O. Howard of the Freedmen's Bureau to speed payment of government bounties to black veterans. Mygatt warned that the "rebels are making use of this delay," observing that immediate payment would have "valuable effects" on the black vote in the coming elections. The secretary of the state League council, J. M. Brown, added that the freedmen needed the money badly. In a similar fashion, E. J. Castello wrote Mygatt complaining that freedmen were being evicted for attending Radical meetings in Natchez. "I wish you would see General Gillem immediately and see if something can't be done in regard to the matter," he wrote. Mygatt indeed followed up the complaint. League leaders frequently pressured government officials in this fashion on behalf of the former slaves.[45]

Petition campaigns and lobbying represented only a small portion

43. R. Gleed to Howard, February 21, 1868, in Letters Received SAC Columbus, Box 38, RG 105; N. Condol to Wood, April, 1867, in Records, M826, RG 105; Brandon to Humphreys, June 12, 1868, Gov. Humphreys Papers, MDAH; McGuire to Patton, August 14, 1867, in Gov. Patton papers, ADAH; L. S. Berry *et al.* to Pope, August 17, 1867, in Swayne Papers, ADAH.
44. P. Strobach to Chandler, February 6, 1869, in W. E. Chandler Papers, LC; Montgomery *Advertiser*, December 12, 1867.
45. Mygatt to Howard, July 4, 1867, Brown to Howard, [July 4, 1867], both in Registers and Letters, M752, RG 105; E. J. Castello to Mygatt, June 3, 1868, in Records, M826, RG 105.

of organizers' services to the freedmen. Much activity involved securing access to basic public services, especially education. One Alabama Leaguer wrote, "I have promised the Colored Folks a school in this community [and] I feel anxious about it. If my friend Keffer can find time I feel confident he will give some assistance." Another organizer reported that the blacks in one backwoods area desperately needed help, since they had no schools and were in ignorance of their rights. Still another asked for both a school and a Bureau agent in his vicinity. Black activists, such as T. W. Stringer of Vicksburg and Holland Thompson of Montgomery, also aided the founding of schools in their areas, and later they showed interest in furthering education.[46]

Activists took on a variety of social service roles. For example, Urbain Ozanne, a League leader, wrote the army on behalf of some black veterans near Panola, Mississippi. The freedmen, he found, had been cheated of their army bounties by a Bureau agent. Confronted with an investigation, the agent admitted guilt and resigned his position. John Keffer assisted one freedman in quite another manner. On a speaking tour, Keffer informed the Bureau that "this poor old man, too infirm to work any more, is perishing of starvation." Keffer instructed that he be fed and taken care of. The other organizers also made this kind of personal intervention often, especially when local officials refused relief to freedmen—or Unionists, for that matter.[47] Humanitarian conduct grew out of the Leaguers' political role; it met genuine social needs and was thus an effective way of seeking the freedmen's favor.

Leaguers defended black people's rights, especially in matters touching on politics. The National Council instructed organizers to "bring to the notice of the council, any injustice or oppression," and the council would then seek recompense for the victims. Leaders protected their followers' civil liberties and tried to shield them from

46. Davis to Smith, May 15, 1867, in Gov. Smith Papers, ADAH; Rose to Smith, July 1, 1867, in Swayne Papers, ADAH; W. T. Ewing to Swayne, April 1, 1867, in Records, M809, RG 105; Friar's Point *Delta*, September 29, 1869; Board of Police, Warren County, Minute Book G, September 11, 1869, in Warren County Courthouse, Vicksburg; Rabinowitz, "Holland Thompson," in Rabinowitz (ed.), *Southern Black Leaders*, 252–53.

47. U. Ozanne to Secretary of War, August 25, 1868, in Registers and Letters, M752, RG 105; Keffer to Pierce, August 10, 1867, in Letters Received SAC Demopolis, Box 27, RG 105.

violence, or at least to punish wrongdoers after the fact. For example, a white Alabama activist reported the murder of a black member of his League to the Bureau. The perpetrators, he stated, had been freed by civil officials who were not disposed to do justice. John Keffer received a murder complaint from an anonymous League member. "Believing you to be a friend of the colored race," the man wrote, "the subject would have been divulged to you when you were in this section if I had been at home." The Springfield family in St. Clair County, Alabama, exemplified this vigilance. They were "radical members of the League, ardent friends of the Africans and all that." An opposition paper described their conduct in one episode: "Last winter, in Ashville, a negro was whipped for some offense by a white man, and the Sheriff of the county, a Mr. Brown, stood by and encouraged it. One of the Springfields was there and made some objections, and a lively fight was commenced, which resulted in some bloodshed." The feud eventually resulted in the Radicals raising an anti-Klan militia and engaging in combat with local officeholders. These League leaders, and many others, certainly tried to protect freedmen from Conservative violence.[48]

League leaders, in fact, often acted as auxiliaries for Bureau personnel. One Republican activist wrote that freedmen approached him "with all their complaints and wishes," and as a result he functioned as "a *sort* of an *agent*" of the Bureau. Mississippi's Jonathan Tarbell attended court as "a friend" to one freedman, and after an unfavorable verdict, he informed the Bureau of irregularities in the trial. In Wilcox County, Alabama, two Leaguers asked to be appointed to the Bureau without pay; they wrote Swayne that local freedmen needed their services, and the general appointed one of the pair an agent. Military officials frequently utilized the League network to bolster their own efforts on behalf of the freedmen. For example, one Bureau man sought a position as civil rights commissioner for Arthur Bingham, a League organizer. If Bingham was "clothed with official authority," he could secure freedmen just treat-

48. Edmunds to Conway, April 9, 1867, in Moody Papers, Boston Public Library; J. Lancaster to Smith, September 8, 1867, in Letters Received SAC Opelika, Box 35, RG 105; "An L. L." to Keffer, November 28, 1867, in Records, M809, RG 105; Montgomery *Mail*, July 14, 1870, quoting Chattanooga *Times*.

ment in the contract process. Relations between the League and Bureau agents were not always this harmonious, however. Activists frequently harassed agents they thought insufficiently zealous. One Alabama Bureau official actually resigned his post in protest of a Leaguer's interference. Whether working with the Freedmen's Bureau, or occasionally against it, Leaguers tried to further the interests of the former slaves as conspicuously as possible.[49]

Agriculture constituted the crucial focus of this intervention; basic changes were under way in the plantation system, and these engaged much of the activists' time and attention. For the first time, the former slaves confronted labor contracts, lawsuits, and other pressing legal matters of bewildering complexity. Given the range of new duties liberty brought blacks, they needed access to literate individuals. The presence of the Bureau and the military certainly helped, but there were not enough officials to go around. As H. B. Springfield, a member of the League clan in St. Clair County, wrote for his "Colored friends": "Becose we havent an agent to sea to us the people have been every since the surrender a cheating the darkey out of all that they can make there is not the 25 darkeys in this county that get his pay. . . . [The Bureau agent in] Taladega is two far and we cant write every time that we want assistance." In the hinterland, away from the Bureau and the military, planters abused freedmen, and there was little interference by local civil officials. Blacks clearly needed all the assistance they could get in conducting business with their former masters.[50]

Into this vacuum Republicans moved to help blacks deal with the white power structure. Often this meant corresponding with military officials to lobby for favorable treatment. Radical carpetbagger Joseph H. Speed, for example, repeatedly urged General Swayne to appoint a Bureau agent in Perry County, but his efforts were more far-reaching. Once he wrote the general that "there is another matter of which we spoke when I saw you last. The issuing of an order giving the freedmen a lien on the crop for their wages. *This is abso-*

49. G. Reese to Swayne, May 7, 1867, J. Tarbell to G. W. Corliss, August 15, 1868, Reynolds to Morgan, November 14, 1867, McGogy to Kinsman, June 22, 1867, G. A. Farrand to Pierce, December 2, 1867, all in Records, M809, RG 105.

50. Alf Turner *et al.* to Swayne, September 15, 1867, in Records, M809, RG 105; Mobile *Nationalist*, November 15, 1866, March 14, 1867.

lutely necessary. Many men are now driving freedmen away from their farms as the crop is made on mere pretexts. . . . [W]hen the order is issued let it give the freedmen *the same means of redress that is now given the landlord for rents by the statutes of Ala.*" More common still was the practice of helping individual laborers with business problems. In one Leaguer's words, "The freedmen here are without protection. Complaints come to me daily (being a northern man) in relation to their labors that their old masters are cheating them." Party leaders found their day-to-day activities absorbed by such issues.[51]

The organizers' involvement in agricultural matters led naturally to service as legal advisors. Since they were often the only literate individuals freedmen trusted, these leaders helped decipher contracts and other documents. They also corresponded with the Bureau and gave what help they could when blacks encountered the law. One indication of the importance of this role was the substantial number of activists who practiced law, many of whom served a black clientele. In Mobile, for example, George Harrington and W. W. D. Turner were bounty agents collecting for black veterans; they also figured conspicuously in civil rights litigation. These two "League lawyers" also were expected to give inexpensive legal aid when blacks ran afoul of the authorities. In Meridian, Mississippi, John R. Smith organized a League at the very time he apparently represented numbers of defrauded black laborers. "A lawyer named Smith" conducted suits for them on contingency at low fees, and "in a great number of cases . . . succeeded in getting their pay," according to a Bureau report. Freedmen's satisfaction with his performance probably encouraged them to accept his political leadership.[52]

Even individuals without legal training gave what advice they could. Organizers pored over contracts and other materials as a regular part of their political leadership. One Republican wrote that freedmen looked upon him as a friend; they "frequently come to my office, and meet me when attending their sick as a physician, and insist on my looking over their 'papers' to advise them what to do. In

51. J. H. Speed to Swayne, September 1, 1867, A. B. Collins to Pope, October 18, 1867, both in Records, M809, RG 105.

52. Sunderland to Preston, February 2, 1867, in Letters Sent SAC Meridian, Vol. 199, RG 105; Mobile *Register*, July 25, 1869.

many cases they have been badly swindled." He further observed that lawyers declined such cases without cash in hand, which none of the freedmen had, so the responsibility fell to him to do whatever was possible. D. H. Bingham also undertook this kind of paralegal intervention, and though he was not a lawyer, he continually involved himself in the freedmen's complaints. In one instance, Bingham wrote a letter for a freedman and signed the man's name, informing the employer that "under legal advice" the freedman would resist eviction; Bingham then reported the case to the Bureau. This League activist demonstrated acute sensitivity to the problems of agricultural laborers. In August, 1867, he wrote General Swayne that after voter registration, planters began "discharging and driving off hands who have contracts to work for a part of the crop, for the express purpose of getting their interest in the crop for a mere trifle, and to force the negro to vote in accordance with their wishes." He also complained that planters were fleecing freedmen in their accounting of supplies provided on credit. Organizers such as Bingham, by the very nature of their role, became familiar with a variety of freedmen's economic and legal needs. League leaders, especially those who were white, mediated between newly emancipated freedmen and a hostile power structure.[53]

The conduct of Daniel Price of Sumter County, Alabama, illustrated these wider aspects of League leadership. This schoolteacher became involved in the blacks' agricultural affairs, acting as something of an ombudsman for the freedmen. Price corresponded with the authorities on unjust crop settlements and other grievances. He wrote to the Bureau that local tax collectors harassed blacks who rented land and farmed on their own. Price also directly lobbied officeholders when necessary. In one case, a woman was assaulted and her husband driven off a plantation without pay, and Price intervened when the nominally Republican probate judge recommended letting the matter drop. Only a "good deal of persuasion" from Price induced the judge to bring charges. Even when the Klan

53. G. W. Graves to Swayne, August 10, 1867, in Letters Received SAC Demopolis, Box 27, RG 105; Burnet Houston to G. S. Houston, August 7, 1867, in George Smith Houston Papers, William R. Perkins Library, Duke University, Durham; D. Bingham to Swayne, August 7, 1867, in Swayne Papers, ADAH.

drove Price into exile, his interest in the freedmen's economic wel-
fare did not flag. He wrote his old comrades that wages were higher
and repression less intense across the Mississippi line. He urged
them to join him in Meridian, and some four hundred reportedly
took his advice. Price's League activities led him to perform often on
behalf of the freedmen, and he tried to increase their freedom from
planter domination.[54]

Of course, once League activists were installed in local offices,
they were in an even better position to aid their constituents. Their
help was badly needed, especially after the expiration of the Freedmen's Bureau in late 1868. For example, William Miller of Eutaw,
Alabama, reported that after being elected probate judge, he was
"utterly overrun" with freedmen's troubles. He was doing his best to
help, but many had signed such poor agreements that it would ruin
the freedmen to adhere to the terms. Probate Judge W. T. Blackford
performed the same sort of service in Hale County. He had the
freedmen bring their contracts to his office for review. Similarly,
Daniel Price increased blacks' access to the legal system, once he was
elected circuit court clerk. One observer stated that he was the only
man in Sumter County bold enough to serve court documents
"when justice demands it." Of course, the capacity of local officeholders to impanel jurors, collect taxes, and enforce the law were
just a few of the ways in which sympathetic officials could be of
use.[55]

Some League activists took on a quasi-judicial role themselves,
mediating disputes among the freedmen. Distrusting the courts,
freedmen sometimes chose to use their councils as an informal alternative. In Choctaw County, Alabama, the head of the local League
reportedly was "taking charge of the effects and administering to the
estates" of deceased Leaguers. Across the state in Bullock County,

---

54. Price to Pierce, June 10, April 28, 1868, both in Letters Received SAC Demopolis, Box
27, RG 105; KKK Report, XI, 111. For other examples of Price's work on behalf of the
freedmen, see Adam Dawson to Pierce [in Price's handwriting], December 5, 1867, Price to
Pierce, April 13, 1868, both in Letters Received SAC Demopolis, Box 27, RG 105; Price to
Smith, October 7, 1868, in Gov. Smith Papers, ADAH; and Livingston *Journal*, July 17, 1868.

55. W. Miller to Wilson, November 24, 1868, in Letters Received SAC Demopolis, Box
27, RG 105; KKK Report, X, 1494; [?] to Harris, June 30, 1868, in Letters Sent SAC
Demopolis, Vol. 140, RG 105.

TABLE I
White League Activists' Postwar Employment, Alabama

Occupation	Number	Percentage
Bureau employee	26	16.4%
Planter	22	13.8
Lawyer	20	12.6
State or local officeholder	16	10.1
Schoolteacher	15	9.4
Doctor or surgeon	12	7.5
Federal officeholder or employee	11	6.9
Merchant or storekeeper	7	4.4
Minister or missionary	6	3.8
Editor	5	3.1
Blacksmith	4	2.5
Farmer	4	2.5
Claims agent	2	1.3
Law enforcement	2	1.3
Printer	2	1.3
Banker	1	0.6
Plantation purchase agent	1	0.6
Principal of college	1	0.6
Resort keeper	1	0.6
Shoemaker	1	0.6

SOURCES: Data base compiled from the partisan press, various congressional investigations, Bureau documents, and private correspondence.

NOTES: In this and the following tables, each individual was counted once for every category of occupation held during the period. The vast majority of activists, however, were counted as having no more than two professions. The total number was 176, the number with known occupations was 113, and the total number of reported occupations was 159. Although the activities of some few may be distorted, the basic trend is probably accurate, especially among whites where the evidence is more plentiful. It should also be pointed out that the documentation is substantially better in Alabama than in Mississippi for both white and black activists.

TABLE 2

White League Activists' Postwar Employment, Mississippi

Occupation	Number	Percentage
Planter	9	18.4%
State or local officeholder	8	16.3
Lawyer	7	14.3
Schoolteacher	6	12.2
Bureau employee	5	10.2
Doctor	3	6.1
Federal employee or officeholder	2	4.1
Mechanic	2	4.1
Merchant	2	4.1
Claims agent	1	2.0
Druggist	1	2.0
Overseer or foreman	1	2.0
Minister	1	2.0
Farmer	1	2.0

SOURCES: See Table 1.
NOTES: The total number was 58, the number with known occupations was 36, and the total number of reported occupations was 49.

the leagues apparently held criminal trials complete with punishment. But the activists' role as legal advisors was the most typical and significant, whether they were in or out of office. Organizers counseled freedmen on agricultural matters and assisted them in their litigation. In practical terms an essential feature of League activity, the assistance provided the cement holding the movement together, binding the largely white leadership to the black mass base.[56]

The occupational backgrounds of the activists suggest they possessed skills, power, and resources that freedmen needed. In Alabama, for example, white League organizers had an array of useful abilities. Lawyers, Bureau officials, and other federal employees were leading categories; all could do legal work, and they often had

56. Montgomery *Mail*, December 27, 1867.

influence through official positions as well. Schoolteachers, like Daniel Price, were literate and had other attributes freedmen could use to advantage. Even planters, another significant category, bore a clear relation to blacks' aspirations for agricultural autonomy. The situation was broadly similar among Mississippi's white League activists: planters, lawyers, schoolteachers, and Bureau employees composed the bulk of the individuals with known occupations.

TABLE 3
Black League Activists' Postwar Employment,
Alabama

Occupation	Number	Percentage
Minister or preacher	10	21.3%
All Agriculture (6 farmers, 3 laborers)	9	19.1
All Trades (2 carpenters, 2 shoemakers, 2 tailors, 1 blacksmith, and 1 house builder)	8	17.0
Schoolteacher	6	12.8
Barber	5	10.6
Employees of Mobile *Nationalist*	4	8.5
Storekeeper	3	6.4
Cotton sampler	1	2.1
Musician	1	2.1

SOURCES: See Table 1.
NOTES: The total number was 81, the number with known occupations was 36, and the total number of reported occupations was 47. Difficulties exist in the economic data on black leaders. For example, "minister or preacher" as an occupational category is problematic. Many of these men were local exhorters without an established church; they often derived little or none of their income from their religious calling. Even so, this description does indicate their primary position in the black community, and is thus useful as a means of assessing the nature of their leadership.

TABLE 4
Black League Activists'
Postwar Employment, Mississippi

Occupation	Number	Percentage
Minister or preacher	7	35.0%
Schoolteacher	3	15.0
Lawyer	2	10.0
Barber	1	5.0
Blacksmith	1	5.0
Employee of Mobile *Nationalist*	1	5.0
Gin worker	1	5.0
Merchant or storekeeper	1	5.0
Photographer	1	5.0
Railroad worker	1	5.0
Republican Congressional Committee agent	1	5.0

SOURCES: See Table 1.
NOTES: The total number was 47, the number with known occupations was 16, and the total number of reported occupations was 20.

Noteworthy is the absence of organizers without special skills. Activists clustered in occupations the freedmen needed but could not yet provide for themselves.

Black activists, by contrast, were different. In both states they were largely preachers, teachers, tradesmen, farmers or farm laborers. Their role apparently did not depend as heavily on providing expertise, legal or otherwise. Many were in fact only becoming literate during the period; their leadership grew out of being liked or trusted by their neighbors. This pattern constituted a functional reason why so much of the League leadership was white: these activists' political role was largely service-oriented, and carpetbaggers and scalawags were in a position to be of use.

Overall, the evidence is clear that League organizers provided a host of services as part of their partisan leadership. The organizers furnished the outside assistance freedmen needed to counteract the planters' social influence. The Leaguers gave freedmen access to real power: at first with the Bureau and the military, later with the new Republican governments. If the League splintered into factions, and if the activists were sometimes self-serving, they did provide needed help at the local level. Thus councils often remained vital at the local level, long after the League disintegrated as a centralized political organization.

The freedmen, conscious of the limitations of their leaders, decided that the League activists merited support. From their point of view, the deficiencies of the organizers did not loom large. One·black activist in an Alabama Republican club made the logic of the situation explicit; Bill Sammons told freedmen that they must support the former Leaguer Charles Hays and other Republicans for reelection, for it made "no odds how much Mr. Hays steals or how much whisky Mr. Jones drinks." They were Republicans, and they were the "only men that sticks up for us, and tries to do us good." Unless the freedmen voted for them, warned Sammons, all was lost.[57] Given what the opposition had to offer, and also the services the leaders could provide, the choice was understandable.

57. *House Reports*, 43rd. Cong., 2nd Sess., No. 262, pp. 405–406.

FOUR

Freedmen and the Republican Ideology

The public discourse of the Union League reveals much about the movement's appeal to the freedmen. It is of course difficult to extract from written sources what nonliterate people thought, but examining the rhetoric that they found persuasive provides one line of approach. The explosive growth of the League itself indicates how attractive Radical polemics were to the freedmen. Black enthusiasm for the League resulted from a desire to preserve and extend their freedom; they thought that Reconstruction would guarantee liberty in quite practical terms. League organizers encouraged this belief, casting the Radical ideology in terms the former slaves found powerful. The League's articulation of the freedmen's desires in a culturally accessible fashion was an essential factor in the growth of the Republican party.

Radical political rhetoric was bound up with social conflict over the future of the plantation. Former slaves perceived that the agricultural regime resembled slavery and also that planters held fast to its repressive features. Freedmen viewed the League as a means of resisting the reconstitution of servitude. The movement developed out of a broad-gauged agrarian upsurge, and much of the League's discourse revolved around blacks' resentment toward the plantation system. The politics of dignity, access to land, and resistance to reenslavement propagated by the League all fit a single pattern: they enunciated a quest for greater autonomy incompatible with a coercive labor system modeled on plantation slavery. The ideas of the League insurgency were a partly symbolic expression of blacks' desires for basic changes in agriculture—and in particular of their revulsion against authoritarian plantation management. Agrarian revolt found ideological expression in this reformulation of the antebellum "Free Labor" creed.

In order to discuss what the League's appeal to the freedmen was, we must first emphasize what it was not. The older view, associated with the Dunning interpretation of Reconstruction, stressed the League's clandestine character. The organization's secret ritual was seen as luring the superstitious former slaves through their love of "midnight mummery." Weird initiation ceremonies, in Fleming's words, made the freedman "feel fearfully good from his head to his toes." But the blatantly partisan nature of the League's ritual undermines this elitist view. The political overtones of League meetings were quite evident, and freedmen certainly realized that the movement supported Reconstruction. The ceremonial aspects of the order may have piqued some freedmen's interest, but they all understood that the goal was to help the Radicals and secure black uplift generally.[1]

In some respects, the ritual associated with council meetings was typical of the ceremonials of other secret orders. It resembled that of the Masons, from which it clearly derived; like those of many fraternal organizations, it extolled civic virtue, universal brotherhood, and other worthy causes. The League differed from these other organizations, however, in its being overtly partisan. Meetings were intended both to impress and to indoctrinate the freedmen. For example, present on the model podium were to be symbolic representations of Republican liberty, which included an altar, a Bible, the Declaration of Independence, a flag, a censer, a sword, a gavel, and a ballot box. Also present were to be a sickle, a shuttle, an anvil, and other emblems of industry. Initiations were solemnly pretentious, often subjecting the prospective Leaguer to a sermon on the merits of liberty and nation. The organization proclaimed its goals to be preserving

1. Fleming, *Civil War and Reconstruction in Alabama*, 559–60.

the Constitution, maintaining the Union, safeguarding loyalists, and securing the elevation of the laboring man. The catechistic function of the League ritual was overt, and it was clearly intended to inculcate Republican beliefs in the audience.[2]

The oath taken by initiates was straightforward, and it indicates much about blacks' motivations in joining. The new member pledged to do all in his power to "elect true and reliable Union men and supporters of the government, and none others, to all offices of profit and trust." Initiates obligated themselves to protect and defend worthy members of the League, and never to divulge League proceedings to outsiders. Associated with the oath were passwords and hand signals called the Four L's—Liberty, Lincoln, Loyal, and League were the code words. Planter sources depict the freedmen refusing to divulge these secrets under pain of death, the argument being that the League vow of silence was enforced by threat. This may often have been an excuse for withholding information from inquisitive whites, yet it seems clear that freedmen took the oath with some seriousness. In Fleming's words, "After passing through the ordeal, the negro usually remained faithful."[3]

The freedmen's political intentions in entering the League appear evident, since they could hardly have failed to recognize that joining would antagonize their employers. It would have been foolish indeed to risk reprisals for a simple social club. Moreover, the characteristic decentralized development of the League would have been impossible if the freedmen had not grasped its basic goals. The nature of this structure was shown by the instructions the Alabama State Council issued to organizers. "When you desire to establish a council of the U. L. A. at any point," advised the League, "go there or send an assistant. Assemble nine or more loyal men, explain to them the objects, and, as far as you think proper, the principles of the Union League of America." The members would elect officers after their initiation, and the new council would act autonomously from then on. The belief was that the mass of freedmen had some idea of the League's aims, and agreed with them sufficiently so as to need little

2. *Ibid.*, 561.
3. *Ibid*; Fleming (ed.), *Documentary History of Reconstruction*, II, 12.

outside direction. The organizers' confidence in the political acumen and Radical inclinations of the former slaves proved well placed.[4]

The evidence indicates that freedmen basically understood the League's objectives. For example, a rank-and-file League member, testifying before a congressional subcommittee, related detailed information about Radical activity in north Alabama, but could remember almost nothing of the League's ceremonies. He recalled simply that he and his comrades swore to vote Republican, but "not without they wanted to." Conservative sources admitted occasionally that the freedmen knew what they were doing. One Democrat called them willing agents of the Radicals, carried away with the grandeur of a one-forty-millionth part of governing the nation. A northern traveler reported similar enthusiasm when he asked a rural laborer near Montgomery how he had voted. "Voted for mass' Mc Leod, an' de 'Publican party, and the United States, an' de Congress," his respondent replied. The northerner observed that he was "constantly astonished at the quickness with which the freedmen pick up the catch-words and slang of politics. . . . I hazard little in saying that, in these matters, they are apter than any class of whites."[5]

The motivations were largely political, but they were a bit nebulous. Most freedmen initially held only indistinct notions of what the Reconstruction Acts meant. Explaining the enactments was the first order of business for the leagues, and the local councils never entirely lost this pedagogic function. Reading Radical newspapers aloud was a mainstay at League meetings. Suffrage itself was something of a mystery to the former slaves. Freedmen joined the League more to further black progress than to engage in the specific job of electing candidates. The politicization of the freedmen grew directly out of the crisis of production in the countryside, and it reflected acute anxiety over their emerging status. The League mobilization was thus political in the widest sense: it channeled a collective aspiration to restructure the contours of black life starting with

4. Walter Lynwood Fleming, *The Union League of America*, Documents Relating to Reconstruction, No. 4 (Morgantown, W.Va., 1904), 15.
5. KKK Report, VIII, 864; Stephen Powers, *Afoot and Alone: A Walk from Sea to Sea by the Southern Route* . . . (Hartford, 1871), 67. Powers apparently visited Montgomery in 1867.

agricultural labor. Basic issues of power on the plantations were involved in the Radical movement, and these illustrated the interconnection between political insurgency and labor concerns in League-sponsored mass activity.

Prospective land redistribution has often been described as a central part of the League's appeal to freedmen. Fleming and other historians of the Dunning school stressed this concept in their various state studies; many post–World War II revisionists agreed, but emphasized that demands for confiscation were positive and reasonable. An evaluation of the actual evidence, however, reveals this often-made claim to be a half-truth. Tremendous interest existed among freedmen in confiscation, but the leagues were not the source of this agitation, at least not in Alabama and Mississippi. Dissatisfaction with agriculture certainly underlay blacks' enthusiasm for Radical rhetoric, but their aspirations went beyond land redistribution.

Freedmen certainly would have liked to receive land as a result of Military Reconstruction, and many hoped at first that Radical governments would pursue such a policy, but League organizers soft-pedaled the issue. The League hierarchy was strongly influenced by congressional leaders who, after initial hesitation, decided that talk of confiscation hurt them with the northern electorate. The emphasis on land redistribution in the historical literature on the League oversimplifies a more complex set of issues. The freedmen's desire for forty acres and a mule extended to any sort of access to land, including rental or purchase. Former slaves wanted to farm, without white oversight, in any way they could. This larger question was central to the League's appeal to the freedmen. What planters identified as a League-inspired goal of confiscation was actually a ground swell of revulsion against prevailing agricultural practices, as well as a desire for any kind of independent farming. An exclusive stress on land redistribution thus clouds the actual social process that the leagues encouraged: the breakdown of centrally directed plantation management, largely in response to labor unrest.

Emphasis on the League's alleged advocacy of confiscation began as part of the Democratic attack on the Republican party. Much of the press denounced the leagues on this basis. Thus the Vicksburg

Times commented that for three successive Januaries, freedmen had looked for the land promised by "old Mygatt, and the loyal league villains." A journalist in Montgomery reported that all Leaguers were assured they would receive a grant of confiscated land. Another correspondent stated that Thaddeus Stevens' confiscation speeches were being read aloud at League gatherings. Such assertions were prevalent in the Democratic press, and for years "forty acres and a mule" remained an abiding feature of Conservative political discourse. Even as late as 1869, the Mississippi leagues were alleged to be circulating membership cards that entitled freedmen to share in land redistribution.[6]

That these claims were widely credited by planters is indicated by their private correspondence. An Alabama planter was so unnerved by his field hands' talk of land redistribution that he contemplated leaving for California. Another thought that "every negro would vote for such a proposition." George Haywood, from the Alabama plantation belt, wrote that "the blacks all want land, dont wish to leave here & hope to get it by confiscation, but I will not write more on any such unpleasant subject as this the condition of the Southern States." A Mississippi planter found his worst fears confirmed by a discussion with one of his leading hands. The man assured him that all the freedmen believed that the Radicals, once safely in power, would issue them land and provisions. One observer summed up the prevalent southern view, claiming that the freedmen clung to a belief in land redistribution, despite the disappointments they had experienced.[7]

Many planters also thought that the Leaguers were conspiring to appropriate land and other property by force. Despite the paucity of evidence of any such intent, southern whites often discussed the possibility of an insurrection, perhaps under Radical guidance.

6. Vicksburg *Times*, January 5, 1868; Talladega *Watchtower*, June 19, 1867, quoting Washington *Intelligencer*; Mobile *Advertiser and Register*, June 22, 1867; Mobile *Register*, November 5, 1869.

7. J. Parrish to H. Watson, August 6, 1867, A. Bruners to S. Watson, September 3, 1867, both in Henry Watson, Jr., Papers, William R. Perkins Library, Duke University, Durham; G. W. Haywood to Ernest Haywood, May 21, 1867, in Ernest Haywood Papers, UNC; Susan Sillers Darden Diary, June 25, 1868 (MS in MDAH); S. Matthews to J. Matthews, September 19, 1867, in S. Matthews Papers, MDAH.

Some landowners were so disturbed by the threat—as well as by that of confiscation—that they joined the leagues themselves to prove their loyalty or to find out what was going on. The belief in a black attempt to seize lands at Christmas, 1867, was reported across the region. In Mississippi these rumors seemed so threatening that they alarmed civil and military officials. The gravity of these fears was well illustrated by the panic such reports evoked.

Late in 1867, commanding general E. O. C. Ord began receiving reports of possible uprisings from various portions of Mississippi; the harvest of that year had been a disaster, and many planters feared any signs of black restiveness. From Meridian and Marion came newspaper reports of League raids on merchants, or of conspiracies to the same end. A judge in Hinds County wrote Ord that unmistakable proof existed that freedmen intended a racial war. The local "Black Club" was engaged in various plots, including organized depredations upon planters' livestock, and they were ultimately planning to commandeer plantations throughout the region. The freedmen were "hoping that Congress will arrange a plan of division and distribution, but unless they find this done by January next they will proceed to help themself." In response, Ord sent a Bureau agent, who found nothing amiss, but the profusion of such accounts convinced the general that the state stood on the brink of massive bloodshed. "From all sides," Ord noted, "appeals reach me for troops to protect the whites." He concluded that the freedmen must be disarmed.[8]

Ord issued a proclamation accusing outside agitators of fomenting rebellion among the freedmen, and he urged the (white) citizenry to increased vigilance. The general also ordered military personnel to "arrest promptly all incendiaries, regardless of party or position." Ord explicitly stated that his soldiers would kill blacks attempting to occupy planters' property. He thought the situation so grave that he telegraphed General Grant in Washington of impending danger, warning that the freedmen would try to take whatever they wanted. This message proved to be Ord's undoing. When nothing of the sort

8. Meridian *Gazette*, December 4, 1867; A. L. Dabney to Ord, November 13, 1867, H. R. Williams to M. Barber, December 29, 1867, both in Records, M826, RG 105; Ord to Grant, December 7, 1867, in Registers and Letters, M752, RG 105.

actually transpired, the general asked to be relieved of command and was replaced by Gillem. The point, however, is that such fears appeared plausible to normally responsible men.[9]

Conservative whites recognized that freedmen desired confiscation, and they blamed outside troublemakers for encouraging this hope. Planters also feared that the leagues incited extralegal land seizures. These concerns were understandable; given that some congressional Republicans were openly discussing confiscation, the widespread conviction that Leaguers propagated that sort of talk was natural. But the question remains of the truth of such beliefs. Were Radicals actually promising confiscation, or leading freedmen to believe that it would occur? Did freedmen join the organization expecting to receive land? The data preclude a simple answer. Many freedmen hoped for land redistribution, and some entered the League with this in mind, but local councils seldom encouraged such expectations. Confiscation was not generally promised to members, nor were they prodded to take direct action through the local organizations.

One point about the League and the confiscation issue is clear: despite the prevalence of reported attempts at seizing lands, few if any such accounts are verifiable. Leagues often participated in mass actions—sometimes quite militant ones—but these had to do with self-defense or involved issues other than land. After all, permanent possession of land by force is not easily attained, and the freedmen had little wish to confront Yankee troops in battle. Not a single authenticated seizure of planters' lands by the League occurred in either Alabama or Mississippi, and even Conservatives were likely to treat such tales with skepticism. At the height of the insurrection scare, Governor Benjamin Humphreys of Mississippi wrote Ord: "I cannot believe that conspiracies to any extent exist at this time. . . . Some negroes in every portion of the state believe these promises [of confiscation] will yet be complied with. And some may be so foolish as to threaten 'to go to war . . . ' but I doubt whether any considerable number entertain such sentiments—they rely more upon the ballot box, than by the cartridge box and may be conspiring to make

9. Jackson *Clarion*, December 24, 1867; Ord to Grant, n.d., in Ord Papers, UC Berkeley.

their power tell in that way." Humphreys' judicious observation applies equally well to both states. In spite of all the press speculation, freedmen did little to initiate conflict.[10]

If freedmen did not intend to rise en masse to gain land, planters did have reason for concern. Given the talk of land redistribution, and the freedmen's obvious dissatisfaction with agricultural practices, landowners naturally read blacks' unaccustomed behavior as presaging revolt. Moreover, many freedmen still hoped for confiscation, as was understandable in view of the earlier rumors that the government would issue forty acres and a mule at Christmas, 1865. After all, the Freedmen's Bureau actually promised land to freedmen for several months after the war ended. It was to be expected that some blacks remembered the idea long after, and persuasive evidence exists that many desired confiscation under Radical rule. For example, an Alabama Bureau agent reported from the cotton belt that the freedmen did not intend a racial war and bore no ill-will toward their former masters; however, they still hoped "something may turn up that they may be apportioned 40 acr[e]s land mule & c." A Radical leader wrote Swayne, asking for information about federal homestead legislation, commenting that he needed to placate his followers who still wanted their land and mules. One League member and planter attested to such hopes in a particularly striking fashion. S. Hillyer asked the Alabama Bureau for advice about the confiscation rumors rampant among the freedmen in his area. His employees were refusing to contract for another year, giving as their reason that they were finally going to receive farms. Hillyer wrote, "Of course if any good is to befall them I would not have the fact of it kept back nor object to their having it." This Leaguer thus confirmed the prevalence of confiscation talk, for he half believed the rumors himself.[11]

There are also indications that some Radical leaders, especially in isolated areas, were leading blacks to believe in the possibility of confiscation. Peres Bonney of Pike County, Mississippi, was said to have made such pledges while running for election to the constitu-

10. B. Humphreys to Ord, November 26, 1867, in Ord Papers, UC Berkeley.
11. William S. McFeely, *Yankee Stepfather*, 97–98; D. J. Fraser to G. Sharkey, January 14, 1868, in Letters Received SAC Selma, Box 36, RG 105; P. Jones to Swayne, July 8, 1867, in Records, M809, RG 105; S. Hillyer to Pierce, January 5, 1868, in Letters Received SAC Demopolis, Box 27, RG 105.

tional convention. According to his opponents, Bonney's later defeat for higher office resulted from disillusionment with those unfulfilled pledges. C. P. Simmons supposedly won election to the Alabama Constitutional Convention on the strength of the same promise. Some important League leaders also talked about confiscation favorably in private. Future Alabama congressman C. W. Buckley thought such measures appropriate as early as 1865, but political ambitions later seem to have moderated his stand. Mississippi's Jonathan Tarbell thought the Rebels deserved the worst that Thaddeus Stevens would inflict upon them. Some Radical leaders made such statements openly; for example, future congressman Robert S. Heflin of Alabama flirted with advocacy of land redistribution just after passage of the Reconstruction Acts. Military officials asked the Bureau agent in his area to investigate reports that Heflin was plotting insurrection. The Bureau man denied the rumor in the following terms: "I have no hesitation in saying that the fears . . . are groundless. It is true that Judge R. S. Heflin sometimes makes speeches to the freedmen, and also participated in the organization of Union Leagues, and that he is in favor of confiscation; but it is not true that he induces the freedmen to believe that the rebels property will be confiscated and divided among the freedmen. He only says that it ought to be done." The agent apparently had second thoughts about sending this description of Heflin's activity to Swayne. He crossed out the final line, replacing it with the comment that he had never known Heflin to make an inflammatory speech.[12]

But if some few Leaguers urged or promised confiscation, the organization as a whole did not. Leading spokesmen refrained from making land redistribution a major component of their speeches. Many activists disavowed the concept, suggesting that blacks' desire for land would be met in other ways. The League's public rejection of confiscation was so forthright that it seems unlikely that most freedmen joined the League in hopes of land redistribution. The League hierarchy so muted the whole issue, in fact, that such promises were only an occasional feature of League rhetoric. Much of the

12. Jackson *Clarion*, June 4, 1868; Eliza McNabb to Ott, August 2, 1868, in Eliza McNabb Letters, MDAH; Russell to Smith, October 19, 1867, in Swayne Papers, ADAH; Philadelphia *Inquirer*, June 17, 1865; Tarbell to Ord, July 20, 1867, in Ord Papers, UC Berkeley; R. T. Smith to Kinsman, June 19, 1867, in Letters Sent SAC Opelika, Vol. 133, RG 105.

reason for this cautious approach lay in Washington. The National Council and its president James M. Edmunds stood close to moderate Republicans in Congress, and not to Stevens, Sumner, and other Radical proponents of land redistribution. Centrist Republicans, after all, bankrolled the organizing campaign through the Union Republican Congressional Executive Committee, and Edmunds and his fellow Leaguers naturally followed the judgment of their backers on the political situation. Senator Henry Wilson of Massachusetts, one of the most powerful men in Congress, epitomized the mainstream Republican view. During his southern speaking tour in the spring of 1867, he declared that confiscation was not contemplated and that only if the former Confederates sabotaged the Reconstruction Acts could it ever happen. Wilson hoped thereby to gain planter accessions to the Republican party. The League publication, the *Great Republic*, adopted precisely this line and promised that white participation in Reconstruction would forestall confiscation. Even this tentative use of the issue disappeared after a few weeks, for it became clear by early summer that the northern electorate rejected such measures. The National Council began denouncing the idea in any form and denying that its members had ever considered confiscation a real possibility.[13]

League leaders at the state level demonstrated similar caution. This is hardly surprising, given their extreme dependence on outside support. Money, patronage, and other aid were essential to the very survival of the fledgling party. Southern Republicans solicited the views of their congressional allies and, as a result, responded quickly to national trends. In April, 1867, for example, the Alabama State Council adopted resolutions similar to the views then prevalent in Washington: "If the pacification now proposed by Congress be not accepted in good faith by those who staked and forfeited 'their lives, their fortunes, and their sacred honor' in rebellion, it will be the duty of Congress to enforce that forfeiture by the confiscation of lands, at least, of such a stiff-necked and rebellious people." This statement— barely within the accepted boundaries—was as close to endorsing

---

13. Benedict, *A Compromise of Principle*, 257–62; Washington *Great Republic*, June 20, 1867; David Montgomery, *Beyond Equality: Labor and the Radical Republicans* (New York, 1967), 335–86.

confiscation as the League ever came, in either Alabama or Mississippi. When the northern situation became more sharply defined, even this kind of statement grew rare.[14]

By summer, League leaders distanced themselves from the land redistribution issue. If Congress opposed confiscation, then responsible activists recognized that further agitation would only hurt the Republican party among the freedmen. Furthermore, several League leaders, black and white, received financial assistance from the URCEC, a factor that likely moderated their utterances on this critical issue. For example, Keffer repeatedly denounced confiscation. Freedmen would earn their homes by hard work, he intoned, and expecting to get them any other way was folly. Albert Griffin's *Nationalist* was the most fervent Radical sheet in Alabama, but he editorialized against such hopes. "We have always opposed confiscation," the paper stated, "and until lately did not imagine that it ever would be advocated by any considerable number of men." Traveling organizer Thomas W. Conway told thousands of freedmen throughout both states that confiscation would never occur and that they should look to helping themselves by means of their own exertions.[15]

Black spokesmen pursued a similar course, often seeming more willing than were white leaders to disavow confiscation. John Mercer Langston addressed League gatherings often during his tours with the Bureau's Education Division. In Natchez he told his audience that they should have farms but only earned by their own toil and economy. The government would not issue them land. The leading black politician in Mississippi, James Lynch, denounced confiscation, in keeping with his moderate stance, and Alabama's black Leaguers took an identical position. L. S. Berry of Mobile declared that he was as opposed to confiscation as was any Rebel, and Holland Thompson of Montgomery spoke similarly. The militant L. S. Speed of Bullock County "neither favored nor desired confiscation, but advised the colored people to buy their land and pay for it that they might enjoy it in peace." W. V. Turner of Wetumpka also dis-

14. New York *Tribune*, April 10, 1867.

15. KKK Report, X, 1713; Mobile *Nationalist*, June 20, April 4, 1867. The Montgomery *State Sentinel* (January 9, 29, 1868) represented the sole exception in the region's Republican press. Before the February, 1868, elections, the paper again called for confiscation of lands that belonged to planters who economically coerced voters.

avowed the goal of dragging whites into poverty; he merely wished that blacks be permitted to move upwards too.[16]

This restraint was virtually universal among black leaders who made public statements on the matter. Only one prominent black leader in either state appears to have called for confiscation, Matthew T. Newsome of Mississippi, and he is not known to have been a League member. It is of course possible that some of these leaders talked differently in secret council gatherings, but if they did so, no evidence exists. Many activists were engaged in factional struggles for supremacy in their councils, and if confiscation was a critical goal, someone would likely voice it publicly. Yet nothing of the sort occurred. This very absence undermines the argument that confiscation was the central League demand. Had land redistribution been the cry of the rank and file, black leaders would have been saying so, given the organization's democratic internal structure.[17]

This was demonstrated clearly at the Mobile Freedmen's Convention in early May, 1867. One of the first and most influential black meetings after the beginning of Military Reconstruction, the convention was called to endorse the Republican party, and it attracted delegates from all over Alabama. White Republicans went to great lengths to ensure politically expedient resolutions. The National Council's Conway spoke, and Albert Griffin also received an invitation to address the freedmen. Griffin told the delegates he opposed confiscation, but if the Rebels adopted a "vote as I say or starve" policy, a different course would become appropriate. The resolutions adopted by the freedmen showed the results of such advice. Along with praising the growth of the Union League, the delegates resolved: "That in the event of the threatened discharge of colored people from their places of employment throughout the State, because of their unwillingness to become the political tools of their employers we will . . . demand . . . further legislation looking to the punishment of treason, as the necessities of the end may demand, even to the confiscation of the property of the guilty." The distinct

16. Natchez *Democrat*, July 6, 1867; Panola *Star*, October 5, 1867; Montgomery *State Sentinel*, July 23, 1867; Connolly to Smith, August 8, 1867, in Records, M809, RG 105; Montgomery *State Sentinel*, May 15, 1867.

17. Harris, *The Day of the Carpetbagger*, 104.

implication was that if the planters behaved themselves, they could keep their lands. Certainly the Republican leadership lobbied the freedmen to adopt this position, but the important point here is that they seem to have done so without much opposition. As the delegates scattered throughout the state they generally used this exact formulation in their respective local leagues.[18]

The overemphasis on confiscation is clear if we examine those few leagues that actually called for such measures. The members were mostly native white yeomen, not freedmen. A League leader from one up-country area wrote, "The people here are generally in favor of Congress, and are in for a confiscation of the property of the secessionists." The promise of land redistribution, he added, also won support from lukewarm former Rebels. Another Leaguer reported that some poor whites were dissatisfied with Reconstruction because it did not include the confiscation of land, and similar reports appeared in the press. In the words of future senator Spencer, "Winston, Walker, Fayette, Franklin, Blount, Marshall, De Kalb, Jefferson, and Morgan [counties] are almost unanimously in favor of Stevens' confiscation policy. This Congressional District would give a five thousand majority for his policy." These counties were overwhelmingly white. Such open assertions by yeoman Unionists did not emanate from the League's black councils.[19]

In sum, the whole confiscation issue has been overblown—at least in Alabama and Mississippi—as far as the Union League is concerned. The League did not promise the freedmen land, and it certainly did not encourage the freedmen to seize acreage by force. The Dunning school's depiction of confiscation as central to the League's appeal is misplaced, for the League downplayed it as a political demand. Freedmen certainly wanted land, and their restiveness worked major changes in plantation agriculture. But the reason for their new militancy was not a League pledge of forty acres and a mule. Rather, they were dissatisfied with the legacy of slavery on the plantation, and they were determined to achieve greater autonomy

18. Washington *Great Republic*, May 5, July 26, 1867; Mobile *Nationalist*, May 9, 1867.

19. W. T. Stubblefield to Smith, June 20, 1867, in Swayne Papers, ADAH; T. M. Peters to R. M. Patton, August 29, 1867, in Gov. Patton Papers, ADAH; Montgomery *State Sentinel*, August 24, 1867; Spencer to Keffer, July 12, 1867, in Swayne Papers, ADAH.

through collective effort. Emphasis on confiscation as the major issue for blacks oversimplifies a broader revolt against the coerciveness of postbellum agriculture.

Freedmen's motives for joining the League rested less upon hopes of possible confiscation than upon immediate responses to the rhetoric of citizenship and equality. Emancipation so pleased them that they needed little persuasion to vote for the party of freedom and Union. Radical discourse tapped the democratic impulse extant in black religious and community life. The appeal for black advancement took various forms, but consistently the goal was to preserve and extend freedom. Symbolic assertions of equal rights evoked strong reactions in people who recently had been slaves. The trauma of their shared past provided impetus for political action, as well as an obvious goal around which to coalesce. Freedmen responded to the League because it addressed their aversion to slavery and contrasted future autonomy with past subordination.[20]

Given this vital feature of black motivation, it scarcely comes as a shock that much of Reconstruction Era politics revolved around freedom, if somewhat indirectly. An excellent illustration was the freedmen's support for public education. Educational opportunities obviously benefited former slaves, for whom reading and ciphering were practical necessities. But learning had an emotional appeal too. In W. E. B. Du Bois's words, the very "feeling of inferiority which slavery forced upon them fathered an intense desire to rise out of their condition by means of education." Even Fleming agreed with this assessment, seeing the lure of formerly forbidden privileges as an incentive for school attendance. This was not emulation of white practices for their own sake. Freedmen saw ignorance as part of their former servitude and embraced knowledge as the badge of freedom. In this, as in other aspects of their behavior, blacks enjoyed their new rights and opposed the survival of even the symbols of slavery.[21]

Blacks' mass actions during Reconstruction were also assertions of

20. Many historians have seen aversion to the practices of slavery as a central feature of the freedmen's motivation. See, for example, Kolchin, *First Freedom*, xix; Ransom and Sutch, *One Kind of Freedom*, 65–66; and Roark, *Masters Without Slaves*, 142.

21. Du Bois, *Black Reconstruction*, 638; Fleming, *Civil War and Reconstruction in Alabama*, 458.

self-respect. Councils in Mobile, for instance, confronted whites about the city's segregated streetcar lines, a surprising move since few freedmen could afford to use the system often. Anything suggesting subordination was freighted with memories of slavery, and matters of racial etiquette became politically charged. Henry W. Barry of Mississippi reportedly told Leaguers "never to take off their hat to a white man." After the League spread through the countryside, freedmen seemed to become much less deferential. For example, in Sumter County, Alabama, a planter reported that bad feeling arose as soon as the leagues were created. Freedmen stopped moving off the sidewalks to allow whites to pass. Subtle changes in conduct had explosive implications. After one such occurrence, a melee broke out in Auburn, Alabama, when a college student clubbed a freedman with a fence post.[22]

Much of the "sass" or demoralization reported of the blacks was precisely an assertion of equality. Freedmen flaunted their altered status before their former masters. No other interpretation is possible of such conduct as one planter described: "At night they would pass, talking not only loudly but almost menacingly. Women and children were alarmed. I have known colored men to stand right in front of my house and shoot in the direction of the house at a mocking bird in a tree. These men were all connected with what was called the Union Leagues or Loyal Leagues, and they were all armed. . . . I have heard these parties, when passing my house at night, denounce me in very strong terms." Such behavior afforded freedmen a great deal of gratification. League leader G. W. Albright recalled with pleasure, even fifty years later, how much black militia drills had infuriated planters. The prevalent practice of bringing guns to League meetings, even before the Klan arose, suggests that this attitude was widespread. The freedmen's publicly brandishing firearms became an important sign of emancipation.[23]

The assertiveness in the face of prevailing norms, the studied

22. [?] to Ord, December 11, 1867, in Records of the Fourth Military District, Department of Civil Affairs, Box 1, Pt. 1, RG 393; *Monroe Eagle* (Claiborne, Ala.), October 22, 1869; John L. Hunnicutt, *Reconstruction in West Alabama: The Memoirs of John L. Hunnicutt*, ed. William Stanley Hoole (Tuscaloosa, 1959), 50.

23. KKK Report, VIII, 432; George P. Rawick (ed.), *The American Slave: A Composite Autobiography: Supplement Series 1* (Westport, Conn., 1977–), IV, 17–18.

defiance of the customs of slavery, became common after the League's advent. It was especially apparent on the farms; advocating equality in the abstract was the intellectual counterpart of hostility to the centralized plantation. As planters rejected blacks' pleas to rent or buy land, freedmen's restiveness became more apparent. Thus the League could politicize an already dissatisfied work force. Black organizer G. W. Cox demonstrated the League's impact in the countryside soon after his arrival in Tuscaloosa. Freedmen sought him out at crop-division time for advice on how to sue their employers, and his assistance to them soon earned Cox the enmity of local whites. In another location, a planter discovered how tense matters were on his estate when he disciplined a League member. The hand wanted to attend the elections two days in succession, and when the planter announced that there would be a fine for lost time, the freedman "commenced swearing and cursing, making use of language and remarks disrespectful saying that he was as free as I was, that he was not going to come to me and say Master shall I go anywhere. I then told him he had better shut his mouth, that before receiving such abuse as that I would go to the house and get my gun and shoot him. [He] replied that he had a gun and could shoot too." League rhetoric stirred thousands of freedmen to stand up for their rights; conversely, the impasse on the plantations made freedmen receptive to oratory about equal rights. Blacks reacted strongly against anything that even smacked of slavery, including the ritual obeisance required under the paternalist norms of the old regime.[24]

The League utilized the identification of equal rights rhetoric with the rejection of slavery to gain black votes. Freedom itself was the issue, as was implicit in all public discourse. In the words of one League document, a true Radical "desires that slavery should be abolished, and that every disability connected therewith should be obliterated." Former slaves perceived the remnants of slavery in the regnant order of the plantation system, and they associated legal inequality and segregation with the attempt to keep as much of servitude as was practicable. Republican oratory consistently linked these issues. The Tuskegee *News* reported that "the gist of what all

24. Montgomery *State Sentinel*, August 7, 1867; Deposition of William M. Christian, in G. W. Corliss to Greene, November 25, 1867, in Records, M826, RG 105.

the speakers said, was to glorify the millennium of negro equality—freedom, free schools, free ballot box, free jury box, free everything." The paper identified the central theme correctly; freedmen so thoroughly detested the memory of slavery that the concept of liberty had a tremendous emotional resonance for them. It was a winning issue for the Radicals.[25]

League oratory on the superiority of free labor also played upon that sentiment. Even before the war, Republican speakers invoked a producer ethic. Eric Foner pointed out in *Free Soil, Free Labor, Free Men* that it was "a common idea in both economic treatises and political pronouncements that labor was the source of all value." This was part of the whole Republican critique of slavery as regressive; during Reconstruction, Leaguers directed similar arguments to the freedmen. Republican appeals to the dignity of labor found immediate favor. Former slaves recognized that it was the "colored people who worked and made the money with which the white folks bought the land," in the words of one Natchez freedman. Talk of this sort often surfaced: "The negroes were told of their sufferings in slavery," an Alabama Democrat recalled of the League. "They were told, 'All this property that you see here, these lands, were cleared by you; you made all these fences; you dug all these ditches; and you are the men they belong to.' That was the style of speaking." This observer thought that such rhetoric encouraged hopes of land redistribution, but freedmen approved the traditional Republican stress on the moral value of labor regardless. It appealed to their self-esteem and was consistent with their own conviction that slavery had been an enormous wrong.[26]

The propaganda distributed among the freedmen is revealing. A campaign document that Democrats referred to as the Loyal League Catechism typified Radical arguments. Actually entitled "A Dialogue between a White Republican and a Colored Citizen," it received extensive circulation in 1867 and 1868, often being read aloud in League councils. The pamphlet explained that Radical Re-

25. Fleming (ed.), *Documentary History of Reconstruction*, II, 14; Montgomery *Mail*, July 29 (quoting Tuskegee *News*), May 29, 1867 (quoting Auburn *Intelligencer*).

26. Eric Foner, *Free Soil, Free Labor, Free Men: The Ideology of the Republican Party before the Civil War* (London, 1970), 12; KKK Report, VIII, 384.

publicans had freed blacks, upheld their rights, and therefore merited their support:

Q. What are the most prominent principles advocated by the Republican party?
A. Equal rights before the law and at the ballot box for all men without regard to race or color; that is, that every man shall have the same rights and liberties as any other man.

The aegis of Lincoln and other popular Republicans was invoked, but the crucial argument was that the freedmen should "shun the Democratic party as they would the overseer's lash and the auction block."[27]

Of course, League spokesmen discussed other issues, but even these often revolved around the symbolic negation of slavery. For example, councils emphasized public education, as did the catechism. One version of the League ritual instructed literate Leaguers to teach their fellow members how to read: "We must thus banish ignorance from our Councils." Leaguers lobbied the Bureau for schools in their neighborhoods, and a large number of organizers were themselves teachers. But if education and similar forms of black uplift were discussed, freedom dominated political rhetoric. Even the more esoteric local issues, such as occasional back-to-Africa talk, centered on defending their endangered liberty.[28]

That freedom had the premier role in blacks' political activity is clear in one argument that appeared repeatedly in Radical speeches. Conservatives reported that fear of literal reenslavement moved freedmen to vote Republican. Much credence must be granted this claim, for vast numbers of freedmen believed their liberty at stake in the first elections after Military Reconstruction began. As early as April, 1867, according to one Mississippian, "mischievous persons are already at work here endeavoring to sow the seeds of dissension in the minds of the colored population against the white. They are told that the Southern people are their enemies and will in due time endeavor to enslave them again." Other Democratic sources depicted

27. Fleming (ed.), *Documentary History of Reconstruction*, II, 16–17.
28. Fleming (ed.), *Union League Documents*, 31; Montgomery *Mail*, May 2, 1867, September 8, 1868; Parrish to Watson, September 3, 1868, in Watson Papers, Duke University; Davis to Smith, May 15, 1867, in Gov. Smith Papers, ADAH.

this statement as the League's critical argument. One paper stated that it inflamed the blacks; the Jackson *Clarion* frequently stressed how common reenslavement rhetoric was. In the recollection of Mississippi's former governor Humphreys, "Carpetbaggers made this color line and ever true to it called the 'colored man and brethren'—under his oath bound obligation—up to it as his only salvation from a return to slavery under Democratic rule."[29]

The League made this argument openly. The catechism stated that the Democrats would "disfranchise them, and if possible return them to slavery and certainly keep them in an inferior position before the law." Further, it maintained that freedmen should starve rather than aid in their own reenslavement, and it quoted Patrick Henry's famous "Give me liberty or give me death" to illustrate the point. It exhorted them to remember their former condition and to vote Republican so as to avoid a return to chains and slavery. Radicals proclaimed these charges in public. One speaker read the relevant portions of the catechism at a meeting when Democrats were present, and Keffer included the argument in his set speech on his organizing tours. Frederick Speed, a League organizer in Vicksburg, recalled that the charge was "reiterated time and time again" at Republican meetings.[30]

Freedmen widely believed the League's charge that reenslavement could happen under Conservative rule. One planter reported that his "own family negroes . . . asked me was it possible for them to be put back into slavery." The planter identified the source of such fears as the speeches by a local League leader. According to another landowner, the leagues spread all sorts of similar rumors before elections. A third noted that after Alabama's 1870 campaign, some of his former slaves returned to their old quarters. "Well massa," said one, "what house must I go into? I understand that the Democrats have succeeded, and that we are slaves again." As late as 1875, the story was reportedly still circulating in Mississippi, and one observer said

29. E. G. Baker to Sherman, April, 1867, in John Sherman Papers, LC; Jackson *Clarion*, June 24, 1868; Royall, *A Reply to "A Fool's Errand,"* 24; Humphreys to Lamar, January 3, 1875, in L. Q. C. Lamar Papers, MDAH.

30. Fleming (ed.), *Documentary History of Reconstruction*, II, 16, 18; KKK Report, IX, 1346; Union Springs *Times*, September 25, 1867; *House Reports*, 43rd Cong., 2nd Sess., No. 265, p. 236.

that the Democrats' victory that year resulted partly from the declining believability of such claims.[31]

The effectiveness of reenslavement as a political weapon can be discerned in the Democrats' denials of any such intention. "Nobody in this country desires to re-enslave you," stated one spokesman, "and when the Radicals tell you that we do, they lie most basely." The Conservative Livingston *Journal* also disavowed such goals, though admitting that freedmen might lose their vote if they continued voting Republican. Conservative spokesmen would obviously have avoided so defensive a tone had it been possible, but the freedmen's alarm was too intense. In Mobile such fears were so pressing that Conservatives needed to respond. Just prior to the 1868 presidential canvass, they issued a broadside informing the freedmen they could rest easy in their free status.[32]

Conservatives depicted the Radical charges as sheer demagogy. Knowing that literal reenslavement was unlikely, they saw using these arguments as dishonest and somehow unfair. They, and the Dunning school after them, saw blacks' belief in these rumors as proof of their credulity. Fleming commented satirically, "The chiefs of the League sent agents to the plantation negroes. . . . They were told they would be reenslaved and their wives made to work the roads and quit wearing hoopskirts." Fleming disparaged such fears as foolish, and his depiction is typical of those scholars hostile to Reconstruction. To such observers, the freedman's fear of reenslavement demonstrated that he was incapable of intelligently exercising the franchise.[33]

Actually, freedmen's fears contained a good deal of substance. The Thirteenth Amendment terminated slavery, but it by no means ended efforts to preserve coerced labor under different legal titles. James Roark summarized the planter mentality: "They sought to be realistic and practical, but their early efforts clearly reflected their continued faith in slavery. . . . Their inability to give up their pref-

---

31. KKK Report, IX, 1347, VIII, 298–99; Baskin to Middleton, August 19, 1875, in Ellis Scattergood Middleton Papers, MDAH.
32. *Henry County Register* (Abbeville, Ala.), August 10, 1867; Livingston *Journal*, January 4, 1868; Broadside in Johnson Papers, Duke University.
33. Royall, *A Reply to "A Fool's Errand,"* 24; Fleming, *Civil War and Reconstruction in Alabama,* 514.

erence for compulsory service meant that they strove to reinstitute their authority in the freedmen's lives and labor. Rebuilding plantations along familiar lines required the continuation of work gangs, white supervision, task systems, clustered cabins, and minimal personal freedom for blacks. Subservience and regimentation were the planters' goals. Unable to accept the implications of emancipation, they sought to keep blacks as nearly slaves as possible." Freedmen were not attorneys; to them, slavery meant continued subservience in their daily life on the plantation—gang labor, overseers, whippings. The practices freedmen thought demeaning were the very ones planters seemed intent on keeping. While literal slavery was dead, the attempt to preserve its substance emphatically was not, as the Black Codes demonstrated. Systematic legal and social discrimination—which the freedmen identified with slavery—showed no sign of disappearing.[34]

Reenslavement therefore furnished freedmen an apt metaphor for the process actually under way; it reified their diffuse concerns. Planters, through the Black Codes and their refusal to rent or sell land, frustrated freedmen's desire for greater autonomy. They tried to institutionalize a labor system that was blatantly repressive in practice. Freedmen responded to the League's charges of reenslavement because the program for farming-as-usual seemed essentially the same thing. The history of the South after Redemption demonstrates that they were not far wrong. Thus the prevalence of reenslavement talk illustrates freedmen's acuity rather than their ignorance. They had a better idea of what was at stake than did many of their critics.

Much has been written in the last two decades on retrieving the history of the inarticulate. The problem is acute in the case of the freedmen, but one can glean something of what they thought from the political rhetoric they found persuasive. If the former slaves responded strongly to what League leaders said, then it can be assumed that these spokesmen dealt with concerns relevant to the black populace. A detailed exploration of the Radical appeal to the

34. Roark, *Masters Without Slaves*, 141.

freedmen reveals the centrality of personal autonomy, from control of their labor to education and equal rights. The memory of slavery shaped the black political response and provided an emotional impetus toward collective action. The rapid spread of Radical ideology itself resulted from the freedmen's dissatisfaction with the stalemate on the plantation; autonomy as a goal appealed strongly to people who perceived their aspirations as frustrated by the planters' refusal even to rent them land. Freedmen found the rhetoric of equal rights persuasive because it expressed their central goal: the determination to oppose reimposition of a coercive labor regime.

The data suggest a clear relationship between Radical ideology and the freedmen's hopes and fears. Blacks seized upon the traditional free-labor rhetoric and invested it with a meaning of their own. The relationship is similar to one described in another context by Elizabeth Fox-Genovese and Eugene Genovese: "A new vocabulary, imperfectly circulated among an imperfectly literate population can serve as a major catalyst for legitimating angers, perceived injustices, and time-out-of-mind hostilities, and for directing them toward political action. In a generally inflammatory situation, the words need not mean the same things to all participants. It is the momentary convergence of discrete dissatisfactions upon a common language that provides a political context for private miseries and permits common action among widely disparate individuals." The Radicals' egalitarian ideology asserted that the new status quo violated blacks' humanity at a basic level, just as slavery had. It thus provided a language for the widespread labor revolt in the region.[35]

35. Elizabeth Fox-Genovese and Eugene D. Genovese, *Fruits of Merchant Capital: Slavery and Bourgeois Property in the Rise and Expansion of Capitalism* (New York, 1983), 239.

FIVE

Land, Labor, and the Loyal League

The Union League significantly influenced plantation agriculture. Although its overt role was as a partisan organization, the League incorporated elements of a broad-gauged agrarian movement. Dissatisfaction with the coercive nature of cultivation provided the social impetus for politicizing the freedmen. The League appeared at a time of ferment in the cotton belt, and the evidence suggests that it heightened the restiveness of the labor force. Strikes and boycotts accompanied the Radical mobilization as freedmen applied slogans of liberty and equality to their situation as laborers. Leagues thus became involved in blacks' desires for greater autonomy and, particularly, in efforts to gain for the freedmen access to land.

There are many views on what caused the changes in the postwar agricultural system. According to some scholars, market forces broke up the centralized cotton plantation. Others stress the freedmen's aspirations as critical. The evidence presented here supports the latter emphasis, for it demonstrates that black pressure on the plantation system was intense. Anger at the coercive work regimen made freedmen ripe for Radical agitation, and their politicization in turn undermined work discipline. The freedmen seized on the League and its rhetoric to protest continuation of the labor system derived from slavery.

To comprehend the interrelationship between the League mobilization and southern agriculture, we must first sketch the postwar evolution of cotton production. Alabama is the focus of observation, though Mississippi followed a substantially similar pattern. Political insurgency among the freedmen did not arise in a vacuum, but instead reflected acute economic derangement and social discontent. Little organized agitation occurred among laborers before 1867, and open confrontations with white authority were sporadic, but increasing restiveness was evident even prior to Military Reconstruction. Along with the agricultural disarray, the politicization of the freedmen concentrated discontent and thus made managing plantations far more difficult.

Indications of future conflict became visible during the Civil War, with slavery gradually unraveling as a labor system. Wartime demands sapped the capability either to coerce or to reward slaves. Central Alabama escaped becoming a battlefield until the spring of 1865, but in the changed situation, slaves tended to reduce the work they did. The "general strike" of blacks that Du Bois described was something of a gradual transition to freedom. The area along the Tennessee River farther north underwent even greater disruption than did the central Alabama cotton belt; this plantation region became a war zone from 1862 on, and slaves escaped to the Yankees in large numbers.[1]

Planters, attempting to rebuild a postwar labor system along lines familiar to them, faced an already disorganized work force. Their political response was clear. During the nearly two years of Presidential Reconstruction, public policy demonstrated a widespread consensus among the elite. Freedmen were to be forced back into the fields and on the planters' terms. Through the Black Codes, state power substituted for legal slavery to give landowners leverage over their hands. The Black Codes included harsh vagrancy statutes and a pass system. Alabama lawmakers also tried to discourage freedmen from renting farmland. They even attempted to ban court testimony by blacks against whites, an exclusion that would certainly leave freedmen vulnerable to fraud and violence. However, pressure from military authorities eventually dissuaded the lawmakers. The Black

1. Du Bois, *Black Reconstruction*, 55; Armstead L. Robinson, "'Worser dan Jeff Davis': The Coming of Free Labor during the Civil War, 1861–1865," in Thavolia Glymph and John J. Kushma (eds.), *Essays on the Postbellum Southern Economy* (College Station, Tex., 1985), 11–47.

Codes represented the scaffolding for rebuilding agriculture on the pattern of the old regime: overseers, obtrusive discipline, gang labor, women and children in the labor force, and even a return to physical coercion. In addition, wages were to be kept at a minimal level.[2]

The former slaves resisted this program in several ways. There was a widespread effort to shorten the hours of work. The proverbial "day clear to first dark" shrank, and the work week fared similarly, as Saturday afternoons become a subject of controversy. A Tennessee Valley planter, requesting the aid of the Bureau, wrote:

My hands are beyond my control. Yesterday all men but four refused to take care of mules—would not even feed them & Saturday noon did not get back to work on time by a long ways. This morning I called them to work at 5 minutes before 5 O'clock. The first hand got to work 8 minutes after 6 O'clock, the last one . . . to work 11 minutes after 7 O'clock. I can't get but part work at a time. They are all the time swearing this is worse than Reb times & this won't do for free niggers. . . . [W]ithout your assistance I am gone up the spout.

One Conservative paper argued that augmenting the tendency to reduce hours were the increasingly prevalent "sharecrop" (payment in kind) wage arrangements, which encouraged freedmen to look on themselves as partners and therefore properly independent of white control. In recent years, quantitative historians have used census data on acreage in cultivation to estimate the shortfall in black labor. The figures derived by Ransom and Sutch generally support the opinion of the Alabama planter who thought it would "take three now to do the work that two did formerly."[3]

A related trend in the black community was for women to withdraw from cotton cultivation, thus insulating them from harassment by planters and overseers. According to Gerald Jaynes's calculations in *Branches Without Roots*, almost one-third dropped out of the full-time work force on cotton plantations by 1867. It is not clear whether black men or black women took the lead in this movement. Kolchin

2. Fleming, *Civil War and Reconstruction in Alabama*, 378–83; Nieman, *To Set the Law in Motion*, 92–94.

3. E. G. Black to Callis, May 12, 1866, in Letters Received SAC Huntsville, Vol. 58, RG 105; *Henry County Register* (Abbeville, Ala.), March 27, 1869; S. L. Arrington to A. H. Arrington, April 8, 1866, in A. H. Arrington Papers, UNC; Ransom and Sutch, *One Kind of Freedom*, 44–47.

argues that the men were responsible, because they wanted their wives to stay at home just as white women did. Contemporary accounts, however, also picture black women as increasingly assertive. "My negroes give very little trouble," one planter wrote, "with the exception of the *women* who . . . are very obstinate." Either way, blacks' distaste for the work standards of slavery is clear, and they expressed this hostility in other ways as well. Planters who used the whip now faced possible violence in response, or at least a risk that the laborers would report the incident to military authorities. Freedmen's Bureau records contain many such complaints.[4]

But the central issue during the early postwar period was access to land. Freedmen wanted to farm under their own supervision. Owning land offered a modicum of independence, which held great appeal for former slaves. The rumors of confiscation prevalent in late 1865 doubtless manifested a general desire to be self-employed with one's own forty acres and a mule. When it became clear that land redistribution would not occur, freedmen tried to purchase small farms themselves. Since they were poor, however, some form of renting seemed a necessary first step toward landownership. But planters were seldom willing to rent under any arrangement. The conflict that often ensued is illustrated in the journal of Octavia Otey, a north Alabama planter. Soon after the war ended, one of her leading hands asked to rent land. She told him she expected to run the farm herself; besides, she did not rent to Negroes. Over the following years, Otey recorded the freedmen's deteriorating work habits and insubordination. After unsuccessfully attempting to secure white laborers from Tennessee, she finally relented in late 1867, feeling "much troubled about letting land to negroes, and making arrangements for the New Year. I would not let any land to negroes if I could help it."[5]

Planters avoided renting land to freedmen for various reasons. The Huntsville *Advocate* expressed the opinion in 1865 that there

4. Jaynes, *Branches Without Roots*, 229; Kolchin, *First Freedom*, 62; W. M. Polk to "Sister," March 17, 1867, in Polk Family Papers, UNC; Jones, *Labor of Love, Labor of Sorrow*, 58–68. Jaynes derived his figures from data for Louisiana, but the results are probably similar for Alabama as well.

5. Octavia Otey Diary, December 20, 1865, December 28, 1867 (MS in Wyche and Otey Family Papers, UNC).

were "few negroes who could be relied upon as tenants," at least until they acquired some capital. In the Tennessee Valley it was "generally believed" that because of recent legislation planters could not rent land to freedmen "without becoming responsible for their behavior & c & c & many who had contracted to rent are now refusing to close contracts on account of it." Those landowners who rented to freedmen confronted great social pressure from their neighbors; the prevailing belief was that such individuals were diminishing the perquisites of being white. Whitelaw Reid observed this prejudice in the Mississippi Valley, but his comments apply to Alabama as well: "The feeling against any ownership of land by the negroes is so strong, that the man who should sell small tracts to them would be in actual personal danger. Every effort will be made to prevent negroes from acquiring lands; and even the renting of small tracts to them is held to be unpatriotic and unworthy of a good citizen." This bias is not surprising, for planters viewed independent farming by blacks as tantamount to anarchy.[6]

The few freedmen who actually obtained lands met outright hostility. When a freedman began farming a small tract in central Alabama, for example, a neighbor threatened to blow his brains out. Landowners even organized to prevent the practice of renting land to blacks. One planters' association was created in part to stop land rental; its resolutions observed that the "vice of this arrangement is, that the negro in his anxiety to be free from all restraint of the white man, is now thrown . . . upon his wits for support." The result would be theft and pilferage by the incompetent freedmen. The Mobile *Nationalist* pointed out that these agreements were widespread; the average freedman was discouraged because "combinations are formed against him, in many portions of the country, to prevent him from obtaining a home for himself, or having the management of his own affairs." As evidence, the paper cited the "treatment of the colored people at Bladon Springs, as well as in Sumter and Marengo counties, as also in many other places."[7]

6. Huntsville *Advocate*, November 16, 1865; A. W. Preston to Goodfellow, December 28, 1865, in Letters Received SAC Huntsville, Vol. 57, RG 105; Contract Book 1865–66, SAC Huntsville, Vol. 81, RG 105; Reid, *After the War*, 564–65.

7. Complaint Book, March 4, 1867, SAC Demopolis, Vol. 141, RG 105; Mobile *Advertiser and Register*, February 3, 1866; Mobile *Nationalist*, January 11, 1866.

An impasse resulted from this conflict. Planters farmed much as before, with only minimal concessions to the changed circumstances. Whippings were less frequent, largely because of Bureau intervention. Planters also shifted from cash to sharecrop wage arrangements because of scarce credit, as well as in the interest of redistributing risk to their hands. But planters overall tried to act as if they were still masters, and this contributed to abysmal crops in 1865, 1866, and 1867. Conservatives blamed the freedmen for the poor harvests. Other factors would include bad seed, poor stock, and ruined fences. Heavy rainfall resulted in flooding and in insect invasions. The armyworm, for example, commonly destroyed two-thirds of the bolls on infested plants. Whatever the cause, poor yields combined with declining cotton prices to create hard times; planters found themselves deep in debt, and the price of land fell precipitously. Freedmen, suffering from the economic stringency, made little beyond supplies during these years. Seldom did they receive more than a nominal sum at reckoning time, and very often they found themselves in debt. This reality, coupled with an understandable—and often accurate—conviction that they had been cheated, increased their already severe disaffection with the labor system.

Such was the situation at the onset of Congressional Reconstruction in March, 1867. To freedmen, the agricultural order resembled servitude and, furthermore, was unremunerative. The former slaves shortened their working hours, withdrew women from agricultural labor, and were insubordinate. Their resentment increasingly centered on an insistent desire for land. When confiscation faded to improbability, they tried to buy and rent land, and they were, for the most part, unsuccessful. Thus recruiting freedmen into the League did not upset a smoothly functioning labor system but sharpened existing tensions. Blacks were ready for the Radical appeal because they remained nearly slaves in crucial aspects of their lives and because they had failed to achieve more than minimal changes in the plantation regime.

Events in Hale County, Alabama, provide a revealing glimpse into the social processes set in motion by Congressional Reconstruction. An area of large plantations with a heavy black majority, the county demographically typified the central Alabama cotton belt. Political activity began there soon after the Reconstruction Acts passed. The Bureau agent reported in April, 1867, that freedmen were "visiting him in committees, in squads, platoons & companies" asking for information on their new rights. They requested that he make a public address, setting forth their legal status. He obliged with political speeches, as did other Bureau officials and Radicals in the vicinity.[8]

The Union League was organized in May, 1867. A mass rally was called, and among the scheduled orators were two delegates returning from the Mobile Freedmen's Convention who knew the League ritual. These men had been sent, expenses apparently paid by their neighbors, to find out about the blacks' political status. On the appointed Saturday, four thousand freedmen flooded into the county seat, Greensboro. After hearing talks representing a variety of viewpoints, the freedmen adopted resolutions in support of Radical Reconstruction. They also elected delegates to the approaching statewide Republican convention in Montgomery. After this public meeting, tension increased in the countryside. The Bureau received several reports of planters fining or discharging laborers for attending League meetings or registering to vote.[9]

In June, violence erupted when a prominent freedman was shot down on the streets of Greensboro. Alex Webb, just appointed a voter registrar for his district, was a saddler by trade and relatively prosperous. He had been active in organizing the Republican party in his neighborhood. He was killed by one John Orrick, a white who boasted that he "would never be registered by a nigger" and who was, it seems, interested in the same black woman who had attracted Webb. At all events, city officials took Orrick into custody after the shooting but immediately allowed him to escape. That night, large numbers of angry freedmen came in from the countryside, armed with guns, pistols, and clubs; some threatened to burn the town.

8. S. P. Spann to Pierce, April 12, 1867, in Letters Received SAC Demopolis, Box 27, RG 105.

9. Complaint Book, May 8, 1867, SAC Demopolis, Vol. 141, RG 105; Pierce to Spann, April 28, 1867, in Letters Sent SAC Demopolis, Vol. 139, RG 105; Mobile *Advertiser and Register*, May 26, 1867; Complaint Book, May 27, June 26, July 27, August 14, 1867, SAC Demopolis, Vol. 141, RG 105.

The authorities panicked at this situation that "threatened a serious outbreak." The sheriff appointed several hundred freedmen as a posse and sent them after Orrick. They scoured the area for days, searching several houses, but could locate only one individual they thought implicated in Orrick's escape. The excitement did not die down. The evening after the shooting, a leading black spokesman in the area, James K. Green, urged the creation of a freedmen's militia in preparation for the next such incident.[10]

The freedmen took Green's advice. By August, a correspondent reported that "several Union Leagues in the county" had a distinctly military character, and the council in Greensboro numbered some five hundred. Leagues were set up under the general guidance of Green and a native Unionist, Dr. W. T. Blackford. Two whites teaching schools in the countryside also engaged in political organizing. But if the shooting of Webb galvanized the freedmen to Radical activity, it also affected whites' behavior. At the height of the disturbances, whites "secretly armed themselves for the fight if it did begin." Afterward, Green and Blackford were threatened and harassed, and one freedman who had led the posse in search of Orrick had to flee his home. When the Klan spread through the region some months later, Hale County witnessed a great deal of nightrider activity.[11]

The assassination of Webb, and the turbulence that followed, played havoc with plantation discipline. Six days after the shooting, overseer D. Drake complained that the freedmen were "so much excited they have done but little work since." His hands actually joined the throng marching on Greensboro. The disturbances delayed work on the crop, and Drake's difficulties multiplied as Radical agitation convinced local blacks that they were of "some impor-

10. Pierce to Swayne, June 28, 1867, Records of the Third Military District, Office of Civil Affairs, Box 4, Pt. 1, RG 393; Dorman to Swayne, June 14, 1867, in Swayne Papers, ADAH; J. Parrish to Watson, June 20, 1867, in Watson Papers, Duke University; Mobile *Times,* June 20, 1867; Mobile *Advertiser and Register,* June 7, 1867; Gadsden *Times,* July 3, 1867.
11. Carrollton *West Alabamian,* August 21, 1867; Demopolis *Southern Republican,* June 2, 1869; Gadsden *Times,* July 3, 1867; W. T. Hendon to Swayne, November 13, 1867, in Records, M809, RG 105; D. Drake to P. B. Cabell, June 20, 1867, in Cabell Family Papers (acc. no. 38–111), University of Virginia Library, Charlottesville, hereinafter cited as UVa; Pierce to G. A. Farrand, September 10, 1867, in Letters Sent SAC Demopolis, Vol. 140, RG 105.

tance." In September, Drake wrote that the hands had been idle for weeks because of "so much politicks"; he described a dispute over whether they would be loaned mules in order to attend a dinner in Greensboro. Drake denied the request, and so the freedmen stayed home, but they did "little work." Some weeks later the freedmen prevented the overseer from shipping cotton from the place, demanding that their share be used to buy clothes and shoes, as the weather was getting cold. At year's end, they also accused Drake of fraud. They refused to contract with him for another year's labor, or to leave without an explanation of the settlement. Their discontent finally forced the overseer's replacement early in 1868, but even this did not end the unrest.[12]

Similar troubles spread throughout the countryside. One planter observed in October that his hands refused to take care of the mules on his place, and they also disputed his reckoning of accounts and were "seizing upon what they assume to be their portion of both cotton & corn." The planter requested that the Bureau intervene against the rebellious blacks. On another plantation, conflict grew out of a fight between the planter's son and a black child. When the case went to court and the black child received a forty-day jail sentence, the freedmen called upon League leaders to petition the military for relief. Soon the planter found that his freedmen were very "turbulent and disorderly," coming and going when they chose, working when they felt like it. In another neighborhood, freedmen prevented arrests by authorities, and the local magistrate despaired of apprehending a suspect without provoking conflict. As one Bureau official summed up the situation in Hale County, "Without great caution difficulty with the freedmen will be inevitable." He blamed the League's leadership for the potential of bloodshed.[13]

Contemporary observers noted a change among the workers. One Conservative paper reported a general loss of control over the labor force, which was the League's fault, and it urged importing German

12. D. Drake to P. B. Cabell, June 20, August 5, September 3, 18, December 28, 1867, January 1, 186[8], all in Cabell Family Papers, UVa.

13. J. C. Henderson to Pierce, October 14, 1867, in Letters Received SAC Demopolis, Box 27, RG 105; James K. Green *et al.* to Pierce, September 3, 1867, in Letters Received SAC Demopolis, Box 27, RG 105; G. A. Farrand to Pierce, December 2, 1867, in Records, M809, RG 105.

farmhands as a countermeasure. "In that way," urged the Carrollton *West Alabamian*, "the planters of the South would be—as they *should* be, *masters of the situation.*" Labor issues appeared just below the surface of politics, as the activities of the Bureau agent at Greensboro indicate. Captain H. G. Claus, Bureau officer and ambitious Radical, systematically refused to approve annual labor contracts for 1868 such as were "made last year" in the vicinity. He thus sought favor for recognizing blacks' dissatisfaction with the whole process of signing on as gang laborers.[14]

The effects of the politicization of the freedmen can be seen on two Hale County plantations. On both the Henry Watson and the Paul Cameron places, a similar evolution away from prevailing agricultural practices occurred. The cases were not identical, but they demonstrated the impact of wider political events on the conflict between landowners and laborers.

Unrest began on the large Watson place immediately upon the Union army's arrival in the area at the end of the war. The freedmen undertook several partly successful work stoppages, insisting upon the firing and the eviction of their overseer. They refused to sign the contract that the planter drew up, which included such provisions as requiring permission to leave the premises. Only when a Bureau agent assured them that the rewritten contract was satisfactory did the freedmen resume their labors. Even after that, however, Henry Watson and his associates perceived an impressive range of misbehavior. Women would no longer work in the fields, saying they wanted to be supported by their husbands as white women were. Nor would hands do labor that did not directly increase their portion of the crop. Watson complained that "we cannot get them to shell corn to take to the mill for their own food, to feed the hogs which are to make the pork that is to be divided among themselves."[15]

The freedmen were equally discontented. They found that their one-eighth share of the crop came to $6.06 per hand for the year 1865. By Watson's figuring, most of them wound up in debt, despite

14. Carrollton *West Alabamian*, August 21, 1867; D. H. Smith to Swayne, January 27, 1868, in Records, M809, RG 105.

15. Parrish to H. Watson, June 25, 1865, Settlement Memorandum dated December 19, 1865, Contracts dated June 26 and 30, 1865, Henry Watson to "Julia," December 16, 1865, all in Watson Papers, Duke University.

having received no cash advances during the season. Not surprisingly, the entire work force deserted him early in the new year, and he reported great difficulty in replacing them. His neighbors, he thought, were making undue concessions to the freedmen: "The more like a negro the Employer is the greater has been his success in getting hands, the best masters have made the greatest failures and an impossible fellow with a bottle of whiskey and liberal promises can entice all the labor from any one of them."[16]

Throughout 1866, difficulties continued as hands remained scarce. "I am in the midst of a large and fertile cotton growing country," Watson observed, "many plantations are entirely without labor, many plantations have insufficient labor, and upon none are the laborers doing their former accustomed work." He thought that freedmen accomplished only half as much as they did when they were slaves. In conjunction with the bad weather and the army-worm, this resulted in a crop that was "almost a complete failure." Watson estimated that he, along with most of his neighbors, lost thousands of dollars that season for the second straight year.[17]

Despite the turmoil and the poor seasons, Watson still attempted to manage the plantation as he had before the war. A few planters in his vicinity rented land to freedmen early in 1867, but only later in the year did Watson begin to consider similar changes. He did so in the midst of the League's mobilizing his work force. Watson's brother-in-law wrote that the League was advising the Negroes "to ignore the Southern white man as soon as possible. Not to work with or for him, or be controlled by him, but to set up for themselves." Setting up for themselves, of course, meant farming independent of white control. He further observed that every freedman within ten miles had entered the League. By mid-summer, Watson was warned that a "*war* between races" would likely result from the League organizers' activities, and he was so discouraged by these reports—along with the poor crop—that he fully intended to let his land lie fallow the next year. An increase in the price of cotton, however,

16. Fragment dated December 19, 1865, H. Watson to J. A. Wemyss, January 26, 1866, both in Watson Papers, Duke University.
17. Watson to Iselin, March 7, 1866, Watson to W. A. & G. Maxwell & Co., July 11, 1866, April 12, 1867, all in Watson Papers, Duke University.

changed his mind. Watson decided to subdivide his plantation and rent it to freedmen, who would work under their own supervision. The arrangement was satisfactory, and his manager soon reported that "the negroes are working very well this year. We have them divided off into squads." Such work squads, as Jaynes points out, often represented the intervening stage between gang labor and family-based tenant farming. Although the armyworm again destroyed Watson's crop in 1868, the planter was convinced that freedmen made admirable tenants, and he thus became reconciled to greater autonomy for blacks in their lives and labor. By the end of 1870 at the latest, freedmen were leaving the old slave quarters and building cabins scattered across his land. A few individuals purchased small plots in the neighborhood, but most would remain sharecroppers for the foreseeable future.[18]

Similar developments took place on the Cameron plantation some miles away. During 1865, overseer W. O'Berry reported the same escalating conflict over terms of employment. The women would not work, nor would the men tend the hogs. The planter's traditional prerogatives rankled the freedmen here too. O'Berry reported them angry because he would not "suffer a gang of negroes in the quarters at night." The overseer corrected the problem by shooting a visitor "full from head to foot" with buckshot. Not surprisingly, freedmen proved unwilling to contract here as well. O'Berry ran the plantation again in 1866 and had a difficult time of it. He was obliged to advance cash to the freedmen to keep them at work. The loss was total— worms again destroyed the crop. O'Berry decided never to loan money to the freedmen again, blaming their poor performance for his misfortunes. Any man, he complained, who had free blacks to deal with "has about as much as he can stand up to." According to O'Berry, some of his neighbors despaired of ever making a profit again. Despite these problems, he determined to farm in much the same manner the next year.[19]

18. Deed dated February 23, 1871, Parrish to Watson, May 28, August 13, November 7, 1867, G. Hugins to Watson, June 5, 1868, Contract dated January 11, 1867, Deed dated October 2, 1869, all in Watson Papers, Duke University; Jaynes, *Branches Without Roots*, 158–73.

19. W. O'Berry to P. C. Cameron, March 3, 1866, November 7, 1865, both in Cameron Family Papers, UNC.

The League's arrival changed the whole situation, for on this plantation lived two individuals who became prominent Radicals in the vicinity. One man served as a delegate to the Republican party's founding convention in Montgomery. O'Berry described this important political influence after his hands returned from registering to vote in Greensboro. Now, they did not move "as well as they did before." Some said they were "to have the land and the growing crop on it, one or two said they understood . . . such things, they all belong to the uion leaugue." The overseer reported considerable confusion among the freedmen as a result. Local planters organized an agricultural association to defend their common interests, but O'Berry cast about for his own solution to the problem. By October, 1867, he decided to reorganize production altogether. From then on, he would work the land "in families" and leave the hands to find their own provisions. Talking to his neighbors, he found a great many considering the same idea. In January, O'Berry divided his force into three squads, all under black supervision, and he withdrew from active control in the making of the crop. Soon he too reported improved work habits among the freedmen. Over the next years the Cameron place was leased and eventually sold to former hands on the plantation. The independent black settlement that developed exists to the present day.[20]

Both these plantations demonstrate similar patterns of political agitation—engendered largely by the League—encouraging changes in the organization of labor. The freedmen saw Radical rhetoric as having immediate relevance to their situation as agricultural workers, and their increasing restiveness encouraged the abandonment of gang labor. Existing evidence is too sparse to indicate whether the League exercised a similar role on neighboring farms. Political unrest was acute through the whole region, however, and the agricultural evolution of the Watson and Cameron places was typical of the area. One overseer complained in May, 1868, that hands were scarce with "so many freedmen working on their own hook." So eager were the

20. O'Berry to Cameron, May, 1867, August 11, September 27, October 20, 1867, January 30, April 6, 1868, all in Cameron Family Papers, UNC; Sydney Nathans, "Fortress Without Walls: A Black Community after Slavery," in Robert L. Hall and Carol Stack (eds.), *Holding On to the Land and the Lord: Kinship, Ritual, Land Tenure, and Social Policy in the Rural South* (Athens, Ga., 1982), 55–65.

freedmen for greater independence that some were actually trying to farm "without horse or plow."[21]

The tendency grew more pronounced the following year. In May, 1869, a Hale County correspondent reported on the transformation that had taken place: "Many planters have turned their stock, teams, and every facility to farming, over to the negroes, and only require an amount of toll for the use of their land, refusing to superintend, direct, or even, in some cases, to suggest as to their management." Those blacks who had been unable to rent land that year had been reluctant to contract as laborers, generally waiting until the inauguration of President Grant in early March. Others, restive but lacking capital, were squatters on unproductive lands. One freedman anxiously asked his employer not to rent a tract to anyone else, promising to pay "as much as enny other person." He requested an immediate answer, so he could "rest contented." Such conduct manifested freedmen's dissatisfaction with the prevailing system of agriculture and their disposition to strike out on their own. In this, Hale County illustrates the prevailing pattern: the freedmen's politicization had strong overtones of agrarian revolt.[22]

Areas across the Alabama cotton belt experienced similar conflict as sharp political upheaval disclosed the underlying social discontent. In other communities where League mobilizations were strong, the pattern was much the same. An examination of Sumter, Macon, and Bullock counties shows the saliency of labor issues. Questions of autonomy, especially access to land, dominated grass-roots politics after the passage of Military Reconstruction.

In Sumter, on the western border of the state, planters reported a deteriorating situation after emancipation. Cotton cultivation continued in the traditional manner, and farm operators made the typical complaints about women not working, plantation maintenance, and the like. Moreover, freedmen gradually improved their bargaining techniques at contract time. A correspondent for the Livingston *Journal* observed, "The negro partner got in 1865 one tenth, in 1866

21. L. L. Singleton to P. B. Cabell, May 2, 1868, in Cabell Family Papers, UVa.

22. Mobile *Register*, May 30, 1869; Albert Goodrum to Mr. Calvin, July 4, 1869, in Cabell Family Papers, UVa.

one quarter, in 1867 one third, [and] for 1868 he demands one half." The author wondered how long the freedman's native modesty would forbid his demanding the other half. The larger planters in the county also complained that irresponsible persons were outbidding them for laborers. The landowners' attitude was typified by the arresting comment of the *Journal* on contemporary Russia: "We think the continued and liberal use of the knout has contributed in no small degree to the usefulness of the emancipated serf as a laborer." The sentiment is positively nostalgic.[23]

Radical activity began in Sumter County in May, 1867. Local freedmen called a mass meeting at which Reconstructionist whites shared the podium with various freedmen. Several of the black speakers took a cautious line; however, one man fresh from the Mobile Freedmen's Convention gave an oration "Radical throughout." In late June, leagues reportedly were forming, and by the time of Keffer's visit in August, they existed throughout the county.[24]

The creation of the League proved less tumultuous here than it was in some other locales, but the beginnings of the movement clearly alarmed planters and their allies. The sheriff wrote that the "colored people of this county are meeting together I suppose for the purpose of joining the Loyal League or holding meetings of that kind. On last Thursday night at Sumterville there were counted by moonlight *Ninety* guns, and on Saturday night there were about the same number. . . . I suppose there was from two to three Hundred present at the two meetings." He predicted that whites would shed blood in the near future and urged that something be done to halt the freedmen's provocative displays. The local press speculated that the Leaguers planned an insurrection, and whether or not many believed such tales, planters certainly noted freedmen's unusual behavior.[25]

One white discovered this change when he rode by a League meeting; sentries challenged him and sent him on his way under guard. A local attorney also recalled a dramatic alteration in blacks'

---

23. Livingston *Journal*, January 19, 26, November 16, 1867; Bevill to Pierce, April 7, 1866, in Letters Received SAC Demopolis, Box 27, RG 105.
24. Livingston *Journal*, May 18, June 22, August 17, 1867.
25. J. J. Bailey to Patton, September 16, 1867, in Gov. Patton Papers, ADAH.

conduct. Before the League existed, a "good feeling" had prevailed between the races, but then "there came men here by the name of Rolfe, and also Hays and Price; and from the time they came here a bad feeling commenced between the white people and the negroes. . . . The negroes, then, became impudent; they would hardly get off the street or sidewalk, or give way to a lady; they jostled them, and they seemed suspicious of the whites. They were soon organized into what they called the Loyal League, and they marched into this town under arms on various occasions." This militancy became strikingly evident on a plantation rented by three white northerners. In debt and in danger of having their cotton seized by creditors, the Yankees turned to the freedmen to protect their crop—along with the freedmen's own share—from the authorities. A lawyer for the creditor was warned that if he "should interfere with, or remove any of such property, the loyal league" would stop him. Taking the threat seriously, the lawyer wrote General Swayne for aid.[26]

The potential influence of League activity upon the labor system was not lost on the planters. Almost immediately, they made efforts to unite against blacks' demands. A call for a planters' association in the local paper coincided with John Keffer's first speaking engagement in the area. At a large meeting of landowners in late October, one subcommittee was appointed to organize the Democratic party in the county, and another drafted the platform for a planters' organization. Resolutions passed, one stating that "the present disorganized and inefficient System of Labor" would bankrupt the region. The planters agreed that there had to be a single wage scale and that employers must not hire men discharged by other planters. This dual response to the League illustrates the outstanding point: planters perceived a simultaneous challenge in the political and the economic realms.[27]

The timing of the transition to decentralized tenant farming in Sumter was similar to that in Hale County. While some few individuals rented or sublet land to blacks in early 1867, the first favor-

26. Livingston *Journal*, October 5, 1867; KKK Report, X, 1623; J. H. Gray to Swayne, December 23, 1867, in Records, M809, RG 105.
27. Livingston *Journal*, October 26, 1867.

able references in the local press appeared in September. Initially, the Livingston *Journal* recommended sale or rental to whites only, telling readers to "sell at what you can get for it, or give away to white settlers, all your land that you cannot cultivate successfully." But since white labor was so scarce, the tenor of the advice soon changed: "We can see no remedy—no real protection to the present owners of land, but a speedy change in the system of employing many hands on one large plantation. We believe it is far better to divide up the lands and place them in the hands of other operators, even if one is not disposed to sell. . . . Faithful men, who have been former slaves of [the] land owner, may be found in some instances." It is significant in this context that the leading white Leaguer in Sumter, Daniel Price, defended the freedmen's right to rent land. Price wrote the Bureau that the tax collector discriminated against independent small farmers. The official had been "set upon them by a lot of scoundrels here who are always trying to break up every colored man that goes off to work by himself. If these men had been working for some rebel they would not have been interfered with." The rental of land emerges here as a political issue: in such a charged situation, independent black farming represented a challenge to prevailing practices.[28]

Gaining access to land also proved a critical issue in the area around Tuskegee in Macon County. Future black legislator James H. Alston helped organize the League during the summer of 1867, and the disorder that commonly attended such activity was reported. Early in 1868 the abandonment of gang labor began, and Alston reported that "many Freedmen in the vicinity of Tuskegee, have rented land (from 10 to 30 acres each)." These changes had an unpleasant sequel, as Alston observed in a deposition. He received a threat from the Ku Klux Klan, ordering him to "notify the colored people that they must leave their rented places on pain of death." Alston described subsequent assaults and harassment upon him and other freedmen, and a Bureau investigation found that he had not exaggerated. "Numbers of freedmen have left their homes on ac-

28. W. Mapiz to Pierce, November 1, 1867, in Letters Received SAC Demopolis, Box 27, RG 105; Livingston *Journal*, September 28, October 5, 1867; Price to Pierce, April 28, 1868, in Letters Received SAC Demopolis, Box 27, RG 105.

count of these threats," an agent wrote from the scene. Tuskegee's Leaguers would be decimated in the coming years, and it is worthy of note that the Klan found renting land to be their first offense.[29]

Bullock County showed in striking fashion the conflict likely to accompany this transition. League-related turbulence was extreme in this isolated rural area, near the eastern end of Alabama's cotton belt. The population was nearly three-quarters black. The potential for social upheaval was tremendous—labor relations were harsher than they were in most other cotton areas. For example, the Bureau arrested a future Democratic leader in late 1865 for continuing to hold his field hands in slavery. Admitting the charge, he argued that the Thirteenth Amendment was of "doubtful validity" and therefore could be ignored, pending court challenge. There were complaints that the authorities were apprenticing minors involuntarily to their former masters, and that taxes were being unfairly levied on freedmen. A planter near Perote, complaining that local officials were biased against blacks, reported that several of his female former slaves were being cheated by their new employer; he asked the Bureau what could be done to help if the magistrates would not enforce the laws.[30]

League agitation began in the late spring of 1867, and it was somewhat unusual in that black leaders were predominant. The authorities became immediately alarmed. The local sheriff reported "regular military organizations of companies & c armed with pistols & guns & all such weapons as they can procure with fife & drum." One freedman was said to be traveling the back roads, establishing militias. Bureau investigators questioned black Leaguer L. S. Speed about these reports, and he replied evasively that parades were part of the rites for deceased Leaguers. The organizer of another militia was more forthright. He wrote General Swayne requesting official authorization for drilling, in the hope of avoiding trouble with

29. Notasulga *Universalist Herald*, August 1, 1867; statement of J. H. Alston in Shorkley to R. T. Smith, April 4, 1868, in Letters Received SAC Opelika, Box 35, RG 105; R. T. Smith to O. L. Sheppard, April 8, 1868, in Records, M809, RG 105; KKK Report, IX, 1016–22.

30. Union Springs *Times*, September 18, 1867; Marjorie Howell Cook, "Restoration and Innovation: Alabamians Adjust to Defeat, 1865–1867" (Ph.D. dissertation, University of Alabama, 1968), 50; I. Johnson to Swayne, July 11, 1867, C. W. Rumph to Swayne, [October, 1867], both in Records, M809, RG 105.

whites. His goal was to "in lighten our people" and to "defend the United States against every rebellion." The area soon had a network of local leagues and quasi-military formations that functioned well into Reconstruction. In 1868 the Columbus *Enquirer* reported that L. S. Speed still directed thousands of men: "A gentleman gives us the following in regard to the strength of Leagues. . . . [O]n Sunday they met at Mrs. Comer's place, below Hatchechubbe, well armed, numbering about six hundred. There is another League at Spring Hill, numbering three hundred; another at Enon, numbering four hundred; another in the neighborhood of Silver Run, numbering five hundred; another at Union Springs, numbering eight hundred; and one near Eufaula, numbering one thousand. They are thoroughly armed and equipped." All these groups operated in an area fifty miles across, representing a mobilization of freedmen perhaps unparalleled in the state.[31]

The impact of this organizational activity upon the labor situation was soon evident. A white correspondent complained to Swayne that the drilling had a "demoralizing tendency" in the region around Midway. At the slightest rumor, freedmen would leave their work, and the result would be the failure "to gather a good crop after having made it." Farm laborers began to show unaccustomed militancy. In July, soon after the start of organizing, a planter named Wiggins had occasion to "correct by whip" a freedwoman in his employ. The next evening, hands from surrounding farms massed on his estate. They broke into Wiggins' house and seized him "without any authority save their radical ideas." What they intended is not clear, but white neighbors claimed that the freedmen were going to lynch him. Armed whites reached the scene. The deadlock was resolved the following morning by the arrival of black reinforcements summoned from miles around. The blacks conveyed their prisoner to the nearest magistrate, who, doubtless intimidated, placed him under arrest. In the aftermath, however, warrants were issued for the freedmen who

31. Royal to Swayne, July 12, 1867, in Records, M809, RG 105; E. A. Broly to Swayne, August 7, 1867, in Swayne Papers, ADAH; F. C. Hall to R. M. Patton, July 3, 1867, in Gov. Patton Papers, ADAH; W. E. Connelly to Kinsman, August 7, 1867, in Records, M809, RG 105; J. H. Young to Swayne, July 27, 1867, in Swayne Papers, ADAH; Union Springs *Times*, July 31, 1867; Mobile *Register*, October 14, 1868, quoting Columbus (Ga.) *Enquirer*.

had led the crowd. Similar disturbances and work stoppages occurred in Bullock County throughout this period.[32]

Actions such as these among the freedmen provoked angry responses. "White men of Alabama," warned the local paper, "get ready to defend yourselves, or be strangled to death in your sleep like a litter of blind puppies." One Radical wrote the Montgomery *State Sentinel* that the chivalry were picking quarrels with black leaders, in hopes of creating an excuse for violence. Threats were made openly; in the countryside, freedmen reportedly had been shot and lynched. Some planters, however, worked out a more sophisticated strategy. They planned a huge barbecue and invited the freedmen to come and hear Conservative speeches. Evoking the old regime's most positive paternalistic features gained the planters an audience. They simultaneously made a determined effort to co-opt the more pliable League leaders. Benjamin F. Royal, one of the most prominent organizers, actually received an invitation to address the throng. Royal, a future state senator who espoused political moderation, used the occasion to mend fences. According to the Union Springs *Times*, he "defended the League against the charge of being a political organization, contending that it was merely a moral and benevolent society, interfering with no man's political or religious rights—declared himself in favor of political equality, but opposed social equality—advocated the preservation of law and order and friendship between the races." At the conclusion of Royal's speech, Democratic leaders vied with one another in publicly shaking his hand.[33]

This *modus vivendi* between League and Conservative leaders did not last long. In late September, when John C. Keffer visited Union Springs, some two thousand freedmen gathered to hear him speak. Many of them brought guns and, when asked why, responded, "By order of General Speed." The freedmen declared that their League

32. E. A. Broly to Swayne, August 7, 1867, in Swayne Papers, ADAH; W. Ivay to McCall, in McCall to Swayne, July 26, 1867, Records, M809, RG 105; Union Springs *Times*, July 31, 1867; Connelly to Kinsman, July 26, 1867, in Records, M809, RG 105; A. Craven *et al.* to Swayne, July 29, 1867, D. McCall to Swayne, July 30, 1867, both in Records of the Third Military District, Office of Civil Affairs, Box 2, Pt. 1, RG 393.

33. Union Springs *Times*, September 25, 1867; G. M. Belser to Kinsman, May 29, 1867, in Records, M809, RG 105; D. A. McCall to Patton, April 5, 1867, in Gov. Patton Papers, ADAH; Montgomery *State Sentinel*, June 1, 1867; Union Springs *Times*, August 14, 1867.

oath bound them to comply with such directives. Keffer was so disconcerted that he ordered all firearms stacked on the podium before he would speak. Keffer's talk was a rousing affair in which he saw fit to disparage Royal's moderation and to praise Speed's Radical sentiments: "In one sentence he counseled love and fidelity from the negro to the Southern planter, and in the next told that negro that the one aim and tendency of that planter's politics was to restore slavery. In his cold cruel voice, he rebuked the present idleness of the black, and then . . . he carried that rude, passionate mind back to that most hated instrument of slave punishment, by telling them, 'You worked better under the lash.' "[34]

Keffer's oratory seems mild enough in retrospect, but local whites found it incendiary, and two men waylaid Keffer on the road out of town. One seized him while the other shot him in the head. Miraculously, Keffer survived and crawled, bleeding, back to Union Springs. Upon news of the attempted assassination, the freedmen regrouped, and by morning, "the 'Leagues' all armed . . . had reached the outskirts of the town." Local whites placated two militia companies by arresting Keffer's assailants, but one remaining League was still "at the time of writing encamped under the bluffs." If freedmen worried that justice might not be done, events confirmed their fears. The primary assailant was allowed to escape as soon as things quieted down, for which the military arrested the local sheriff. The escapee, a Colonel Andrews, turned up many months later and stood trial. The jury found him guilty of assault and battery, and he was fined one dollar.[35]

Tension in the countryside culminated in the Perote disturbances in late 1867, during which black Leaguers apparently set up a de facto government. Trouble in Perote had been imminent since September, when the shooting of a dog nearly provoked a race riot. Sometime about November, a black adventurer named George Shorter arrived from Montgomery. Little is known of him save that

34. Cecil E. McNair, "Reconstruction in Bullock County," *Alabama Historical Quarterly,* XV (Spring, 1953), 91–95; Union Springs *Times,* September 25, 1867; *Elmore Standard* (Wetumpka, Ala.), September 27, 1867.

35. *Elmore Standard* (Wetumpka, Ala.), September 27, 1867; Washington *Chronicle,* September 26, 1867; Bullock County Circuit Court, "Minutes," Book A, in Bullock County Courthouse, Union Springs, Ala.

he came from the northern states originally. Shorter claimed to have orders from General Swayne to set up a local black government, and, aided by skillfully forged papers and a smattering of education, he convinced local freedmen of the truth of his tale. Freedmen were seldom this credulous in political matters, but the isolated region and its polarized atmosphere favored deception. Moreover, it was settlement time after another catastrophic season—"not over one third of a fair crop"—and freedmen looked upon planters with unusual resentment. Appealing to their discontent, Shorter set up his regime. According to the Mobile *Times*, the Leaguers "formed a code of laws to govern the negro population, opened a court officered and organized, arresting by night all blacks who opposed their unlawful proceedings."[36]

As rumors of these events spread, local officials prepared to intervene. The opportunity came when Shorter fell out with subordinates over disposition of League funds. He apparently ordered the seizure of a man who then turned to the civil authorities for protection. The sheriff began arresting prominent blacks around Perote and seems to have apprehended Shorter quickly. However, other activists—still under the impression that Shorter was a legitimate emissary—rallied their followers to resist further arrests. They called for aid, and large numbers of blacks marched on Perote while whites also poured in from twenty miles around. Then someone burned down the local black church. After the fire, panic-stricken whites wrote Swayne that "disorder, riot, insurrection & bloodshed" were in the offing; sixty freedmen were described as defiantly resisting the authorities. The planters requested that a garrison of "twenty men, or ten men or five men" be sent to restore order.[37]

The black population was clearly angry, as one storekeeper in nearby Eufaula found when he eavesdropped on a conversation. "We are going to take them from the cradle up[,] we will soon have a good sup[p]ly of arms and ammunition," said one freedman. A woman

36. Montgomery *Advertiser*, December 12, 1867; Livingston *Journal*, December 21, 1867, quoting Columbus (Ga.) *Enquirer*; R. T. Smith to [?], [December, 1867], in Letters Sent SAC Opelika, Vol. 133, RG 105; Montgomery *Advertiser*, September 19, 1867, quoting Columbus (Ga.) *Enquirer*; Mobile *Times*, December 8, 17, 1867.

37. Mobile *Times*, December 8, 1867; Montgomery *Advertiser*, December 4, 1867; Citizens of Perote to Swayne, November 30, 1867, in Records, M809, RG 105.

agreed, stating that anyone who would not participate deserved the same fate. Bureau agent W. E. Connelly, himself a League organizer, concluded that this report was "perhaps well founded." Although no one seems to have been killed in the Perote episode, it was possibly fortunate that Union troops arrived from Montgomery swiftly, for only then did quiet return.[38]

With the army at his back, the sheriff rounded up more blacks, arresting no fewer than fifteen. Shorter and some leaders were tried and condemned to six months in jail. The rest received reprimands, probably because the Bureau pressed for leniency. Shorter was not a popular man, once the story finally unraveled, and rumor had it that the freedmen might lynch him themselves. His luck seems to have held good, however; he and several comrades broke out of jail, never to be heard from again. (Of course it is possible that nightriders were responsible for their disappearance.) What is important about this incident is that it demonstrates the desperate acts to which the freedmen were being pushed. Significantly, several contemporary accounts portray the Perote upheaval as a labor conflict. One such was the Eufaula *News*:

We have heard from a reliable source of some very bad conduct on the part of some of the freed people near Perote in Bullock County. It seems in several instances not satisfied with the settlement as made by their employers and unwilling to call in anyone else, although the Bureau agent was proposed, they proceeded to help themselves to what they thought they ought to have, regardless of the rights of others, and threatening with death any one who might interfere to prevent them. An intelligent mulattoe woman who witnessed their proceedings and remonstrated with them about their conduct had to fly to save her life. We fear that this is but the beginning.

The Mobile *Times* repeated the story, including the statement that the disturbance stemmed from the crop settlement. Within days of the trouble, moreover, several black leaders journeyed to Montgomery, bearing "terrible complaints" of oppressive working conditions in the county.[39]

38. J. Tamey to Grant, December 5, 1867, in Records of the Third Military District, Office of Civil Affairs, Box 2, Pt. 1, RG 393.

39. Union Springs *Times*, December 21, 1867; Carrollton *West Alabamian*, December 11, 1867, quoting Eufaula *News*; Mobile *Times*, November 28, 1867; Montgomery *State Sentinel*, December 13, 1867.

Whether or not the Perote affair arose from a labor dispute, the disorders clearly manifested themselves on the plantation. The freedmen simply refused to work as they had in the past. Soon after the disturbances, Bullock County's probate judge wrote that there appeared to be "a notion among a portion of the laborers in this section that they will be provided for by contributions from the North or from other mysterious ways if they refuse to work for current rates of wages or shares of crops & c." Some newspaper accounts specifically identified the League as being involved in blacks' efforts to farm independently. The Mobile *Register* reported that freedmen in the county were setting up for themselves and had no capital more substantial than a League certificate.⁴⁰

In the midst of this turmoil, and prodded by another bad crop, planters recognized that some concession had to be made to the freedmen's demands. "Southern farmers are compelled," the Union Springs *Times* concluded, "to change their old routine system of farming and try some other." Although the *Times* at first advocated a variety of agricultural reforms, here as elsewhere the practical solution proved to be renting the freedmen land: "If the negro makes any progress at all, his second step will place him beyond the necessity of being a hireling. The first and great lesson he has to learn is to save part of his earnings—economy. He will invest as a renter, if he can do no better, or, where able, will buy a little land. . . . The home instinct—the yearning after one's own vine and fig tree is the strong actuating motive of labor in this age. The man who has not this instinct and desire will be found of little use to society." By the spring of 1868, the paper noted that numbers of freedmen had rented land. Reports soon filtered in that the freedman was "decidedly improving as a laborer." That year's crop turned out well, and for the first time since the war, planters made substantial profits; this stabilized tenantry as the norm of agricultural cultivation.⁴¹

The argument here is not that the leagues were the decisive cause of the emergence of decentralized tenant farming, in Bullock County

40. McCall to "Asst. Commissioner of the Bureau," January 10, 1868, in Records, M809, RG 105; Mobile *Register*, March 16, 1868.
41. Union Springs *Times*, September 18, November 30, 1867, May 2, 1868; Mobile *Register*, March 16, 1868.

or elsewhere. A multiplicity of economic and social forces undermined centralized management in cotton, and the politicization of the freedmen represented just one factor. It is plausible, however, that the political upheaval influenced the timing of the shift to tenant farming. The agitation certainly reinforced the sense of crisis for the planters, and it thus encouraged them to depart from prevailing agricultural practices. The point is that many local leagues took on a pronounced agrarian character, and the movement acquired much of its impetus from black resistance to coercive forms of plantation management. The League thus figures as a crucial factor in labor resistance, aimed at reordering conditions of work in ways more satisfactory to the freedmen.

The Loyal League interacted similarly with plantation agriculture in the rest of Alabama as well. While the League was not avowedly a rural labor organization, its mobilization had something of the same effect. Access to land and conditions of work were important in the League's appeal to the freedmen. At times, Radical activity even took on a more explicit labor function. The memory of slavery united freedmen and roused them to action against the status quo on the plantation. The whole point of League rhetoric was against the planters' trying to retain coercive control over the freedmen. This emphasis could only erode plantation discipline.

League spokesmen frequently addressed agricultural issues, and land acquisition in particular represented an important concern. Organizers often lambasted the plantation system as undemocratic, and defended the right of freedmen to rent or own farms. The influential editor Albert Griffin wrote several articles decrying the reluctance of whites to rent land. Griffin's vision of the future differed vastly from that of the planters; the large plantations were "destined soon to be cut up into small farms, to be controlled by their owners and their sons. Hired labor will become more and more difficult to procure, yet a laboring, self-reliant, and intelligent population will multiply all over the country." W. E. Connelly of Eufaula expressed similar views. Working large numbers of freedmen on one plantation had failed, and some planters were now renting small farms to industrious freedmen. Connelly praised the idea and "urged all parties to adopt it." He also hoped that all citizens would soon "have an opportunity to secure a homestead, and the latent wealth of the state will be brought to the surface and distributed among the people."[42] This, Connelly thought, was the practical application of the principles of the Republican party.

These goals were not limited to party ideologues: grass-roots black leaders frequently avowed similar hopes. For example, when George Washington Cox traveled to rural Tuscaloosa to organize the League, he became very interested in agricultural issues. This former slave noted and approved of the freedmen's tendency to settle on their own in the woods, and raise corn, potatoes, wheat, cabbage—anything but cotton:

The fact is, the colored people are very anxious to get land of their own to live upon independently; and they want money to buy stock to make crops. And we are aware . . . that the only way to get these necessaries is to give our votes to the party that are making every effort possible to bring these blessings about by Reconstructing the State.

Charles Leavens, one of the founders of the Mobile League, found freedmen in southwest Alabama determined not to work as they had done. The freedmen, who were "cramped in making their contracts for land to cultivate," now awaited substantial change. Their new resolution Leavens depicted in sympathetic terms.[43]

On his organizing tours, John C. Keffer also addressed labor concerns and agricultural conditions. After one of his speeches, landowners became so alarmed that they tried to import labor from outside the state, offering free homesteads just to attract whites into their neighborhood. After another such talk, a newspaper reported an unusual amount of poor work and insubordination among the farmhands, which it blamed on the "pernicious doctrines inculcated by Keffer and others at the barbecue. Many of the negroes returned with the belief that they are soon to be placed in possession of the lands now owned by their employers." This account exemplifies a characteristic of contemporary attacks against Keffer and other Leaguers for confiscation talk: it does not clearly differentiate be-

42. Mobile *Nationalist*, October 31, November 22, 1866; W. E. Connelly to Kinsman, August 1, October 1, 1867, both in Records, M809, RG 105.
43. Montgomery *State Sentinel*, August 7, 1867; Mobile *Nationalist*, October 10, 1867.

tween forcible redistribution of acreage and the simple desire to rent or buy land. A planter, commenting upon Keffer's speech at the barbecue, insisted that expectations of free land were widespread among freedmen and quoted as verification a question put to him by one of his own hands: "'When your plantation is divided out between us will the colored people in your employment all be dealt with alike as to the quality and quantity of lands they will get?' " The question, of course, could have referred to tenancy as well as ownership. It seems likely that such evidence was often deliberately misinterpreted in order to alarm white voters. Whatever Keffer had actually said—or the freedmen heard—there can be no doubt that his speaking tours upset agricultural production. In the words of the Union Springs *Times*, cotton lands were currently a bargain for buyers, but only if Keffer did not return.[44]

League organizers in the Tennessee Valley also precipitated labor unrest. John B. Callis of the Bureau and Daniel H. Bingham, a militant Unionist, set up League councils and dispensed aid and advice to the freedmen. Callis particularly raised the ire of Conservatives. George S. Houston, the future Redeemer governor of the state, said that if Callis retained his position, it would "tend to break up the farming and planting." The landowners would rather "let their land go uncultivated than to be under unending trouble through the year & subject to insult and harshness all the while." Houston's complaint grew out of a labor dispute on his own plantation. He had turned off one of his former slaves for attending a League meeting. The man consulted Bingham, who loaned him five dollars and secured an order from Callis permitting the man to return and work his crop. "I have all the rights that you or any other man has [and] I shall not suffer them abridged," the man wrote his former master—with Bingham transcribing the letter. Certainly the continued presence of such a laborer could undermine discipline. Houston reported that after the man returned, he was disobedient and idle, disorganizing the workers by his conduct and conversation. Two laborers testified that the freedman "caused us all to quit our work and go to Athens to examine our contract, by reporting to us

44. Montgomery *Advertiser*, January 5, 1868; *Monroe Eagle* (Claiborne, Ala.), March 26, 1870; Mobile *Register*, August 31, 1867; Union Springs *Times*, September 25, 1867.

that our contract was of no avail, and that Houston could turn us all off at any time he saw proper." The planter's fear that his crop might be damaged seems reasonable, since a single malcontent might have a dramatic impact on the rest of the labor force. For this reason, planters were often willing to boycott Leaguers, despite the prevailing labor shortage. As Bingham put it, planters resorted to every means they could devise to prevent freedmen from joining leagues.[45]

Even some northerners agreed that Bingham undermined necessary discipline. Three Union veterans, engaged in planting near Athens, complained that the freedmen lost "much of their time" at Bingham's League meetings. The northerners were afraid that this agitation would damage their crop. The Leaguers told the freedmen that the civil law no longer existed, advising them not to pay their taxes and making them believe that the lands of their former masters would be confiscated. All this tended to make the blacks dissatisfied and to unfit them for their duties. The agitation caused many minor disturbances in the area, and the Yankee planters feared that a large-scale outbreak might soon occur.[46]

Conservative sources contended that the League hurt plantation labor, and this was a major indictment by the Democrats. As early as April, 1867, the Athens *Post* commented that Radicals "play the old demagogue tricks of antagonizing labor and capital." Another newspaper credited party agents with spreading the impression that freedmen were cheated at settlement time. These reports became commonplace whenever the League stepped up operations. In mid-1868 the Livingston *Journal* reported that the organization was again distracting blacks from work and doing harm in general. The Selma *Times and Messenger* made similar accusations: "We learn that, preparatory to the Presidential campaign, radical emissaries have lately turned up in various counties of the State in the work of reorganizing the negro 'Loyal League,' and that, in some places, the negroes, who had been working well, and whose crops were promis-

45. Houston to Patton, August 26, 1867, in Gov. Patton Papers, ADAH; Callis to J. Danforth, July 31, 1867, Burnet Houston to G. S. Houston, August 3, 1867, G. S. Houston to Callis, August 13, 1867, all in G. S. Houston Papers, Duke University; Deposition entitled "Interrogatories . . . ," in George S. Houston Papers, ADAH.

46. B. J. Spaulding *et al.* to J. Pope, May 15, 1867, in Records of the Third Military District, Office of Civil Affairs, Box 1, Pt. 1, RG 393.

ing, have thrown down the implements of labor and gone into the more congenial, if less profitable, business of President making." Such allegations frequently appeared in Democratic campaign material.[47]

As evidence of actual behavior, partisan claims may have limited validity, but planters in private correspondence made similar observations. Many noted a changed temper in the labor force. A farmer wrote General Swayne that his workers were demoralized by outside tampering, and asked if legal means existed to keep them at home, away from designing persons. A Mobile cotton factor found that his clients dreaded the effects of the elections on the blacks' work habits. James Arrington, a planter in the vicinity of Montgomery, thought that freedmen had performed well for several months after the apparent defeat of the Radical constitution because they had lost confidence in the Radicals, gone to work, and raised good crops. When Congress readmitted Alabama to the Union in mid-summer, 1868, Arrington feared that the situation would change: "We shall soon have the Scalawags and Carpetbaggers installed in office here then they will reorganize their Leagues [and] commence the Presidential Campaign. I fear they will demoralize the negros and we will be troubled to get the crop of cotton picked out." Soon afterward, Arrington decided that the only way to farm in the future was with small squads on the best land, and that the rest of the acreage should be rented out. If the region could "get clear" of carpetbaggers preaching social equality, the freedmen might work better. As matters stood, however, Arrington saw no alternative to changing his method of production.[48]

Bureau officials sometimes echoed the planters' complaints. As early as mid-May, James Christian in Uniontown observed the disruptive effects of political agitation. He heard almost daily that "laborers who had been industrious, cheerful, and efficient, have since these meetings have been held, become idle, dissatisfied, worthless

47. Athens *Post*, April 11, 1867; Mobile *Advertiser and Register*, December 17, 1867; Selma *Times and Messenger*, July 8 (quoting Livingston *Journal*), June 20, 1868; Montgomery *Advertiser*, May 22, 1867.
48. D. S. Harbin to Swayne, August 24, 1867, in Records, M809, RG 105; Wemyss to Watson, March 4, 1868, in Watson Papers, Duke University; J. Arrington to "Brother," June 25, October 25, 1868, both in Arrington Papers, UNC.

and turbulent." His workload increased drastically during the same period, so large was the growth in the number of cases before his office. He went on to cite how unsettling Radical oratory was when the memory of slavery was so fresh. Christian doubted that even the most casual observer could "fail to note the marked change in the tone and temper of the freedmen." Christian apparently found this change so distasteful that he resigned from the Bureau.[49]

Even Radical sources admitted the severity of the problem. Republicans candidly acknowledged that freedmen attended so many rallies, the crops suffered. Party activists sometimes went further, noting that agitation also made the laborers restive. A Radical in Sumter County, for example, observed how prevalent these reports were, and he suggested that it would be well for the military to urge freedmen to greater exertions in the cotton fields. A striking example of politics disrupting agriculture occurred in Montgomery during the campaign to ratify the constitution in early January, 1868. According to the Montgomery *Advertiser*, Keffer urged the freedmen to "make no contracts until after the 4th of February" when the Republicans expected to gain power. In response to the subsequent outcry of the Democratic press, the Republican State Executive Committee noted that reports were "in circulation" in various parts of Alabama that the constitutional convention had directed freedmen not to contract. The committee wished to set the record straight: "We advise all laboring men, especially the colored men, to go to work and make contracts at once." Considerable evidence exists that refusing to contract was often a tactic to pressure planters. Such talk probably manifested a desire for land as much as an actual belief that the League had issued orders not to contract. Certainly the currency of such rumors illustrates the close tie between labor and politics during the period.[50]

The impact of leagues spread beyond their immediate locality, for garbled rumors could undermine discipline as effectively as could the actual creation of a council. The activities of James K. Green and W. T. Blackford in Hale County worried a planter nearly thirty

49. Christian to Swayne, May 15, 1867, in Records, M809, RG 105.
50. Montgomery *Advertiser*, January 5, 1868; Montgomery *State Sentinel*, May 22, September 12, 1867; Mobile *Nationalist*, January 30, 1868.

miles away: "I have recently had a good deal of trouble with the hands. . . . It seems that certain parties in or near Greensboro has been telling them that they ought to receive forty five dollars per month instead of ten, that neither the present crop nor the lands belonged to the Planters, but that they belonged to the Government. . . . Such talk has demoralized them very much & has very seriously impaired what was three weeks ago a beautiful prospect for a crop." In Alabama, at all events, there were few localities untouched by the League. By the fall of 1867, leagues existed virtually everywhere freedmen lived in any numbers, and almost no region of cotton cultivation escaped reports of demoralization among the hands.[51]

In view of the leagues' involvement in the agricultural labor situation, it is not surprising that local councils employed tactics similar to those of labor organizations. Freedman often organized boycotts of offensive Conservative planters. Klan leader John Hunnicutt, for example, faced a concerted boycott because of his avowed killings of League activists. "It got so I could not hire a darkey at any price," Hunnicutt wrote. Another Democratic leader described similar problems in Bullock County, and he was obliged to recruit labor in South Carolina. A Republican paper noted a boycott of objectionable planters in Greene County. Near Bladon Springs, activists reportedly persuaded freedmen to hire out "to none but Loyal Leaguers." According to the Talladega *Watchtower*, the freedmen even intended to "coerce the farmers of this county into the support of Grant and Colfax by refusing to labor for all of those who refuse to support the Radical candidates." The paper countered by suggesting that planters neither employ nor rent land to Grant voters. In addition, white Republicans, and northerners, reportedly encountered fewer difficulties than did others in finding workers—a circumstance that may have helped increase the number of planter-scalawags.[52]

51. E. B. Perrin to Pierce, July 26, 1867, in Letters Received SAC Demopolis, Box 27, RG 105.

52. Hunnicutt, *Reconstruction in West Alabama*, 79; H. E. Stearx, "William C. Jordan and Reconstruction in Bullock County, Alabama," *Alabama Review*, XV (1962), 71; Demopolis *Southern Republican*, February 10, 1869; Montgomery *Mail*, December 27, 1867, quoting Choctaw *Herald*; Talladega *Watchtower*, September 9, 1868; C. C. Colton and M. G. Candee to F. T. Adams, [July 22, 1867], in Swayne Papers, ADAH; Lawrence N. Powell, *New Masters: Northern Planters During the Civil War and Reconstruction* (New Haven, 1980), 49–50, 60–61.

Another tactic freedmen used was seizing crops when they thought themselves likely to be defrauded, and work slowdowns were common. Immediately after the League formed in Talladega, blacks refused to harvest the wheat. "There was an effort made . . . to strike for high wages, and demand exorbitant prices," noted the local Bureau agent. Efforts to fix standard rates were common. In Cherokee County, freedmen bound themselves not to work at harvest for less than two dollars a day and allegedly set a penalty of fifty lashes for those who would not go along with them. At election time in Dallas County, four hundred armed freedmen gathered for the purpose of "explaining some new laws." They reportedly agreed upon a "strike for higher wages," with twelve dollars per month as their demand. One of the black speakers at the meeting stated that anyone who worked for less than five dollars a month should be killed; the freedmen would take their blankets and dwell in the fields before they accepted such a wage.[53]

Quieter, and perhaps more effective, was the simple device of laborers squatting at the end of the year. If armed freedmen refused either to contract or to depart, only a bold planter dared evict them from their homes. Several landowners in an isolated part of Russell County feared "much trouble and probable violence upon the part of the freedmen, when they are requested to leave our plantations." Complaining that freedmen had already seized the crop, the planters asked for federal troops. Significantly, a Freedmen's Bureau investigator blamed League organizer J. B. Healy for causing the difficulty. Healy was the local Bureau agent, and it was suggested that a "more efficient" officer would help matters greatly. Similar problems occurred near Demopolis. Squatting was a powerful weapon prior to the advent of the Klan, and political activity and drilling facilitated such militancy.[54]

Republican politicians and editors sometimes endorsed labor activism. David Montgomery has argued in *Beyond Equality* that be-

53. Complaint Book, November 7, 1867, SAC Demopolis, Vol. 141, RG 105; J. L. McGogy to Kinsman, June 5, 1867, in Records, M809, RG 105; Montgomery *Mail*, July 1, 1868; J. Keyser to J. McKellar and F. Lee, January 4, 1868, Lee to Shorkley, January 4, 1868, both in Letters Received SAC Selma, Box 36, RG 105.
54. J. A. Wright to Mills, December 30, 1867, in Records, M809, RG 105, see endorsement.

cause of their support for government intervention in the economy, Radical Republicans often sympathized with the labor movement. Whatever the merits of this thesis for the nation as a whole, it seems to have been true of the Republican press in Alabama. The Mobile *Nationalist* editorialized early in support of labor unions, provided that intimidation of workers not occur. The Montgomery *Alabama State Journal*, the state's leading Republican paper, held that "instead of fewer Unions, more are needed, and more comprehensive and wisely organized." In regard to agricultural strikes, the paper complained not that they were too frequent, but that they were too often unsuccessful. The advice was to prepare strikes well in order to win.[55]

It would not do to overstate the point; the League was not a union, nor did the Republican party engage in labor organizing. The League leadership primarily focused on winning elections, and the labor activities that happened under League auspices were at the local level. Nevertheless, the League's general affinity for labor activism is evident; as the Montgomery *Advertiser* observed, "The Union Leagues lay down as part of their creed sympathy with labor against capital, and the Republican platforms generally do the same thing. In other words that they are the champions of the poor man as against the rich." This tendency was clear in the prominence of former Leaguers in the Alabama Labor Union (ALU), the first group explicitly for farmworkers. This offshoot of the National Negro Labor Union—and thus of the white National Labor Union—was founded in 1870; the economic troubles of the mid-1870s apparently destroyed it. The ALU was one of the strongest such organizations in the southern states, and it was part of the first attempt at a modern agricultural union among blacks. Although real organization of the cotton belt proved beyond the ability of the ALU, and probably the fledgling labor movement as well, it provided a sounding board and a lobby for farm laborers.[56]

Among the delegates to the founding convention of the ALU were

55. Montgomery, *Beyond Equality*, ix–xi; Mobile *Nationalist*, April 5, 1866, April 11, 1867; Montgomery *Alabama State Journal*, May 13, 1870.

56. Montgomery *Advertiser*, July 28, 1867; Montgomery *Alabama State Journal*, January 6, 1871; Philip S. Foner, *From Colonial Times to the Founding of the American Federation of Labor* (New

most of the black leaders prominent in organizing the League. The ALU officers included George Washington Cox of Tuscaloosa and James K. Green of Hale; James H. Alston of Macon and L. S. Speed of Bullock also attended. All these Leaguers had shown concern for issues of land acquisition, and Alston was threatened by the Klan for renting land. Also elected to ALU offices were Holland Thompson and L. J. Williams of Montgomery and Yancey Simms of Talladega. These men had been League leaders, as had fellow delegates William V. Turner of Wetumpka and Allen Alexander of Mobile. This group comprised nearly all the well-known black Leaguers who were alive and active in 1870. ALU policies resembled those of the League, and resolutions adopted at its various meetings brought forward similar complaints. At one such gathering, the Committee on Labor and Wages denounced gang labor as a relic of slavery and recommended buying land on the installment plan.[57]

The obvious continuity between these two organizations underlines an important aspect of the League in Alabama. It was a political movement with strong overtones of labor revolt. Freedmen examined the plantation labor system in light of the Radical rhetoric of equality, as well as their own experience, and found it wanting. Their politicization expressed their hostility to the vestiges of slavery all about them. Only by granting the freedmen more direct access to land, and less supervision of their labor, could planters get them back to work. Thus the Union League emerges as both a political expression of discontent among agricultural workers and a collective means to exact concessions from the planter class.

In Mississippi as well, labor concerns loomed large. The specifics of the interaction between the League and agriculture differed somewhat from those in Alabama, due in part to the divergent structure of the League in the two states. The League grew gradually, and intense local agitation occurred over a two-and-a-half-year period, so

---

York, 1947), 402–408, vol. I of *History of the Labor Movement in the United States,* 5 vols.; John Benjamin Myers, "Black Human Capital: The Freedmen and the Reconstruction of Labor in Alabama" (Ph.D. dissertation, Florida State University, 1974), 212–13.

57. Montgomery *Alabama State Journal,* November 15, 16, 1873; Montgomery *Advertiser,* November 11, 16, 1873.

generalizing about its role is difficult. But in Mississippi too the League encouraged the restructuring of plantation agriculture. There were organized efforts to dissuade freedmen from working for planters who would not rent land. Leagues sometimes boycotted the process of annual contracting for hands and sometimes called strikes for higher wages.[58]

Prior to Military Reconstruction, events in Mississippi were similar to those in Alabama. Planters wrote about flood damage and armyworms in 1865 and 1866, and about the impact of poor cotton prices. Mississippi's planters also complained of deteriorating work habits. Among the freedmen, the expectation of land redistribution was widespread. As newspaperman John Trowbridge noted, however, "The freedmen, who, before Christmas [1865], had refused to make contracts, vaguely hoping that lands would be given them by the government, or leased to them by their owners, now came forward to make the best terms they could." Access to land had the potential to become a political demand, as a sympathetic northern Bureau official found in conversation with a black leader in Vicksburg. The northerner opined that the planters intended to force the freedmen to contract through the Black Codes. The prompt rejoinder was, "What if we should compel them to lease us lands?"[59]

After the organization of the League, denunciations of the existing plantation system became commonplace. Alston Mygatt, the Mississippi League's president, openly demanded change. In his keynote address at the constitutional convention, he stated that under the Republicans "large landed estates shall melt away into small divisions, thus densifying population; cities shall grow, towns spring up, mechanism flourish, agriculture become scientific, internal improvements be pushed on, free schools flourish in every district and loyal men shall rule." As J. Mills Thornton has argued, Radicals saw property taxes as having desirable social consequences and explicitly advocated them as redistributive in character. During the 1869 campaign, in which they finally came to power, Republicans repeatedly claimed that taxes would force planters to sell their land. "This is the

58. Harris, *The Day of the Carpetbagger*, 101.
59. J. T. Trowbridge, *The South: A Tour of Its Battlefields and Ruined Cities, A Journey Through the Desolated States, and Talks with the People* (Hartford, 1866), 362, 368.

promise," stated the *Hinds County Gazette*, "which is now being made to the colored people through the Loyal Leagues and otherwise." The Democratic press devoted much space to refuting this "monstrous" line of argument. In one instance, a set of resolutions, purportedly by black Democrats, appear to have been forged for that very purpose.[60]

State-level League leaders focused on such issues only intermittently, since ensuring changes in the plantation system lay largely beyond legislative recourse. At the local level, however, many Leaguers endeavored to improve working conditions or gain access to land. Gerald Jaynes suggests that local leagues were the "hatcheries" of "radical economic experiments which kept planters uneasy." The activities of one black Leaguer near Natchez provide some support for this observation. H. P. Jacobs, a future legislator, tried to negotiate the purchase of a large plantation on behalf of a company of freedmen. Jacobs explained his idea at a series of mass meetings; the freedmen would finance the venture through the bounties the army owed black veterans. On one of his speaking tours, Jacobs approached a prospective seller who dismissed his offer as having an "electioneering purpose," but the landowner soon realized that the freedmen were in earnest: "They are refusing to work for any one, believing they are to have a place of their own." Despite Jacobs' efforts, the purchase did not take place. The Bureau deemed the leaders of the company unsuitable and withheld the required financial aid.[61]

Freedmen commonly utilized local leagues against planters more directly—in particular, boycotting the annual contract process. A Bureau agent in the wealthy Delta region observed this phenomenon in March, 1868. Freedmen declined to contract as hands, despite the agent's best efforts to get them to do so, and he blamed their intrac-

60. Washington *Chronicle*, July 13, 1868; Jackson *Clarion*, January 8, 1868; J. Mills Thornton III, "Fiscal Policy and the Failure of Radical Reconstruction in the Lower South," in Kousser and McPherson (eds.), *Region, Race, and Reconstruction*, 349–94; Jackson *Clarion*, September 30, November 10, 1869, quoting *Hinds County Gazette* (Raymond, Miss.); Resolutions, "We the Freedmen of Pike County," October 23, 1869, in Mayes-Dimitry-Stuart Papers, MDAH.

61. Jaynes, *Branches Without Roots*, 295; A. Farrar to J. Biddle, February 10, 19, 1868, both in Registers and Letters, M752, RG 105; H. R. Pease to M. Barber, January 28, 1868, in Records, M826, RG 105.

tability on political itinerants. Another Bureau officer found freedmen refusing to contract in Bolivar County, because they were awaiting "new laws for their benefit" from the constitutional convention then in session. According to an army officer, freedmen shunned labor agreements along the Yazoo River, in part because they hoped for favorable action from the convention. Bureau chief Alvan C. Gillem connected political agitation and blacks' refusal to come to terms: "There seems to be a wide-spread belief, which is daily increasing among the freedmen, that land in the state is to be divided and distributed among them, and in some sections of the state this illusion is assuming a practical form by the freedmen refusing to contract for the next year, or to leave the premises they have cultivated this year. It is feared that this course, induced by evil disposed advisors, may lead to collisions the extent and result of which it is difficult to surmise."[62] Annual labor agreements were critical, since planters wanted some mechanism to ensure a sufficient labor force. As a landowner put it, in reference to his hands taking time off for meetings, "The only restraint on the freedmen is the contract & if that is not carried out the rules & threats of the 'Leagues' are all powerful & the Negroes will believe the contracts of no avail." A Mississippi planter complained that his hands would neither contract nor leave their quarters, and such comments became more prevalent each January. Squatting, in particular, proved an effective way of pressuring the landowners.[63]

Agricultural unrest near Meridian illustrated this pattern. During December, 1867, at settlement and contract time, many hungry freedmen became squatters on their employers' land. The situation encouraged both black militancy and white overreaction. According to local whites, the Leaguers arrayed themselves to march on Meridian and Marion, demanding provisions from merchants; they also threatened to seize what they needed. Several arrests of leading freedmen were made by the Bureau, which soon concluded that the stories were exaggerated, but restiveness was indeed pervasive.

62. Preuss to Barber, March 31, 1868, in Letters Sent SAC Greenville, Vol. 148, RG 105; H. R. Williams to Barber, February 10, 1868, in Records, M826, RG 105; Jackson *Clarion*, December 25, 1867.
63. S. D. Lee to G. S. Smith, October 25, 1867, in Letters Received SAC Macon, Box 45, RG 105; R. Davis to Ord, December 27, 1867, in Ord Papers, UC Berkeley.

Black Leaguers were organizing military companies, and many of them were "destitute of food and clothing, refuse to labor and threaten to take what they want by force." The agrarian overtones of this episode are evident. Immediately after the troubles, the Meridian *Gazette* claimed that League agitation would throw thousands of laborers out of work, and that it was "idle for them to think of cultivating farms on their own account."[64]

The freedmen's reluctance to contract as laborers caused planters enormous worry in late 1867. A white in one League stronghold, Yazoo County, made the planter's dilemma clear: he would not feel safe renting an extensive plantation when he was not assured of a single laborer to work it. The freedmen, it seems, had acquired "some *exalted ideas* themselves since they have been allowed to vote & c and frequently express the notion of 'renting lands' '*If* we contract' & c." A nearby planter agreed that the freedmen had no intention of contracting as hands, because they hoped that Congress or perhaps the pending constitutional convention would divide lands.[65]

Vicksburg epitomized the entire process. In early January, 1868, the Vicksburg *Times* noted a prevailing belief that Leaguers were urging blacks not to hire for the year. Not a single freedman had yet signed a labor agreement, despite the fact that several hundred unemployed workers remained in town. Many freedmen still had not contracted as late as May, according to the local Bureau officer: "There is a great demand for laborers, and it is quite difficult to procure hands, not that there are not men to be employed, for there are a great many idlers, in this City especially. And they are kept from laboring by a few leading colored men who belong to the Union League who persuade them from leaving the City because they think they will lose their votes by leaving. And tell them the whites are just trying to get them off to keep them from voting." This depiction of the freedmen as passive pawns of their leaders is suspect. The officer's own evidence suggests a different interpretation. In the same

64. H. Means *et al.* to O. Greene, December 2, 1867, in Records of the Third Military District, Office of Civil Affairs, Box 1, Pt. 1, RG 393; Meridian *Chronicle*, January 22, 1868; Selma *Messenger*, December 11, 1867; Meridian *Gazette*, December 4, 7, 1867.

65. J. C. Caruthers to R. L. Caruthers, November 13, 1867, in Robert Caruthers Papers, UNC; J. McCormack to Ord, January 3, 1868, in Records of the Third Military District, Office of Civil Affairs, Box 6, Pt. 1, RG 393.

letter he observed that "another progressive move is that the freed-men are working for themselves renting lands and making their own crops." Large numbers of planters rented their whole plantations out, which he described as "giving up to the freedmen." This he saw as a dramatic break from the previous year, and he added that freed-men worked much better under the new system.[66]

The evidence is persuasive that in this wealthy Delta area the League pressured planters to rent land to the freedmen. Either plan-ters would agree or their land would lie idle while cotton prices climbed for the first time since the war. The black leader's boast that freedmen would "compel" whites to lease land proved an accurate prophecy. As one local planter observed, freedmen were increas-ingly disposed to become "*landholders* and *tenants*, and not *hirelings*," and he commented that this might have resulted from "loyal league teachings." The issue remained a crucial one in the Vicksburg stronghold throughout Reconstruction. In 1874 a League-like "Farmers' Club" organized blacks in the rural areas outside the city, and once again freedmen began drilling and talking of armed re-sistance. They complained that land rents were too high and also that "the proprietors of land intend combining to prevent the negroes renting land." The club mobilized freedmen to emigrate from areas where planters either refused to lease land or tried to force them to vote Democratic. Freedmen remained intransigent; the threat of the return of gang labor roused them to collective resistance.[67]

The attitude of the Bureau official toward the trends in Vicksburg reveals a larger point: contemporary white observers were credulous about blacks' motives. Freedmen gave all sorts of excuses for not contracting—they understandably wanted to avoid unnecessarily provoking retaliation. They told planters they were waiting for the next election, or the new constitution, or even Grant's inauguration. Planters often took these statements at face value, interpreting them in paternalistic fashion as superstition or ignorance rather than de-

---

66. Vicksburg *Times*, January 10, 1868; J. C. Chapman to S. C. Green, May 6, 1868, in Letters Sent SAC Vicksburg, Vol. 274, RG 105.

67. *Southern Cultivator*, XXVII (1869), 302–303; Vicksburg *Vicksburger*, September 17, 1874.

fiance. A more sophisticated reading would suggest that freedmen manipulated their employers. They shammed stupidity to disguise the pressure they were applying through withholding labor or squatting, for example. Blacks adopted this gambit on other issues. They often cited League orders whenever they wished to skip work for a rally, or carry arms, or do anything that might anger their employers. To read planter sources, one would think freedmen lived in unholy dread of violating League directives. The evidence suggests that blacks feigned much of this. Even the Conservative Jackson *Clarion*, repeating the charge of confiscation, suspected an element of role playing: "There are thousands of idle, vagabond negroes scattered all over the State, refusing to accept employment and awaiting their deliverance from the necessity of labor to obtain their bread, in the real or pretended belief that the 'Convention' will appropriate other people's estates to support them in their idleness."[68]

Whether or not the refusal to contract was a deliberate attempt to pressure planters, many of them throughout Mississippi abandoned gang labor in 1868, opting for some less centralized form of tenant farming. These changes evoked considerable public debate among landowners. The Natchez *Democrat*, commenting upon reports that some planters were renting to freedmen, suggested that the new system was worth a try. The State Central Agricultural Society also endorsed the practice, but its advice did not go uncontested. The Jackson *Clarion* admitted that renting might work for river counties and wealthy areas; however, in the rest of Mississippi it was simply a recipe for handing over control to the freedmen. "It at once breaks up all unity of action, combination of force, precision of calculation, and general progress in the business of the farm," the paper stated. Yet even the *Clarion* admitted in the spring of 1868 that "men are eagerly rushing" into the arrangement.[69]

By 1869, rental to either families or larger groups of freedmen became prevalent, so much so that the Vicksburg *Herald* warned planters against obsolete prejudices in the matter. The press frequently cited League pressure as encouraging this agricultural

---

68. Jackson *Clarion*, February 28, 1868.
69. Mobile *Register*, July 21, 1867; Natchez *Democrat*, June 20, 1867; Jackson *Clarion*, April 1, 1868.

change. The *Hinds County Gazette* wrote: "The Loyal Leagues here-abouts have determined that the colored people shall not hire them-selves to the whites, for plantation purposes, next year, nor shall they crop on shares with the whites; that they shall rent land and plant on their own account, and that not over $1.50 per acre rent shall be paid for land!" The Goodman *Star* stated that local Leaguers urged freedmen not to work for the white people again in any capac-ity, and that the blacks swore to carry out this policy. The Jackson *Clarion*, reporting that a large meeting in Rankin County had pro-claimed similar policies, expressed fear of strikes and turmoil result-ing from Radical influences. The Natchez *Democrat* echoed these sentiments. A "Loyal Labor League" had determined that hands would not "work the coming year except as lessees of land," accord-ing to the *Democrat*, and freedmen were also planning to boycott all landowners who required liens on the growing crop. The *Democrat* feared that "some of the negroes, perhaps many" would hold out for these terms, to the detriment of the planters.[70]

The overall pattern is clear. In Mississippi, as in Alabama, the League took on the character of an agrarian movement—indeed, it generated rural strife almost unequaled in southern history. Labor concerns intersected with the League in a variety of ways. Some activists helped organize black settlements; others arranged boycotts or strikes against planters. A critical issue was independent access to land, and Leaguers were frequently involved in efforts to prevent freedmen from contracting as agricultural laborers. These efforts were not tangential—they were a critical facet of mobilizing the freedmen. League agitation inspired agrarian radicalism among the labor force, and this is central to understanding the nature of the movement. The Radical movement among the freedmen thus formed an integral part of wider resistance against authoritarian conditions on the plantations.

70. Vicksburg *Herald*, October 1, 1869; *Hinds County Gazette* (Raymond, Miss.), September 15, 1869; Forest *Register*, October 8, 1870, quoting Goodman (Miss.) *Star*; Jackson *Clarion*, October 14, 1870; Natchez *Democrat*, December 23, 1869.

※♛※

SIX

The League in Mobile and Other Urban Areas

The League spread into the cities at the same time it swept through the plantation region. League councils in urban centers functioned in a unique environment, but in a sense analogously to the movement in the hinterland. On the plantations, insurgency reflected freedmen's frustrations with postwar agriculture; similarly in the cities, it was often a response to social and economic grievances distinctive to urban conditions. This was strikingly evident in Mobile, where League organizing initiated a broad program of mass activity. In other large communities, leagues also were part of nearby agricultural struggles. One reason was that numbers of freedmen had migrated to urban areas after the war, and many maintained a lively interest in their old neighborhoods. Overall, the political upsurge in the cities became a vehicle for wider social revolt, just as was true in the countryside.

Mobile demonstrated how urban blacks' aspirations and anxieties provided fertile ground for the expansion of the League; it illustrated the manner in which sharp social ills could generate political activism. The city's black population grew from about 8,400 in 1860 to almost 14,000 in 1870, an increase of 62.7 percent in a decade. Most had come to Mobile immediately after the war. Freedmen soon were a large minority of Mobile's population, which set the stage for intense conflict. Indigent freedmen settled in shanties near the wharves and at the outskirts of town. The men worked as unskilled laborers or dockhands, and the women generally became domestics. Because Mobile suffered an economic decline in the postwar period, there were not nearly enough jobs to go around. For years, unemployment was common and hunger widespread. "The negro laborers who now crowd the wharves to unload the boats," the Mobile *Register* reported, "are incapable of doing it from *weakness*. They are all soup-fed negroes, and have not *stomachs* upon which to work." The Democratic paper further observed that "owing to the hard times, the steamboats would not, under any circumstances, be able to employ even the city negroes, but the large crowds of country vagrants now in town render it impossible for the river and bay interest to give a living to even a small modicum." The arrival of nearly six thousand penniless freedmen created for the city's ruling whites an enormous problem of social control.[1]

Mobile's authorities attempted to discipline the black populace through harsh legislation. Vagrancy edicts consigned many freedmen to long service on the chain gang, thereby discouraging new migration and securing cheap labor for road work. Such measures so incensed the freedmen that the Radical *Nationalist* repeatedly warned against liberating the chain gang by force. Blacks could not enter various occupations, and arbitrary enforcement compounded their troubles. For example, in June, 1866, a white was fined twenty-five dollars for assaulting a black "with no cause or provocation." The mayor remarked that he "did not think that the negro was in much danger from an axe in the hands of such a man. . . . [The assailant] was simply 'bluffing.'" Only days later, two freedmen received the identical fine for the crime of playing cards and, lacking any money, off they went to the chain gang. Contrasts of this kind were legion. Clearly, freedmen had ample cause to complain of official abuse.[2]

Other factors also contributed to the League's politicizing the freedmen. One was the presence of the Mobile *Nationalist* and its activists in the city, and another may have been the significant "Cre-

---

1. Kolchin, *First Freedom*, 11; Mobile *Register*, May 14, 1868.
2. Mobile *Nationalist*, January 11, 25, 1866; Mobile *Advertiser and Register*, November 10, 1866; Mobile *Nationalist*, August 9, 16, January 18, 1866; Mobile *Advertiser and Register*, June 21, 23, 1866.

ole"—freeborn mulatto—community that provided leadership and resources to the freedmen. But the critical institutional force mobilizing the freedmen was the black church. After the war, freedmen withdrew from most white-controlled denominations, and several of the new black congregations became embroiled in conflict with white church officials over existing buildings. These legal struggles over church property, along with other irritants, led to tremendous white resentment toward black religious activity. In General Swayne's words, "The city of Mobile appears to be largely under the domination of rowdyism, and actuated throughout by a feeling of hostility to the freedmen. During the past six months four colored churches have been burned." Given this disapproval, religious leaders lost little good will by embracing the Republican cause. Thus the most significant organizations in the black community were ripe for insurgency when Military Reconstruction began.[3]

Church leaders reacted immediately to news of black enfranchisement. Two days after passage of the First Military Reconstruction Act, church and other community spokesmen met with a few white allies to "draw up a platform of principles" for an integrated League. They undertook the meeting independently of Keffer and the State Council. Two white lawyers, George F. Harrington and W. W. D. Turner, emerged as leaders of the militant faction in local politics—they seized the initiative before more moderate Republicans did so. The Radical rhetoric used at this and subsequent meetings drew a strong response from the freedmen, and in the next few days the League grew rapidly. A gathering in one church was full "to overcrowding, hundreds outside being unable to gain admittance." Within two weeks, the League claimed 2,500 members, and even the opposition press conceded some 1,500. Either figure represented a sizable portion of the entire male black population. As the *Nationalist* observed, "The interest in the progress of the Union League recently formed in this city continues unabated. Every meeting is fully—we

3. Washington *Chronicle*, April 17, 1866; Mobile *Nationalist*, July 18, 1867; Mobile *Advertiser and Register*, July 14, 1866. On Mobile's "creole" community, see Kolchin, *First Freedom*, 140–43. For discussion of postwar struggles over church property, see Harry V. Richardson, *Dark Salvation: The Story of Methodism as It Developed Among Blacks in America* (Garden City, N.Y., 1976), 198.

may say overflowingly—attended, and the addresses there are listened to with marked attention."[4]

During this mobilization, racial tension increased. A Leaguer investigating the situation observed that Harrington's inflammatory addresses were calculated to enflame the races against each other. At one League rally, various speakers demanded the right for blacks to sit on juries, hold office, and ride on streetcars. This rhetoric reportedly encouraged freedmen to become less deferential, just as it did in the countryside. "The results of Radical machinations among the negroes," according to a Democratic paper, "are becoming quite apparent by their change of deportment, and their readiness to engage in lawless and riotous demonstrations." One indication of this new temper was publicly brandishing firearms. After the aforementioned rally, Leaguers raised white fears by discharging guns into the air. Such conduct was more than just show. A freedman wrote to the Mobile *Nationalist* that in the event of trouble, "the practice of firing into the air should be stopped," since "throwing away" ammunition deprived one of defenses. Shoot to hit, he counseled.[5]

Escalating labor strife accompanied the growing political agitation. Late in March, 1867, a general strike spread from the wharves to the rest of the city. One abortive work stoppage had occurred the previous year, but this strike provoked widespread conflict. While the League's role in calling the walkout is unclear, it is significant that disturbances began four to eight days after the first mass League meetings. One black Leaguer publicly affirmed his sympathy for the strikers. At a Republican rally, L. S. Berry defended a freedman who was "knocked down and hauled through the . . . streets like a hog, for no other reason than because he would not do a fair day's work for unfair wages." Democratic sources depicted Harrington and Turner as prime movers of the disturbances, because they were giving the striking freedmen legal

4. Montgomery *State Sentinel,* June 26, 1867; Mobile *Advertiser and Register,* June 26, 1867; Mobile *Nationalist,* March 7, 14, 1867; Loren Schweninger, "Alabama Blacks and the Congressional Reconstruction Acts of 1867," *Alabama Review,* XXXI (1978), 185–86; Mobile *Nationalist,* March 21, 1867.

5. J. Silsby to Swayne, April 1, 1867, in Swayne Papers, ADAH; Athens *Post,* April 25, 1867; Mobile *Nationalist,* April 25, 1867; Mobile *Advertiser and Register,* May 16, 1867; Mobile *Nationalist,* April 11, 1867.

counsel. There were "bad white men among us who are at the bottom of these troubles, and find their interest in exciting feuds and perhaps open hostility between the two races with a view to their own political and official advancement." The *Nationalist* agreed that the League lawyers were implicated, but argued that they restrained the freedmen rather than encouraging them. Regardless of which view was correct, the whites active in the League's creation became major participants in the labor struggle too.[6]

The actions were militant. The dockworkers met and demanded a substantial increase in their wages, and they also swore that no white strikebreakers would be tolerated at the wharves. Discussing the scope of the insurgency, one Conservative newspaper said: "For ten days or two weeks past a growing feeling of dissatisfaction and discontent has been manifested among the entire negro laboring population, including alike those engaged on the levees, those employed in the saw-mills, and those who seek odd jobs and day's-work generally. That this is a combined movement is easily discerned by the manner in which the matter has been carried on." The dock strike encouraged other confrontations. When workers struck a sawmill, the employer had a leader arrested for disorderly conduct and for "interfering in matters that did not concern him." A crowd of blacks followed the arresting officer and his captive to city hall. The mayor, intimidated by the angry onlookers, ordered the freedman temporarily released. As the man left he was "accompanied down stairs by all his friends who were in the court room, and was received with silent triumph by many more friends that constituted the assemblage which blocked the street." Later that same day, blacks set out to free the chain gang, but they were dissuaded from actually making the attempt.[7]

After a few days, quiet returned to the docks. Soon freedmen went on the offensive again, attempting to integrate the city's streetcar lines. When the war ended, the transit companies had banned black riders from inside the cars, even though slaves had been al-

6. Mobile *Advertiser and Register*, August 19, 1866, April 2, 11, 1867; Mobile *Nationalist*, April 25, 1867.

7. Mobile *Advertiser and Register*, April 2, 1867, quoting Mobile *Evening News*; Mobile *Times*, April 2, 1867.

lowed inside. Freedmen found this a gross affront, and in mid-April, after the forcible removal of a black female passenger, they began occupying streetcars. Sharp confrontations ensued; a freedman who entered a car was beaten by a white mob, but other blacks managed to return the favor. According to the Mobile *Advertiser and Register*, operations on one of the lines halted for nearly a day. The local Bureau agent cited Radical rhetoric: "The people are told by some of their advisors [apparently Harrington and Turner] that they will only get their rights by making a bold stand; that the law of Congress is a dead letter unless they spur it into vitality. . . . It is not at all improbable that there will be more of them [confrontations] as questions of 'rights' arise, and advice to hasty action receives attention." Leaguers certainly were involved in the streetcar struggle. L. S. Berry led one of these attempts and was arrested. Thereafter he became the first of several Leaguers to sue the car companies under the federal Civil Rights Act. Harrington and Turner's firm provided legal counsel for the plaintiffs in the litigation. League activists demonstrated much initiative in sponsoring such civil disobedience, and the rank and file supported them by pressuring the authorities. Albert Griffin wrote Swayne that the freedmen were "impatiently awaiting an order from you settling the car question."[8]

These collisions were not transient phenomena, but instead marked the beginning of a campaign of civil disobedience that continued for years. Such efforts often succeeded in alleviating racial oppression. Although most gains were reversed after Redemption, Mobile's blacks forced temporary advances through direct action and other means. The disturbances in April, 1867, for example, apparently moved General Swayne to abolish the chain gang, and continuing strikes eventually raised wages for dockhands. The protracted struggle over the streetcar system furnished the best example of the effectiveness of such tactics. After the first sit-in, the companies

8. Mobile *Advertiser and Register*, April 15, 1866, April 21, June 25, 29, 1867; Tracy to Swayne, April 17, 1867, in Swayne Papers, ADAH; Montgomery *Mail*, April 10, 1867; Griffin to Swayne, April 22, 1867, in Swayne Papers, ADAH. Freedmen may have been permitted to stand on streetcar platforms prior to the disturbances. In any case, these events were not unique to Mobile. Soon after Military Reconstruction began, freedmen in Richmond, for example, initiated similar mass protests over almost identical issues. There were also efforts by blacks in Charleston to occupy the city's segregated streetcars. See Peter J. Rachleff, *Black Labor in the South: Richmond, Virginia, 1865–1890* (Philadelphia, 1984), 41–44.

instituted segregated "Star Cars" for blacks, but this did not satisfy the freedmen. In August of the following year, freedmen again seized the cars, this time hoping to pressure the legislature into enacting a bill that would outlaw separate facilities. In the words of a police official, "Our city has been greatly excited for the past three days. . . . From 12N yesterday till 6 P.M. the excitement was intense. Vast throngs of white and black gathered by the various lines of the city railway." Hundreds of freedmen participated in these attempts—several were beaten by whites and many more arrested. In early 1870 a boycott finally proved more successful. The company was "obliged to take these [separate] cars off, for the negroes did not support them, and they were run at a dead expense." The companies then tried having sections in the same cars that were separated by a wire grille, but this concession did not satisfy the freedmen either. Throughout Reconstruction, black men and women initiated legal challenges to and concerted violations of the scheme. The pattern that emerges is one of long-lived and relatively successful mass activity. Clearly the campaign of direct action begun under League auspices constituted an abiding feature of the urban situation. Politicizing the freedmen mobilized them to act upon diverse social and economic objectives.[9]

But if civil disobedience continued, the Union League's leadership in urging such actions did not. Its role changed because of factional struggles within the Republican party. A purge of militant leaders directed the organization toward a more narrowly political focus. The escalation of conflict during the spring of 1867 had alarmed both local Republicans and General Swayne in Montgomery. These men saw Turner and Harrington as opportunists—with some justification, given later events—and decided to take control of the League. Swayne sent John Keffer and an associate to Mobile to reprimand the pair. The state secretary reportedly restructured the League so that Harrington could no longer dominate the proceedings. Keffer arranged to have the Mobile Council placed under more temperate white leadership, notably that of Albert Griffin of the *Nationalist* and future congressman Frederick G. Bromberg. A white League was established under Gustavus Horton, a local merchant. Outside intervention thus transformed a radical social movement into a narrowly political body under moderate direction.[10]

While Keffer successfully reconstituted the League's leadership, these changes undercut black enthusiasm for the movement. As one activist observed, "The organization of the two Leagues gave rise to distrust in the minds of our people." Bromberg noted that under the new leadership the black leagues grew only slowly, though Horton's white council had more success. The white council's increasing prominence troubled black activists, who resented the fact that "only a few white men came into the original League because of a prejudice against the colored members. Those weak-kneed, milk-and-water policy gentlemen determined to form a white League for the benefit of all *quasi* Republicans whose prejudices were stronger than their principles." Small wonder that at the Mobile Freedmen's Convention, held just after the reorganization of the League, the delegates considered resolutions denouncing segregated party organizations. The divisiveness resulting from this purge would trouble Republicans for the remainder of Reconstruction.[11]

A major riot in mid-May provided Generals Pope and Swayne a further opportunity to bolster the moderates, to whom they gave the city administration. On May 15, Pennsylvania Congressman William D. Kelley tried to give a Radical speech, but was interrupted by a drunken heckler. A scuffle broke out, then there were gunshots, and in the melee several people were killed. Although the freedmen's recent restiveness contributed to the disturbances, whites clearly initiated the riot. General Swayne determined that the Conservative city government was at fault, so the military ousted the municipal

10. Silsby to Swayne, April 1, 1867, in Swayne Papers, ADAH; Mobile *Nationalist*, April 4, 1867; Montgomery *State Sentinel*, June 26, 1867.
11. Mobile *Advertiser and Register*, July 27, 1867; Montgomery *State Sentinel*, June 26, 1867; F. Bromberg to Keffer, April 27, 1867, in Swayne Papers, ADAH; Mobile *Nationalist*, May 9, 1867; Alexander *et al.* to Swayne, June 25, 1867, in Records, M809, RG 105; J. Silsby to Swayne, April 1, 1867, in Swayne Papers, ADAH; Athens *Post*, May 16, 1867. Factional alignments were further complicated because they did not mesh with Radical versus moderate divisions at the state level. Albert Griffin, for example, was considered a fiery Radical during 1867 at the very time these events took place.

officers and appointed Gustavus Horton mayor. Other moderate League leaders such as Bromberg and Griffin fared well under the new administration. Horton immediately turned his attention toward strengthening the leagues through patronage. In July, for example, Horton replaced eighteen white—mostly Irish—city laborers with freedmen. The police department drew a disproportionate share of Horton's attention, since the riot had focused concern on the inadequacies of the force. Horton used police jobs to recruit whites to the League while he also met some of the black demands for patronage.[12]

This course of action soon brought Horton into conflict with another recent appointee, Chief of Police C. A. R. Dimon. He was himself a League member, but a relatively conservative one. He reported to General Swayne that many policemen were "joining the L. L. and are truly efficient men," and he asked that he be "allowed discretion" in making removals. Dimon disliked the prospect of a political purge of the police force, and in particular resisted the appointment of a black man, Ovid Gregory, as an assistant chief. In response, Swayne rebuked Dimon for obstructing the mayor's plans, and a full-scale restructuring of the force ensued. Four officers and twenty-eight men were dismissed in July, 1867, alone, and the only reason given was that "they would not join the Loyal League." Actually, more was involved than simple partisanship. One policeman resigned because he would not acknowledge a black man his equal, and other whites who quit gave similar reasons. The removal of the overtly racist policemen, and their replacement by Republicans of both races, had wider social implications.[13]

The restructuring of the police force benefited the League in several ways, beyond providing jobs for political supporters and pacifying militant critics. Policemen were expected to subscribe to the *Nationalist* and even to contribute directly to the paper. In addition, as Dimon noted, "$5 dollars was assessed against them in Jany

---

12. Tracy to Swayne, May 15, 1867, in Registers and Letters, M752, RG 105; Mobile *Advertiser and Register*, July 4, 1867.

13. C. Dimon to Swayne, July 30, 1867, Dimon to Hudson, April 12, 1868, J. O'Brien to Horton, August 10, 1867, all in Copybook of Letters Sent, Mobile City Police Records, University of Alabama, Tuscaloosa.

last to defray the expenses of the Loyal League." But these advantages had their political costs as well—for example, the press violently opposed the removals. Chief Dimon was permanently embittered, eventually joining the opposition. At one point, he "offered resolutions in the 'L L' Meetings that as soon as possible we might change the nature of our organization from one of a private character . . . to one open and above board." Dimon argued that clandestine organizations such as the League were divisive and should be abolished, and a Republican club was formed in the city within several days.[14]

More serious was the continuing criticism by the League activists displaced as a result of Swayne's intervention. Although Harrington was no longer part of the League leadership, he maintained influence with the "less stable portion of the colored people." A militant faction—overwhelmingly black—coalesced around him, and these activists aggressively espoused Radical policies. One petition illustrated their discontent, and it was signed by Allen Alexander, L. S. Berry, M. Lankford, and others, some of whom had been prominent in the creation of the original League. The freedmen, they noted, would not be satisfied with token appointments to the police force, for they could be given half the positions without detriment to the city's interests. They denounced the conciliatory policy "which some of our leaders think best" as pandering to Conservatives at the expense of blacks' legal rights. This was "neither wise nor just."[15]

Even though under the moderates' control, the League became a forum for these complaints. Mayor Horton was "arraigned before the 'L L L' by Harrington Turner & Co for certain of his decisions which he had made in the Mayors Court, and they also demanded the appointment of Mr. Gregory as Asst. Chief." In response to this pressure, Horton strove to keep the freedmen from engaging in direct action while he bolstered his position with whatever concessions he could make. On the streetcar issue, for example, he wanted

14. Dimon to Hudson, April 12, 1868, in Mobile City Police Records, University of Alabama; Dimon to Pope, August 18, 1867, in Records of the Third Military District, Bureau of Civil Affairs, Box 3, Pt. 1, RG 393; Mobile *Nationalist*, August 22, 1867.

15. Silsby to Swayne, April 1, 1867, in Swayne Papers, ADAH; A. Alexander *et al.* to Swayne, June 25, 1867, in Records, M809, RG 105.

the freedmen not to "press the question of their rights" beyond seeking a test case in court.[16]

During the summer of 1867, Horton managed to hold the militant faction in check, but the October elections undermined his position, because they revealed the white League's relative weakness. The orchestrated campaign by the press against the Republicans, and the hostility of most of the white community, proved too strong. For example, Mayor Horton's family gradually became convinced that he was in danger, and a false assassination rumor gave him the ghoulish opportunity to read the letters of condolence. Other Republicans had their problems too: Frederick Bromberg's home was burned down before the election, and the head of a local college had his institution bankrupted by boycott because he joined the League. Bromberg observed that the "election test has proved to us that the oaths of the Leagues, and the pledges of club organizations, are straw in the fires through which loyalty is made to pass here." The Republicans had received less than one hundred white votes in Mobile, which was a bitter disappointment. "Our white league and club have . . . proved miserable failures as election engines," and the titular president of the Mobile League, J. R. Eastburn, had resigned not only his office but his membership.[17] The near collapse of the white League undercut the position of Horton and his moderate clique, since conciliating white opinion was unlikely to bring the freedmen further gains.

Over the following eighteen months, Harrington's faction gradually defeated the moderates. The militants had supported civil disobedience and confrontation since the creation of the League. Now, though, they promoted such actions from outside the organization and with ulterior motive. Under their leadership, what happened on the streets, the docks, and the cars had a different goal—to embar-

16. Dimon to Pope, August 18, 1867, in Records of the Third Military District, Bureau of Civil Affairs, Box 3, Pt. 1, RG 393; Horton to Dimon, June 15, 1867, in Mobile City Police Records, University of Alabama.

17. G. Horton to F. Horton, May 22, 1868, H. W. Robbins to Eliza Horton, November 17, 1868, both in Horton Family Papers, Museum of the History of Mobile; Bromberg to Swayne, October 27, 1867, in Records of the Third Military District, Office of Civil Affairs, Box 5, Pt. 1, RG 393.

rass the moderates in the League and the city administration. The militant faction polarized the situation to advantage through repeated confrontation, and the freedmen's enthusiasm for direct action made this strategy a potent one. An indication of the moderate faction's decline was the fate of Albert Griffin. The *Nationalist's* board of trustees, dominated by militants such as L. S. Berry, fired him. In the bitter struggle that ensued, partisans on both sides attempted to seize physical control of the printing press, and the newspaper apparently went bankrupt as a result.[18]

The political showdown occurred in January, 1869. An unusual alliance of Democrats and blacks on the municipal boards excluded Griffin and his cohorts from most city offices. A Harrington follower defended the maneuver as "only a choice between Democrats." This reverse demoralized the moderates; Griffin soon left for Kansas, and others—Bromberg among them—began dallying with the Democrats. Months later, Harrington, who had secured election as Speaker of the Alabama House, persuaded the legislature to abolish the existing city administration. Governor Smith appointed Harrington mayor in early 1870, on the recommendation of various "prominent Democratic citizens" who apparently hoped that their business interests would benefit. During 1869 and 1870, there occurred "the worst municipal scandals, and the credit of the city . . . was pledged for railroads which were never built," according to one source. The Grand Trunk line received $1.5 million but was not completed until the twentieth century. These bond measures bankrupted the city to benefit railroads owned by the "oldest and best known" of its Democratic businessmen, and Harrington himself apparently had personal interests in various railroad corporations. About a year later, the Democrats swept to victory over a divided Republican opposition.[19]

18. Carrollton *West Alabamian*, August 18, 1869, quoting Mobile *Register*; Mobile *Register*, December 12, 1869, A. W. Jones, "Alabama," in Suggs (ed.), *The Black Press*, 23–24.

19. Mobile *Register*, January 14, 19, 1869, February 12, 1870; Mobile *Nationalist*, January 18, 1869; J. A. Bragg to Bromberg, November 20, 1869, in Frederick G. Bromberg Papers, UNC; Peter J. Hamilton, *Mobile of the Five Flags* (Mobile, 1913), 349; Montgomery *Alabama State Journal*, November 6, 1869, January 22, 1870; Frederick G. Bromberg, *The Reconstruction Period in Alabama*, Iberville Historical Society Papers, No. 3 (N.p., 1905), 8, 10, 17; Moore, "Railroad Building in Alabama," 436–37; KKK Report, VIII, 231; *House Reports*, 43rd Cong., 2nd Sess., No. 262, pp. 605–606.

The Union League was not a vital participant in these later factional struggles, nor did it lead the mass activities such rivalries helped inspire. The moderates maintained control of the League, but that undermined its significance as a vehicle for mass activism. The Mobile Council acted as the moderates' organizational arm among the freedmen, and the various factions began their own competing organizations to influence black voters. One activist wrote in mid-1868 that Grant clubs were being formed to counter the carpetbaggers' influence, specifically that of Griffin. The white Horton Council functioned through 1868, and according to the Mobile *Register*, the black council was still active as late as June, 1870. Eventually, however, the leagues seemingly changed into Republican clubs, as did other councils throughout the region. The Horton Council, for example, apparently evolved into the "4th Ward Republican Warriors" by 1870. The Mobile leagues, bureaucratized into the party structure, gradually disappeared as a separate entity.[20]

The League's uneventful later career does not detract from the importance of its initial radical impetus. Despite the complexity of factional maneuvers, the social impact of politicizing the freedmen was clear. Blacks flocked to the League in the spring of 1867 because they believed that it would act upon diverse grievances. The League was as much an economic and protest movement as a partisan one, and it manifested this in confrontations on the docks, the streetcars, and elsewhere. Just as rural councils became enmeshed in the crisis of agricultural production, the urban councils expressed black frustrations in an economically depressed setting. The leagues expressed wider social concerns and encouraged labor insurgency.

The movement in the region's other urban centers contrasted with that in Mobile, for leagues elsewhere demonstrated a more complex mixture of concerns of the city and the countryside. Mobile dwarfed most other cities, and its size imparted a distinctively urban flavor to its politics, as did its geographic isolation from the cotton belt. At the same time, Mobile's unique social characteristics made the League upsurge more militant there than it was elsewhere. League councils

20. W. C. Johnson to Smith, June 26, 1868, T. Thompson *et al.* to Smith, September 22, 1870, both in Gov. Smith Papers, ADAH; Mobile *Register*, June 1, 1870.

in places such as Montgomery, Selma, and Vicksburg acted on the interests of freedmen in the hinterland, as well as those of city blacks. Thus if Mobile's leagues participated in a social movement parallel to the one in the countryside, other urban councils intervened directly in the struggle in agriculture.

Freedmen in many postwar cities echoed the complaints of Mobile's black population. Municipal authorities often responded to black immigration with repressive measures. In Jackson, it was common practice to hold vagrants without trial. When some freedmen passing through town were arrested for stopping overnight, police detained them a week to dig holes for a fence around the jail. A Jackson newspaper observed, "We must keep the ex-slave in a position of inferiority," and recommended laws to make him feel his lesser status. Vicksburg's officials took stern measures against idleness, enforcing an ordinance that anyone without employment for three days could be arrested. The Montgomery *Daily Ledger* expressed the prevailing opinion that the city was intended for white people. The paper advised freedmen to go into the country and cultivate the soil, since that was the employment for which "God designed them." Black religious institutions felt the force of white displeasure and, in Montgomery and Vicksburg, were repeatedly harassed. One Montgomery paper proclaimed, "The negro church is a nuisance; and the authorities should see that the noise they make, not only Sunday but daily, be stopped! God is not deaf! If any of the preachers or the flock believe that it is necessary to make their voices reach the stars in order to be heard, it will be well for the policemen to teach them better." General hostility motivated such complaints as much as did specific grievances. The antagonism prodded black religious leaders toward political activism. Clearly, many of the social irritants present in Mobile also existed throughout the area.[21]

Soon after blacks received the vote in early March, 1867, League agitation began in many urban areas. For example, Montgomery's

21. R. Gardner to Preston, June 30, 1867, in Records, M826, RG 105; *Nation*, November 15, 1865, p. 609, reportedly quoting Jackson *News;* Minutes of the Council of the City of Vicksburg, February 20, 1868, Vicksburg City Hall, Vicksburg; Howard N. Rabinowitz, *Race Relations in the Urban South, 1865–1890* (New York, 1978), 24, quoting Montgomery *Daily Ledger,* September 23, 1865; Page to Gillem, June 25, 1867, in Records, M826, RG 105; Montgomery *Mail,* May 15, 1866.

Leaguers claimed six hundred black members within the month. By April, councils were under way in Natchez, Selma, and Huntsville. The movement awakened considerable enthusiasm among urban freedmen, and it was widespread. In Montgomery, "they had half a dozen league rooms—several at least—in our city," according to a Democratic politician. Vicksburg Leaguers organized several councils on the basis of neighborhoods, and these local clubs persisted for years.[22]

Once Military Reconstruction began, black resentments inspired social activism, though on a more modest scale than was the case in Mobile. The freedmen became assertive in defending themselves and their rights. Soon after the League formed in Natchez, for instance, the beating of a freedman provoked a melee when black bystanders started shooting at the assailant. In Meridian, "some excitement" ensued when the town marshal killed a man resisting arrest. Labor strife also grew during the spring of 1867. Selma newspapers reported that "an association of freedmen had been organized . . . whose principal object is to enforce the pay of $20 a month." A hotel workers' strike developed out of this movement. Throughout its life, the League intervened occasionally in labor-related activities. In Montgomery, a "corps of league negroes" took control of a workingmen's meeting attended by freedmen, and they succeeded in giving the gathering a Radical orientation, according to the opposition press.[23]

Despite these episodes, League organizing in other cities did not initiate the social turmoil evidenced in Mobile. Elsewhere, strikes and mass insurgency under League auspices were infrequent, one inhibiting factor being the cautious League leadership. Mobile's experience was unusual in that factional infighting dominated politics. The restraint practiced by Montgomery's black leaders, for example, was more typical. When a black Democratic convention gathered there, rumors circulated among angry freedmen that the delegates

22. Mobile *Nationalist*, March 28, 1867; Selma *Messenger*, April 11, 1867; Natchez *Democrat*, April 4, 1867; Lakin to J. Chalfant, April 16, 1867, in Freedmen's Aid Society Correspondence, ITC Archives; KKK Report, VIII, 227; *House Reports*, 43rd Cong., 2nd Sess., No. 265, pp. 186–87.

23. Natchez *Democrat*, June 13, 1867; Mobile *Advertiser and Register*, July 21, 1867; Montgomery *Mail*, March 7, 1867 (quoting Selma *Times*), October 25, 27, 1868.

might be mobbed. Holland Thompson, a black Leaguer, urged the freedmen not to interfere with the Democrats, telling them that this mob spirit should be "stopped at once." Other Leaguers, G. W. Cox and L. J. Williams, dissuaded a crowd from attacking a black Conservative, and had they not intervened, "the infuriated crowd probably would have killed him." The temperate style of the Montgomery activists showed again when spokesmen called upon General Swayne to lobby for the appointment of black policemen. Swayne said the timing was politically inopportune, and he persuaded them to his view. The freedmen thereupon told their comrades to "be quiet and calm for a few weeks longer, and when we ratify the Constitution then *we can demand our rights.*" And, indeed, by the following year, almost half the police force was black. Most League leaders sought, by defusing urban social conflicts, to direct the black community's energies toward the electoral process.[24]

There were other reasons for the League's limited social activism in the cities, and a primary one was economic. Railroad construction altered the cotton trade to the advantage of plantation belt towns such as Meridian, Selma, and Montgomery. As Howard N. Rabinowitz pointed out in *Race Relations in the Urban South*, "In the postbellum period it was the railroad rather than a choice water location" that brought economic success. Robust growth, with the employment opportunities it brought, apparently diminished black dissatisfaction. The smaller size of these communities prevented the concentrated misery that existed in commercially depressed Mobile.[25] Furthermore, in the smaller interior cities, many rural freedmen turned up at council meetings, which were the natural focus of agitation there. League leaders thus had to address the concerns of these agricultural laborers, diluting the urban activism distinctively present in Mobile.

This pattern was most evident in Vicksburg, where Leaguers urged field hands to boycott yearly labor contracts. In Natchez, a black Leaguer tried to purchase a plantation on behalf of a group of

24. Montgomery *Mail*, December 27, 1867, August 8, 1868; Montgomery *State Sentinel*, September 5, 7, 1867.

25. Harold D. Woodman, *King Cotton and His Retainers: Financing and Marketing the Cotton Crop of the South, 1800–1925* (Lexington, Ky., 1968), 269–73; Rabinowitz, *Race Relations in the Urban South*, 4.

local freedmen. Huntsville's League often assisted with the farm-workers' problems, and its leading spokesman, future congressman John B. Callis, attained influence through his services as a Bureau official. Leaguers in urban areas frequently helped rural comrades when trouble threatened; a willingness to intervene represented a sustained feature of the movement. In Meridian the League was reorganized in early 1871, when Klansmen from Alabama abducted agricultural workers under the pretext that they had fled labor contracts. The Leaguers confronted the terrorists directly, with at least temporary success. Freedmen in Montgomery demonstrated like tendencies in June, 1870. When J. H. Alston, a black legislator, was shot in Tuskegee, a posse formed to go by train to that city. This may have been the "business of the courts and not of the Union League," in the *Mail's* words, but freedmen clearly viewed the troubles of their cotton-belt comrades as matters of urgent importance.[26]

Certain other functions of the urban councils were significant, particularly in political terms. In some communities, the leagues developed into corrupt urban machines, much like Harrington's faction in Mobile. Sheriff Furlong's "Courthouse Ring" in Vicksburg misgoverned Warren County for years, according to Harris in *The Day of the Carpetbagger.* Furlong and his followers apparently combined espousal of civil rights with large-scale graft. Other Leaguers acted more conscientiously, once elected to public office. Montgomery's Holland Thompson demonstrated concern for his constituents. According to Rabinowitz, he was "largely responsible not only for the inauguration of Negro schools but for white schools as well. . . . And . . . sought to maintain equal school appropriations. . . . [H]e was responsible for the hiring of Negro police, the grading and opening of new streets in black areas, the supervision of soup kitchen relief, and repairs to the city hospital. By his second term he was one of the leaders of the [City] Council." The political development of the city leagues was similar in many respects. Since the League was the first black political organization, demands for civil rights often were channeled through it. As a result, leagues often became the

26. Trowbridge, *The South*, 362; Vicksburg *Times,* January 10, 1868; Chapman to Green, May 6, 1868, in Letters Sent SAC Vicksburg, Vol. 274, RG 105; Montgomery *Mail*, June 30, 1870. Local officials prevented the posse from reinforcing Tuskegee.

basis of the party's Radical faction in their respective municipalities, which occurred in Montgomery, Huntsville, Vicksburg, Meridian, and probably elsewhere. Thus the political evolution of Mobile's leagues can be seen as unique. In no other city did moderates gain control of the organization and purge their adversaries. But beyond the Radical stance, few generalizations about the League and urban politics apply. Its role evolved differently from community to community.[27]

In essence, urban freedmen suffered discrimination, but in most communities such grievances did not engender militant social activism such as initially occurred in Mobile. Rather than concentrate solely on urban problems, most of the councils acted on rural freedmen's needs as well. Leaguers protected their fellows in the countryside from Klan violence, an intervention that was an important facet of urban councils' activities. In political terms, the movement in Mobile also differed from that in other cities; most urban councils were Radical, but it was the moderates who took over the Mobile leagues. Overall, the League in other cities bore more resemblance to the movement in the countryside than to the urban activism of the Mobile Council.

The Union Leagues in the cities differed from those elsewhere in one major respect: the League in urban areas largely stalemated the Ku Klux Klan. Freedmen everywhere resisted political violence, but conditions in the city let them fight on favorable terrain. The more urban the setting, the less did typical Klan techniques succeed. The factors making the Klan effective in rural areas—preponderant force, secrecy, and isolation—were not present in the city. Freedmen utilized the League as a military body and defended themselves, and Klan activity created explosive conflict. Freedmen did not win all the showdowns, but they often held their own. This relative success meant that urban struggles did not resemble those in rural areas. If Democrats attacked the freedmen, the result was riot rather than the successful intimidation typical in plantation regions.

The Ku Klux Klan spread rapidly through Alabama and Mis-

27. Harris, *The Day of the Carpetbagger*, 98–99; Rabinowitz, "The Search for Social Control," II, 687.

sissippi during the spring of 1868. This movement affected urban as well as rural areas, since city blacks were considered particularly unruly. The Klan's goal was intimidation as much as actual violence, so Klansmen sought publicity for what they did in urban areas. In Jackson, for example, several "artistically printed notices posted through town" announced the Klan's presence. These communiqués were generally composed of solemn nonsense, but the message was ominous enough. The first notice in Montgomery issued from the Great High Cyclops, and it proclaimed "the dark and dismal hour will soon be" and warned traitors to beware. Democratic newspapers promoted the organization, printing their announcements and highlighting Klan activities. The Selma *Messenger* illustrated that sort of encouragement: "The following notice comes to us, we know not from whom, nor from whence, with an order to publish it. If the Ku Klux Klan is an order after the style of the defunct Sons of Malta, the publication of the notice may contribute to the innocent enjoyment of some good souls;—even if this mysterious thing be all it is alleged to be by those who fear it, the notice can do no harm; for the Klan may be called together to work in other ways—therefore we print the notice." With such assistance, Klans appeared almost simultaneously in Mobile, Huntsville, Natchez, and elsewhere. The organization was active in virtually every urban center except Vicksburg, where the vast numbers of blacks in the vicinity made operations too dangerous.[28]

Klan efforts in the region's cities met with only limited success, despite how widespread the movement was and the prevalence of white support. The difficulties encountered by the Klan in this environment were similar everywhere, but they were described strikingly in one urban newspaper. The Montgomery *Mail* printed enthusiastic stories about Klan exploits beginning in early March, 1868. "These secret societies are much to be deplored," it commented, "but we infinitely prefer the K.K.'s to the U.L.A.'s [Union League of America]." Soon Klan notices and rumors of nightriders appeared, and on March 25 the first firm sighting in town occurred. The newspaper reported that "one or two . . . dressed in the 'sacred

28. Jackson *Clarion*, March 24, 1868; Columbus (Ga.) *Sun*, March 21, 1868, quoting Montgomery *Mail*; Selma *Messenger*, March 31, 1868; Harris, *The Day of the Carpetbagger*, 382.

garb' have been seen in the neighborhood of the dark corners where the Loyal Leagues are supposed to assemble. As a consequence some folks are badly frightened." But the tenor of these accounts soon changed dramatically, as freedmen demonstrated the capacity to defend themselves and their allies.[29]

The day after the Klan appeared in the city, gangs of freedmen intervened in assaults on white Republicans. The *Mail* thereupon warned freedmen to mind their own concerns, cautioning that "if they allow themselves to be made the means of shielding the carcasses of the carpetbag and renegade rascals who are using them only for selfish purposes, they will regret it only once, and that will be as long as they live." Freedmen disregarded this warning, published under the headline "Word to the Negroes," and, with white Leaguer Robert Barber as leader, organized to meet the Klan. Over the next few days, conflict escalated on the streets. It became clear that blacks were winning these affrays, and the *Mail* revised its editorial position. It denounced "armed organized bodies of men parading the streets at night" and proclaimed them illegal "whether as Leaguers, anti-Ku Kluxes, or what not." With some irony the paper stated that these efforts were unnecessary, since there was "no such organization as the Ku Klux in Montgomery." Within weeks of its initial activities, the local Klan seemingly disbanded. As Allen W. Trelease observed in *White Terror*, this brief period was its only real appearance in Montgomery. In essence, the League drove the Klan from the city permanently.[30]

Leaguers in other urban communities successfully resisted Klan violence, though sometimes the cost was considerable. In Natchez, Union League members reportedly took some nightriders prisoner. "The colored men halted them in regular military style," a Republican paper stated, "forced them to uncover their faces and disclose their names, and chastised one of them so severely that he kept his bed for some days." Although such incidents occurred frequently, League-led resistance seldom deterred white violence as thoroughly as in Montgomery. In Mobile, for example, blacks soon rid the city of Klansmen, but racial conflagrations continued inter-

29. Montgomery *Mail*, March 10, 19, 22, 25, 1868.
30. Montgomery *Mail*, March 26–29, 1868; Trelease, *White Terror*, 81.

mittently for the entire Reconstruction period. In organizing against the Klan, freedmen so antagonized the whites that they risked all-out battle. In Huntsville, 150 mounted Klansmen entered town and rode around the courthouse where the League was in session. They took no further aggressive action. As the Klansmen left, however, a dispute broke out in the heavily armed crowd that had gathered. One of the several casualties was a prominent white Radical. Thus urban self-defense was a double-edged sword, for it could easily increase bloodshed.[31]

The events leading to the Meridian riot of March, 1871, exemplified these dangers. Freedmen struggled against the Klan and, in so doing, fatally escalated racial hostility. Some months before the riot occurred, white activist Daniel Price arrived in Meridian, having fled his home in Sumter County, Alabama. He got a job as a schoolteacher, and wrote back to his former League comrades that conditions were better across the Mississippi line. Several hundred freedmen joined him, deserting labor contracts in the process. Soon bands of armed Alabamians, mostly Klansmen, appeared and claimed the right to return the blacks to their employers. These men effectively acted as kidnappers, since they had no legal authority for such seizures in Mississippi. After one illegal arrest resulted in the serious shooting of a black man, a group of "Loyal League Ku Klux" took countermeasures. The next time Alabamians entered town, freedmen—apparently led by Price—captured Adam Kinnard, a black Leaguer-turned-Democrat who now acted as a Sumter County deputy sheriff. The disguised men "handled him pretty roughly" and administered a sound thrashing. Then Klansmen poured across the border in earnest at the request of local whites. Two black county supervisors were assassinated along with other prominent freedmen, and tension mounted as the stage was set for large-scale violence.[32]

These Klan depredations resulted in a renewal of League activity. The local council had fallen into disarray after the fall, 1869, elections, but now freedmen reactivated it with enthusiasm. One former

31. Natchez *Democrat*, May 18, 1868, quoting an unnamed Jackson paper; Trelease, *White Terror*, 81; KKK Report, VIII, 115, 818–20.

32. Jackson *Clarion*, March 31, 1871, quoting New York *Tribune*; KKK Report, XI, 6–7; Harris, *The Day of the Carpetbagger*, 396–99; Trelease, *White Terror*, 290–93.

Leaguer reported that from the time the border incidents began, blacks organized themselves. This was "not the original Union League, it was in some other shape . . . [perhaps] a local organization of their own," he noted. Such activity increased after blacks sent a delegation to Governor Alcorn and found no aid forthcoming. Black legislator J. Aaron Moore urged that they "take the sign and signal of the old Loyal League" and mobilize themselves. Oratory at the freedmen's gatherings took on a militant flavor; black leader Warren Tyler spoke of the number of "his friends that had been killed and wounded in the county in the last twelve months, and asked the members of the Loyal League if they would all stick up to one another; they responded, 'Yes;' and he said that was right; let every man come, white or black, so they could keep the county quiet; and so that every man could lie down of nights without fears of being killed." Tyler even commended the American Indians for their idea that if one could not locate the perpetrator of a specific crime, perhaps any white would do. Such threats exacerbated racial fears, but certainly demonstrated the freedmen's willingness to fight against the Klan.[33]

After a packed meeting on the night of March 4, at which Moore and Tyler urged a militant posture, a fire broke out downtown. Each side blamed the other for the blaze, but one inebriated black activist proclaimed the town might just as well burn. Jittery Republican officials thereupon took several freedmen in custody for "inflammatory" speech. At the trial two days later, a fight broke out in the courtroom. One shot was fired, and well-armed whites immediately opened up on the defendants from the rear of the building. The blacks scattered—several leaders were already dead, and the freedmen were too disorganized to resist. For several days the Democrats rampaged, killing five prominent freedmen. According to Trelease, "The white mob, organized into companies or posses . . . took over the town searching from house to house for leaders of the black community and confiscating weapons." The repression was startlingly thorough: when whites realized that Representative J. Aaron Moore had escaped, they burned down his home and what they

33. KKK Report, XI, 48, 77, 136–37, 157; Garner, *Reconstruction in Mississippi*, 349–50.

thought was his church. One party even commandeered a train and pursued Moore fifty miles toward Jackson. Members of the mob also committed at least one rape. Thus was Meridian "redeemed" from Republican rule. Anti-Klan activities could fail and thus redound to the freedmen's disadvantage.[34] While urban freedmen had a far better chance than did rural freedmen to defeat Klan terrorism, success was hardly inevitable.

Overall, the League in urban areas had points of similarity and contrast with the movement elsewhere. In Mobile, the initial League upsurge was a social movement, and the organization was involved in strikes, streetcar occupations, and other forms of direct action. In other smaller cities, this was less evident, and leagues in places such as Montgomery and Meridian remained closely tied to the social conflicts of the agricultural hinterland. In all urban areas, however, the League's performance was analogous to that of the movement in rural areas. Political activity reflected a wider social movement to redress black grievances.

34. Trelease, *White Terror*, 293; KKK Report, XI, 38, 67–68, 78, 97–98.

SEVEN

Planters' Response to the League: The Emergence of the Klan

During the spring of 1867, the League mobilization alarmed planters, and they moved to reassert their imperiled influence over the freedmen. At first, these efforts were disorganized and tentative, often directed simply at finding out what transpired in secret League gatherings. Then planters turned to more earnest efforts at control, and a succession of failures eventually drove them toward violence. The emergence of the Ku Klux Klan culminated this process; the Klan's growth in early 1868 had complex causes, but counteracting the Union League was one of its major political goals. The spreading terror dismantled the League relatively quickly, and it thus sapped one of the Republican party's sources of strength among the freedmen. Repression permanently altered the social and political balance of power in the countryside.

The passage of Congressional Reconstruction in March, 1867, provoked little initial reaction among planters, for they took a rather detached view of the unprecedented events in Washington. A Mississippi landowner noted that "people are going on as if no Military Bill has been passed." Another informant found perfect indifference to be the prevailing attitude. Gradually some politicians and planters came to the conclusion that steps should be taken to control the new voters. Reconstructionist conservatives hoped to marshal the freedmen under their banner, thus preempting a Republican appeal. Other whites wanted no part of such maneuvers, preferring straightforward rejection of black suffrage. "Representation in Congress . . . ," noted a Democrat, "will not be a particle of benefit to the reconstructed states. Our true policy is to do nothing to carry out the Radical programme as set forth in the Sherman bills of reconstruction. Our only hope is in a reaction that may possibly take place in the northern mind." Until League organizing began, many planters espoused this policy, which they saw as one of masterly inactivity. Once Radical activities commenced in their areas, however, most lost their composure.[1]

Alerted by widespread press coverage, planters immediately discerned a threat in League gatherings and many feared actual uprisings. Anxious landowners tried to discover whatever they could about the movement. They pumped their laborers for information, generally with scant success. A Democratic lawyer observed that he "never heard" of a freedman revealing what went on at League meetings. Parties of whites roved the countryside, trying to locate these secret assemblies, and commonly freedmen confronted those who managed to find them. In Alabama's Wilcox County, for example, a League sentry was shot after he challenged intruders, and a racial battle nearly resulted. Democrats also gained access to leagues through subterfuge, and in several instances they managed to eavesdrop successfully. In Sumter County, Alabama, an editor and several of his friends secreted themselves next door to a council meeting. "I was there three or four nights, probably more than that," he stated. Another white supposedly crawled beneath the floorboards of a house where the Republicans met. One Klansman even claimed to have disguised himself as a freedman and entered a meeting. The planters spied on meetings, stole documents, and kept the newspapers apprised of what they discovered.[2]

Planters also tried to interdict Radical activity in their localities, for many hoped to control the freedmen through the authority they

1. A. Murdock to Humphreys, April 2, 1867, in Gov. Humphreys Papers, MDAH; [?] to "Cousin Bettie," March 11, 1867, in Hairston and Wilson Family Papers, UNC; T. L. Brothers to M. P. Blue, June 2, 1867, in M. P. Blue Papers, ADAH; Perman, *Reunion Without Compromise*, 229–65.

2. KKK Report, X, 1637; Mobile *Times*, December 27, 1867; Vicksburg *Herald*, June 26, 1868; KKK Report, X, 1688; Hunnicutt, *Reconstruction in West Alabama*, 79; J. E. Robuck, *My Own Personal Experience . . . During the Period of Reconstruction . . .* (Birmingham, 1911), 76–82; Montgomery *Advertiser*, July 24, 1867.

retained as employers. A Bureau agent in Mississippi noted, "It is the general opinion here among the whites that they can influence the colored vote the way matters now stand." These efforts took several forms. League organizer C. W. Pierce described attempts to "mislead the Freedmen by circulating reports that if they register [to vote], they would be put in the Army, pay more taxes etc. This is done by hints and insinuations." In another Alabama community, local officials fabricated a tale that Leaguers were charged two dollars for initiation. Besides spreading rumors, planters also took advantage of the freedmen's political inexperience and limited literacy. During the first elections, they tried to mutilate Republican ballots or substitute Democratic ones, but the freedmen caught on. Soon, as a Klansman stated, "you could not fool a Negro on a ticket." Moreover, the Radicals devised effective countermeasures—taking the freedmen to the polls in large groups, for example, and inspecting their ballots frequently. Conservatives thus accomplished little at first, except to reinforce freedmen's distrust of their late masters. [3]

Reconstructionist blandishments were useless to counteract the Radical appeal, and playing on blacks' unfamiliarity with politics proved self-defeating. These failures caused some planters to despair; others dreamed of a massive immigration of Chinese farmworkers. One prominent planter even recommended deporting the freedmen, but pragmatic individuals saw other choices. The stakes were simply too high to surrender power without a struggle. Landowners were still wealthy, educated, and influential, elements that might yet yield electoral results when utilized correctly. If mild measures did not work, then perhaps more drastic ones would. [4]

3. Eldridge to Preston, July 31, 1867, in Records, M826, RG 105; Pierce to Kinsman, July 18, 1867, in Records, M809, RG 105; Deposition of Emanuel Wright, included in Peck to Kinsman, July 5, 1867, in Swayne Papers, ADAH; Huggins to Preston, June 30, 1867, in Records, M826, RG 105; Hunnicutt, *Reconstruction in West Alabama*, 74.
4. John S. McNeily, "War and Reconstruction in Mississippi, 1863–1890," *Publications of the Mississippi Historical Society, Centenary Series*, II (1918), 380; Marion *Commonwealth*, July 15, 1869, quoting Selma *Times and Messenger*; A. W. Dillard to Johnson, January 24, 1868, in Johnson Papers, LC.

Some planters attempted to cope with the League by joining it themselves. They could then observe council meetings and possibly gain influence over the blacks as well. Living amid a sea of freedmen, large landholders possessed a vested interest in their doings. "A movement was started from below," according to one planter, "for all parties to join the League in order to find out what it was. They feared it was incendiary, and parties did join." The threat of confiscation also intimidated some landowners; they hoped membership in the League would demonstrate loyalty, and at all events it could do no harm. Even some elements of the Conservative press toyed briefly with the idea. How many landowners were involved is difficult to gauge, but the number was substantial during the spring and summer of 1867. One activist wrote that he found "many of our Rebel brethren inclined to join the League. . . . [T]hey think that the title to their lands might be strengthened by their availing themselves, but we are cautious and will not grant them amnesty yet." Another organizer noted that whites in his plantation area were getting anxious to enter the League. Not all individuals seeking admission could join, he wrote, but most professing to support Reconstruction were welcomed. Many wealthy and influential planters entered the organization during this period. In Alabama's Greene County, for example, two of the richest men in the region actually led the League.[5]

The motives of these recruits remain problematical. Many who attended League meetings told their neighbors—then and later—that they were thereby containing the Republican menace. One stated afterward that he entered the League only to break it up. A striking instance occurred in the small town of McKinley, Alabama, where several Conservatives claimed to have taken over a council. They joined, in their leader's words, "to see what it was, and to keep the negroes in a quiet and subdued position." These gentlemen displaced the Unionist blacksmith who originally created the League, and they elected one of their number as president. Soon they advised the freedmen that "there was no necessity of meeting, and they had better quit it; it was taking them away from their work, and getting them mixed up in politics." The council disbanded as a result. Successful sabotage of this sort was rare, but some Leaguers apparently joined to subvert the organization.[6]

Another motive for entering the League had to do with agriculture, for planters were hard pressed financially and faced a shortage of cooperative labor. Some individuals seem to have used Republican politics for public relations purposes, to secure a more contented work force. League activist Charles Hays had "quantities of open land, and to secure laborers for another year he must render himself popular," according to the Tuscaloosa *Monitor*. The Radical sheriff of Barbour County, Alabama, was accused on the stump of becoming a Republican to secure cheap labor, and the freedmen present reportedly agreed with this assessment. In another area, a planter became a "friend" to the freedmen, standing up for their rights. Despite a scarcity of field hands, he had little trouble attracting workers, and his neighbors so resented him that he later suffered Klan troubles. Colonel W. B. Jones, a wealthy and well-educated Confederate veteran, was elected mayor of Demopolis, Alabama, after the war as a Democrat. In 1866 he rented land to freedmen long before others in his vicinity. Enraged neighbors began nightriding to drive his tenants off, and Jones issued guns to his hands and led them in drills. The polarization presumably contributed to Jones's emergence as a League organizer the following year.[7]

The movement of large property holders into the League was brief. Conservatives became suspicious of neighbors who attended council meetings. In one rural area, for example, a white who proposed joining the League to reveal its secrets was dissuaded by community pressure. "We will not trust those men who aver that they seek the companionship of Leaguers in order to see what they are about," the Tuscaloosa *Monitor* declared. "The very same fellows are

6. KKK Report, IX, 1346, 1383.
7. Tuscaloosa *Monitor*, November 27, 1867; H. E. Stearx, "William C. Jordan," 71; Ziegler to Smith, October 3, 1869, in Gov. Smith Papers, ADAH; KKK Report, VIII, 539; C. W. Pierce to W. B. Jones, May 5, 1866, Complaint Book, Vol. 141, RG 105.

more apt to be spies against us than for us." Newspapers began printing the names of suspected Leaguers, challenging them to reveal their politics. Faced with an emerging hostile consensus among the planter class, many members extricated themselves with whatever grace was possible. Notices of withdrawal became common in the press, as did denials of having been associated with the organization. By September, the Livingston *Journal* wrote: "The brethren of weak nerves, who have gone into the Union Leagues to escape the dangers of confiscation, can now come out—shake off the unwholesome atmosphere of the Council Chambers and conduct themselves like white folks. The cloud has gone by, and they have been more damaged in person [that is, reputation] than property."[8]

Some large landowners resisted the pressure of their peers and, from either conviction or self-interest, became open Republicans. In one cynical observer's words, southerners had "gone into the Leagues with a view of seeing whether any mischief was intended to the white people. . . . [A]fter some of them got there, they saw it was the surest road to office and remained." Even after most landowners had dropped out of the League, enough held on to render planter-scalawags a potent force within the party. A Mississippi woman noted that many of her neighbors voted Republican to get some control of affairs, and this was common in some areas. Freedmen, viewing such converts as bringing needed respectability and resources to the movement, at first welcomed landowners despite their sometimes vacillating political commitments. Colonel W. B. Jones again furnishes a vivid example. Jones won election to the Alabama Senate as a Leaguer, but in mid-1868, abruptly went over to the Democrats and campaigned against Grant. He privately explained that "when a gentleman's social relations are assailed, when his family are compelled to seek enjoyments only at home, when associations are no longer his . . . it is no more than right something should be done to remedy such unfortunate evils. . . . No one unless a political fool could stand such [hostility]." Jones eventually found his way back to the Republican party. Such planter-scalawags often proved unreliable allies because of the conflicting pressures upon

8. KKK Report, X, 1637; Tuscaloosa *Monitor*, March 24, 1868; Grove Hill *Democrat*, August 8, 1867, quoting Mobile *Times*; Livingston *Journal*, September 21, 1867.

them, but they were nonetheless an important component of the Republican coalition.[9]

Planters opting for the Radicals were rewarded with considerable power. "Scalawags from black counties were highly influential in the Alabama Republican party," according to historian Sarah Woolfolk Wiggins, and a similar situation obtained in Mississippi. An indication of such influence was how many were elected officials. One quantitative study of Alabama's local officeholders showed that during the period 1867–1868 approximately 94 percent of the Republicans were white. Of these, 85 percent had resided in the state before the war and many seem to have been well-off individuals from the cotton regions. Planter-scalawags certainly received a proportion of offices far beyond their minuscule percentage of the Republican electorate. Such leaders were thus in an excellent position to restrain freedmen's political demands. As one historian put it, black belt scalawags exerted a "moderating influence on the state Republican party."[10]

Planter-scalawags exercised their power within the party in a variety of ways, but their resources gave them one particularly effective means of restraining their comrades. High bonds were required to assume most local positions. Few Radicals could raise much capital, and they had to rely upon moneyed allies to endorse their bonds. Property owners thus had considerable leverage. For example, Charles Hays, the wealthiest Republican in his section of Alabama, rendered "valuable service in kindly making the bonds of newly elected officers." His generosity reportedly contributed to his own election to Congress in 1869. Planter-scalawags demonstrated their power in Sumter County, Alabama. A freedman, Richard Harris, nominated "against the remonstrances of the better part of the members of [the] League," lost his office because no whites offered to help and he himself "could not make a good bond for five dollars." This turn of events angered the black community, which, despite increas-

9. Annie E. Harper Manuscript, October, 1876 (in MDAH), 66; KKK Report, IX, 1346, X, 1452; John Witherspoon DuBose, *Alabama's Tragic Decade: Ten Years of Alabama, 1865–1874,* ed. James K. Greer (Birmingham, 1940), 87–89; W. B. Jones to Smith, August 17, 1868, in Gov. Smith Papers, ADAH.

10. Wiggins, *The Scalawag in Alabama Politics*, 128; Cash, "Alabama Republicans During Reconstruction," 111, 381, 383.

ing militancy, could not force white Republicans to come to Harris' aid. In Woodville, Mississippi, Mayor William H. Gibbs was embarrassed by the sudden withdrawal of his bond endorsers. John C. Keffer actually lost his lucrative post as register in bankruptcy because his backers dropped him. Frederick G. Bromberg of Mobile once even tried to forge official bonds, and his exposure caused him a great deal of difficulty. The financial strength of wealthy Republicans, combined with other resources at their command, clearly gave them considerable power.[11]

Even if landowning scalawags could exercise disproportionate influence through the Republican party, most planters rejected this option. The freedmen demanded far too many concessions to civil rights for most of them to accept. At first, wealthy landowners had joined from fear of confiscation or in order to monitor the doings of the blacks. Steadily increasing white disapproval, and the growing threat of violence, soon caused many to rethink their position. By the fall of 1867, planters as a group turned to forcing the freedmen to leave the League, rather than trying to neutralize its political impact from inside the organization. They rejected co-optation for confrontation as the means to control the freedmen's vote.

By the summer of 1867, economic pressure to counteract the Union League became the prevalent strategy for Democratic victory. Conservatives boycotted individual League activists and relied upon planters' control over their laborers. When elections approached, Democrats called for landowners to fire Republican field hands, and many employers did so. Results, however, fell far short of their desires. Once exposed to the League, freedmen voted overwhelmingly Radical, despite the threat of retaliation and despite damaging their own financial interests. The black community united behind the Radicals and put tremendous pressure on defectors from their own ranks. Economic intimidation seemed only to reinforce freedmen's determination to defy their former masters. The eventual

11. Demopolis *Southern Republican*, June 23, 1869; Marion *Commonwealth*, June 24, 1868; J. C. Gillespie to Patton, June 6, 1868, in Gov. Patton Papers, ADAH; Price to Wilson, November 18, 1868, in Letters Received SAC Demopolis, Box 27, RG 105; Selma *Messenger*, July 8, 1868; Livingston *Journal*, April 25, July 17, 1868; Montgomery *Mail*, January 12, 15, 1868; Swayne to Bromberg, September 12, 1867, in Frederick G. Bromberg Papers, LC.

failure of this strategy would set the stage for the shift to armed repression.[12]

Republican activists presented the most obvious target for economic punishment. For example, the head of Mobile College, Amos Towle, joined the League and his institution suffered boycott. "Down upon him like the vultures," noted one observer, ". . . pounce the three rebel papers of Mobile. Away goes his reputation and his scholars." Within weeks, the formerly prosperous college closed, and Towle left the state. Such campaigns were common against Radicals in business. The Mobile *Nationalist* suffered a boycott of its advertisers. In Tuscaloosa a Conservative paper urged readers to shun the Loyal Leaguers' shops, and it succeeded in damaging their trade. Economic intimidation could also mean refusing needed services to Republican clients. In McNutt, Mississippi, a bitter former Confederate was the only physician in the area. After one election he declared that freedmen would be "sunk in hell" before he ministered to them again, reportedly causing much distress.[13]

Democrats relied mainly upon the economic leverage they held as employers over the freedmen. One paper advised that "employers may prevent employees from voting by a firm judicious stand in their business relations," and the Democratic press urged full utilization of this power. The Oxford *Falcon*, for example, reported the names of all local blacks who voted, saying they should go to the Radicals for work or starve. The influential Montgomery *Mail* likewise recommended public disclosure and boycott of laborers joining the League. Some merchants espoused a similar policy. In one Mississippi community the local retailer threatened to stop dealing with any farmer who let Republican blacks stay on his place. Planters' groups also echoed these appeals. A meeting in Raymond, Mississippi, resolved that without intending to interfere with anyone's political rights, "we will not hereafter employ . . . . any man, white or black, who is known to belong to the Loyal League." Other plant-

12. Trelease, *White Terror*, xli.
13. Mobile *Nationalist*, April 30, 1868; J. J. Gillette to A. O. Gillette, October 28, 1867, in Gillette Family Papers, LC; Tuscaloosa *Monitor*, February 12, August 11, 1868; Mobile *Nationalist*, January 25, 1866; C. T. Lawson to M. Barber, November 20, 1867, in Records, M826, RG 105.

ers' associations complained that freedmen skipped work to attend League rallies and recommended disciplining such employees. Behind this threat lay very real economic power: planters could fire laborers and could evict them from their homes as well.[14]

Such economic pressure became widespread. One agricultural contract actually provided that laborers "not attach themselves, belong to, or in any way perform any of the obligations required of what is known as the 'Loyal League Society' or attend elections or political meetings without the consent of the employer." The more common practice was fining freedmen for attending League functions. In labor agreements generally, those who missed work could have their wages docked. Planters now used this power for partisan ends. In Uniontown, Alabama, a landowner levied "unreasonable charges [of] 100 per day for *all* lost time & 500 for registering [to vote] & c." Bureau records indicate that these cases multiplied during campaigns. A Mississippi Leaguer observed that during a canvass, he heard many such complaints each day.[15]

Dismissal of workers represented the ultimate economic sanction, and both the threat and the action itself occurred frequently. Obviously planters could not fire all their workers, but large numbers went as far as they could. One Mississippi planter reportedly evicted a freedman and said he would be damned if he would employ Leaguers. A Bureau agent observed that three-quarters of his cases after one election involved dismissals for voting. Another agent reported that "many complaints" were made daily by freedmen who had been "driven off because of their attending political meetings. The freedmen go to these meetings, through ignorance, connecting them with registration & voting." Another organizer found planters in his region unwilling to hire Leaguers or even freedmen who registered to vote. Written labor contracts provided little protection—

14. Tuscaloosa *Monitor*, January 28, 1868; Montgomery *Mail*, August 18, 1868; Montgomery *Advertiser*, November 9, 1867; Oxford *Falcon*, June 28, 1868, quoted in *House Miscellaneous Documents*, 40th Cong., 3rd Sess., No. 53, pp. 171, 208; *Hinds County Gazette* (Raymond, Miss.), August 28, 1868; Jackson *Clarion*, December 5, 1867. The *Mail* article referred to urban freedmen, but the editorial was widely reprinted in rural newspapers throughout the state.

15. J. Black to Thaddeus Stevens, February 22, 1868, in Stevens Papers, LC; Complaint Book, November 12, 1867, SAC Demopolis, Vol. 141, RG 105; J. S. Morris to Gillem, November 16, 1867, in Records, M826, RG 105.

indeed, they often encouraged political firings. A southeastern Mississippi planter noted that his contract was "explicit that any laborer who leaves my place refusing to work . . . is liable to be turned off forfeiting all that may be due him." This landowner, deciding to make an example of one worker, seized the man's entire cotton crop for a single absence at a League gathering. The Mississippi Bureau chief, General Gillem, upheld this action, stating that the freedman had no legitimate grievance. Even if many contracts lacked such provisions, employers commonly drove freedmen away by abuse or by cutting off their rations, thus forcing them to leave or go hungry. Many freedmen abandoned maturing crops because of these forms of pressure.[16]

That cotton farming was seasonal facilitated politically motivated evictions. The heaviest plantation work occurred during plowing and cultivation followed by a lull of six weeks or more. Planters profited by dismissing laborers after the crop was "laid by" early in summer, then hiring others to pick the cotton in the fall. Thus immediate financial gain united with perceptions of civic duty to foster political intimidation. In organizer D. H. Bingham's words, planters resorted to "every means at their command to prevent them [the freedmen] from joining Leagues—even to turning [them] off when they could." He observed that they evicted laborers in early summer, just after the heavy work ended, and numbers of Bureau documents confirm this pattern. These reports escalated when political campaigns coincided with the slow season, as in Mississippi's elections to ratify the Radical constitution in late June, 1868. The Republican leader W. H. Gibbs observed that "now that the crops are fairly made, there is the dishonest incentive of gains by getting rid of the laborer as well as the incentive of political hatred, under which the planter acts." Similar complaints from across Mississippi strongly suggest that the timing of the election encouraged a rash of

16. Deposition of Allen Agee, in G. W. Corliss to Greene, November 25, 1867, in Records, M826, RG 105; Complaint Book, September 23, 1867, SAC Demopolis, Vol. 141, RG 105; D. H. Bingham to O. O. Howard, August 3, 1867, in Records, M809, RG 105; S. D. Lee to Smith, October 25, 1867, see endorsement of G. S. Smith, dated October 28, 1867, in Letters Received SAC Macon, Box 45, RG 105; *House Miscellaneous Documents*, 40th Cong., 3rd Sess., No. 53, pp. 146, 171, 173, 180.

evictions. Overall, there can be little doubt that planters widely used their economic power to control the freedmen's votes.[17] Despite these efforts, and despite their relatively extensive resources, planters had little success in dictating how freedmen cast their ballots. The Vicksburg *Herald* complained that freedmen would "talk fair, and scrape their feet and say yes, massa, but they will vote just as . . . the League bids them." A measure of this failure was precisely the necessity of firing so many laborers, for an effective threat obviously need not have been carried out so often. In combination with terror, economic pressure could prove effective, but employers' threats by themselves did not coerce the freedmen. The situation faced by former Alabama governor Benjamin Fitzpatrick was typical. According to one of his neighbors, "All but three of Gov. Fitzpatrick's [employees] have voted, so if the Gov. is firm he will have to ship a good many." Many other planters were "in the same fix," he added. On one zealous Democrat's place, a black foreman approached the planter and informed him the hands were going to town to vote. If loaned a wagon, the foreman could have the freedmen back that evening; if not, they would lose considerably more time. It was a hard choice for the violently partisan planter, but the laborers got their ride. Freedmen, too, could use economic power for political ends.[18]

Over time, property owners recognized that economic pressure left the freedmen unmoved. The experience of a planter near Athens, Alabama, illustrates how this recognition was forced upon

17. D. H. Bingham to W. H. Smith, August 7, 1867, in Swayne Papers, ADAH; Preuss to Preston, July 31, 1867, J. D. Moore to Preston, July 31, 1867, W. H. Gibbs to Howard, July 4, 1868, W. Sprague to J. Tyler, July 2, 1868, all in Records, M826, RG 105. For a detailed description of cotton cultivation from the point of view of the farmer, see James Agee and Walker Evans, *Let Us Now Praise Famous Men* (New York, 1939), 295–315. For a revisionist restatement of the argument that a labor shortage doomed economic intimidation, see Trelease, *White Terror*, xli. And for evidence on the 1868 Mississippi campaign and the prevalence of political firings, see *House Miscellaneous Documents*, 40th Cong., 3rd Sess., No. 53, pp. 94, 108, 115, 142, 144, 146, 171, 173, 180, 235. Finally, the position argued here is the opposite of that of Fleming, who maintained that "whites were complaining loudly because of the scarcity of labor, and few would discharge a negro laborer" (*Civil War and Reconstruction in Alabama*, 544).

18. Forest *Register*, December 10, 1870, quoting Vicksburg *Herald*; C. D. Oliver to Hall, February 5, 1868, in Hall Family Papers, ADAH; DuBose, *Alabama's Tragic Decade*, 110. DuBose's account seems to be of his own experience as a planter.

them. After refusing to allow a scheduled League meeting on his land, he evicted and threatened to shoot a League activist. Freedmen petitioned the Bureau for aid, and soon an agent arrived to see that the League met unmolested. "We organized a Council and initiated thirty seven Col'd and one white member," the agent reported. The planter had only alienated the freedmen and antagonized military officials in the process. This result was typical; economic sanctions reinforced the freedmen's distrust without actually preventing them from voting Republican.[19]

Several factors contributed to this failure. Enthusiasm for the League obviously was a major one, and another was the presence of the Bureau protecting freedmen's access to the ballot. But critical was the tremendous pressure the freedmen could bring against defectors. One black Mississippi activist testified that freedmen "ostracise them; we won't associate with them, nor treat them with that respect and courtesy that we do other men. Other than that we have nothing more to do with them." At a council near Huntsville, leaders urged sympathetic black women to have no social relations with Democrats, and one reportedly hit her husband with a brick for voting incorrectly. Freedmen who publicized their Democratic politics faced particular trouble. In Montgomery, a black Conservative speaker was chased through the streets by a mob of Leaguers, and similar events occurred frequently in the countryside. One League member later testified that the only reason freedmen did not beat defectors was that "we was afraid to"—that is, they feared white retaliation. These threats did not generally emanate from the leadership; instead, violence grew spontaneously from freedmen's hostility to defectors. The Leaguers hated black Conservatives because they themselves supported the Republicans so zealously. The prevalence of this feeling reinforces the critical point: planters' economic intimidation failed because freedmen were convinced that their highest hopes depended on the success of Reconstruction. That con-

19. D. H. Bingham to Callis, May 22, 1867, in Letters Received SAC Huntsville, Vol. 59, RG 105; Callis to McKimmer, May 23, 1867, in Letters Sent SAC Huntsville, Vol. 64, RG 105; R. Bassell *et al.* to Callis, June 10, 1867, in Letters Received SAC Huntsville, Vol. 59, RG 105; Danforth to Callis, May 29, 1867, in Records, M809, RG 105.

viction outweighed the threat, and the reality, of economic retaliation.[20]

Thus planters' recourse to economic intimidation miscarried. Property owners tried hard to counteract the League, by boycotting activists and discouraging freedmen's attendance at council meetings. Even the threat of dismissal did not work, however. The freedmen adhered to the party of Lincoln so emphatically that planters' attempts to dominate them only aroused greater opposition. Democratic efforts at courting the black vote accomplished surprisingly little in areas where League organizing had taken place. Faced with the overt failure of their strategy, planters ran short of alternatives to outright violence, at least if they seriously hoped to contest Republican control of the black vote. Physical coercion replaced financial pressure as the chief method for opposing the League. The ineffectiveness of economic intimidation led directly to the emergence of the Ku Klux Klan.

After Military Reconstruction began, physical intimidation occurred occasionally, but full-fledged terror against the freedmen only emerged during the spring of 1868. A vast literature exists on the Klan, and it need not be summarized here; the point is that the nightriders targeted the League and with devastating results, particularly in rural areas. Klan techniques enabled Democrats to intimidate freedmen with minimal fear of retaliation, since its clandestine methods closed off effective resistance in most cases. The Klan rapidly destroyed the Union League as an effective political organization. This repression had a major impact on the future of Republican rule and on the balance of power on the plantations. The Klan's demolishing the Radical network presaged the eventual overthrow of Reconstruction and also the emergence of an increasingly coercive labor regime.

Soon after the League appeared, there were scattered efforts to

20. KKK Report, XII, 725, IX, 684; Fleming, *Civil War and Reconstruction in Alabama*, 565; KKK Report, VIII, 228; Montgomery *Advertiser*, September 6, 1867. For other instances of actual or threatened violence against black Democrats, see Tuscaloosa *Monitor*, August 25, September 8, 1868; KKK Report, IX, 878, 1072, 1077–78; *House Miscellaneous Documents*, 40th Cong., 3rd Sess., No. 53, p. 180.

counteract it by force. An organizer's report for May, 1867, indicates that "some half dozen or more rebels got up a difficulty & fight with members of the Union League, with no other view than to break it up." Another reported troubles in his Alabama neighborhood: "The entire citizens are anti-Leage and they swore there shal not be another meeting & have the freedmen all allarmed." In some localities, the intimidation became intense early. In Paulding, Mississippi, whites fired upon freedmen returning from a political meeting. The attackers reportedly were led by the local justice of the peace. In another small town, a freedman was abducted and killed for no apparent reason other than being a Leaguer. Violence, however, remained at a relatively low level during the first election campaigns. The press and most planters seemed confident that restrained measures would carry the black vote, and they discouraged bloodshed for fear of alienating the freedmen.[21]

When other measures failed, violence became the alternative of choice. Even before the Klan appeared, such conduct was becoming common, especially in Alabama, where the Reconstruction elections proceeded swiftly. In Bullock County, Alabama, whites mobilized soon after the Perote disturbances. Ben Royal wrote that the "Rebels are forming into clubs to prevent the colored people from voting the Radical ticket." Events in Limestone County, in the northern part of the state, demonstrated the changing political climate. In May, 1867, D. H. Bingham complained of hostility against Leaguers, but thought that "men like myself are in no danger." Eight months later, the elderly organizer was brutally beaten on an isolated road and subsequently died. A few days after Bingham's death, both the vice-president and the secretary of the local council published withdrawal notices. "We advise you all to do the same," they wrote, "for it is calculated to do nothing else but bring us all into trouble." Other leading freedmen followed suit. When future congressman Thomas Haughey tried to reorganize the League, he was chased from town.

21. D. H. Bingham to Grant, May 20, 1867, De Arman to Swayne, May 27, 1867, both in Records, M809, RG 105; D. A. Self to Smith, May 23, 1867, in Swayne Papers, ADAH; W. V. McKnight to R. V. Montague, October 21, 1867, in Letters Received SAC Natchez, Box 51, RG 105; J. W. D. Lancaster to Smith, September 8, 1867, in Letters Received SAC Opelika, Box 35, RG 105.

Republican vote totals reflected the impact of this political violence, for Radical support declined in Limestone County by two-thirds over the next two elections. Clearly, Democrats in this plantation area repressed the League even before Klan operations became prevalent.[22]

What the Ku Klux Klan contributed to the situation was an effective technique of intimidation. During 1867, freedmen had held their own in riots in Mobile and elsewhere. If Democrats did not wish to hazard a general bloodletting, and also federal intervention, they needed an alternative to open confrontation. The approach first devised in Tennessee provided the solution, for Klan-style nightriding permitted the choice of favorable terrain. Since whites owned horses, they had a tremendous advantage in mobility over the freedmen. They could concentrate overwhelming force on isolated locations, and by wearing disguises, they could prevent victims from identifying them. It was very difficult for either the freedmen or the military to counteract these methods, or to win convictions in court after the fact. Ironically the freedmen's success in renting land dispersed them widely through the countryside, making them more vulnerable to attack. Klan techniques also had advantages that were of political importance. Preponderant numbers permitted operations with minimal casualties, and the Klansmen could kill or whip freedmen as circumstances dictated. The critical point about Klan methods was that they foreclosed resistance. Hit-and-run tactics largely prevented the freedmen from confronting their assailants directly.

To a significant extent, the Klan represented a movement by planters to control their laborers' votes, and the partisan nature of the violence was overt. "The testimony of its victims," according to Trelease, "points to the intimidation and punishment of Republican officeholders and voters as its central purpose." Large landowners

22. Trelease, *White Terror*, xli; B. Royal to Swayne, May 20, 1867, in Register of Letters Received by the Assistant Commissioner, and D. H. Bingham to Grant, May 20, 1867, both in Records, M809, RG 105; Athens *Post*, January 2, 9, 1868. Republican vote totals for the county went from 1,130 in October, 1867, to 789 in February, 1868, and a mere 355 in November, 1868. The League apparently continued to meet on occasion, but its operations were limited. For vote totals, see Athens *Post*, October 10, 1867, February 6, November 7, 1868.

participated fully in spreading the organization through the cotton regions. One Mississippi Klansman noted that in his vicinity, it was "rather the better class, the best men in the county" who joined. Federal Judge Busteed of Alabama agreed, depicting the nightriders as gentlemen of education and intelligence. Even the pro-Klan historian Walter Lynwood Fleming thought that the planters dominated the Klan at first, though he maintained that it later fell into the hands of a low class of men who used it for their own aims. Not all large property owners participated in regulator activities, but many clearly supported them at least passively, especially during the initial upsurge. Since planters had long viewed the Union League as a secret conspiracy, more threatening than the rest of Republican activity, it presented the obvious target. "The only thing we did," stated the leader of one Klan-like group, was to "counteract the efforts of the Loyal League in the county, and to secure the defeat of the republican candidates." His club, he thought, was brought about because of the existence of the League.[23]

Planter spokesmen proclaimed that the League justified Klan terror, and they sometimes avowed their support for repressing councils. One Alabamian testified that the Klan directly counteracted the Radical organization, and another likened the League to a chill and the Klan to the fever that follows. The Selma *Times and Messenger* made this point explicitly, calling on citizens to "organize a Ku-Klux Klan whenever they organize a league." The Mobile *Register* urged: "Organize! Organize! . . . Political clubs should be formed in every neighborhood where ten people can be got together. . . . They may be 'Seymour Clubs,' or 'Blair Clubs,' or 'Liberty Clubs,' or even 'Ku Klux Clubs,' if you choose. . . . The first object of these clubs should be a persevering and systematic movement to break up the 'Loyal Leagues.'" A newspaper in a small town in Mississippi actually changed its name to the *Ku Klux* for election time, and this kind of emphatic espousal of violence was common in the state. One Democratic club in Marshall County resolved that, in order to defeat the pending Radical constitution, Democrats would "use every

23. Trelease, *White Terror*, xlvii; KKK Report, XI, 236, VIII, 323; Fleming, *Civil War and Reconstruction in Alabama*, 666–68; Trelease, *White Terror*, 51; KKK Report, XI, 223.

means in our power" and consider "nothing dishonorable that may contribute to our success."[24]

Perhaps the most explicit espousal of violence against the League emanated from Tuscaloosa. Ryland Randolph, editor of the Tuscaloosa *Monitor*, established and led a Klan of about sixty members. His paper denounced the League repeatedly, asked readers to forward the names of members, and listed several such members, describing them as worthy of Klan attention. Randolph recalled that Klan death threats were "concocted and posted by my own hand, disguised, of course." Writing of League activist and future U.S. senator George E. Spencer, the editor concluded that "there might not be enough boughs from which *all* such characters should swing, but the worst of them could be accommodated." According to a congressional investigation, at least eight Republicans died at the Klan's hands in Tuscaloosa County, and the League councils disintegrated swiftly in the vicinity. "All of the Loyal League game about town" had been used up quickly, reported the *Monitor*, and in some cases was "dead and buried." The Tuscaloosa paper was perhaps exceptional in its unbridled advocacy of violence, but most Democratic publicists encouraged—or at least excused—Klan attacks on the League.[25]

Many planters privately expressed similar enthusiasm for the Klan. One Mississippi planter said a League organizer and local officeholder got what he deserved when the Klan nearly whipped him to death. A Mississippi woman wrote to ask her sister, "How are the radicals getting along in your part of the country[?] [W]e have slain them here in Oakland every vote that was given in here was *Democratic*." She reported that the Klan had shot a scalawag for making speeches to freedmen at night, and thought this an excellent political portent. Prevailing opinion was illustrated by an entry in an

24. KKK Report, IX, 781, 872; Selma *Times and Messenger*, July 31, 1868; Athens *Post*, August 6, 1868, quoting Mobile *Register*; Forest *Register* or *Ku Klux*, September 14, 1871; C. Clark to McDowell, in Records of the Third Military District, Office of Civil Affairs, Box 6, Pt. 1, RG 393.

25. R. Randolph to W. Fleming, August 23, 1901, in Walter L. Fleming Papers, Astor, Lenox and Tilden Foundations, New York Public Library; Trelease, *White Terror*, 85; Tuscaloosa *Monitor*, March 18, August 18, 1868; Fleming, *Civil War and Reconstruction in Alabama*, 705.

Alabama planter's journal: "Democratic Clubs are forming . . .
K. W. C. [Knights of the White Camelia] associations are also becoming numerous. Loyal Leagues and all other such mongrel associations will have to break up and the white skinned portion of the negroes will have to emigrate." Moderate scalawags sometimes sympathized with Klan attacks on the League. For example, Nicholas Davis of Huntsville resented the Radical leaders of the League, so operations against them did not unduly disturb him. Testifying that the Klan was "provoked . . . by what was called the Loyal League," he asserted that League organizers had made speeches against southern men at secret meetings and otherwise behaved outrageously. A planter-scalawag on the Alabama Supreme Court thought the carpetbaggers brought their troubles upon themselves. Many large landowners—some of them Republicans—viewed the League as a threat and, therefore, regulator activities as a solution.[26]

Faced with spreading violence, rural Leaguers endeavored to defend themselves as willingly as their more successful brethren in the cities. Even before the Klan, Leaguers drilled in unofficial militias, and these efforts intensified as conflict grew. More freedmen also went armed to meetings. The attitude of a white Alabama organizer typified their combative reaction. Daniel Price urged defiance in response to Klan threats to break up his council. "They shall not do any such thing," he wrote. "If they resort to force we will meet them with force." A black League member in the area of Huntsville recalled similar declarations: "We made threatenings between us in this way: we said that if we were attacked by the Ku-Klux we would try to defend ourselves. We would say to one another, 'If we are attacked by the Ku-Klux, we will shoot them or fight them inside of our houses.'" Activists sometimes threatened retribution against Democrats generally, or the burning of the nearest town. Leaguers near Union Springs reportedly put up a placard stating that if any members were attacked, then the entire neighborhood would be held responsible. Similar responses to the Klan occurred elsewhere, and

26. M. Crawford to "My Old School Mates," April 15, 1871, in Cameron Family Papers, UNC; S. A. Bunton to Clark, June 28, 1868, in Juanita Brown Collection, University of Mississippi; S. Forwood to W. S. Forwood, September 13, 1868, in W. S. Forwood Papers, UNC; KKK Report, IX, 781, 783; T. Peters to Smith, August 24, 1868, in Gov. Smith Papers, ADAH.

observers took them seriously. "The thing will end in bloodletting," a League leader in Wilcox County, Alabama, warned. "When these freedmen once taste blood God knows where it will stop."[27]

The odds did not favor resistance in rural areas. One difficulty was the lack of legal sanction, for in neither Alabama nor Mississippi were moderate Republican governors willing to arm blacks under state authority. Also, the Bureau's withdrawal and cutbacks in army force levels in 1868 were extremely ill-timed. "Anarchy is surely impending," forecast an officer before the departure of one garrison, and he was only slightly exaggerating the impact of the change. The crucial problem, however, was that freedmen never devised an adequate defense against the Klan's mode of operation, though they often managed to shield prominent activists. A. T. Morgan of Yazoo City observed that after his return from the Mississippi Constitutional Convention, freedmen spontaneously defended his house: "Just outside the sleeping-room, on the porch . . . fully a dozen men, negroes, stood guard all night." Leaders commonly had sentries watching their homes, but these precautions were difficult to sustain for long periods.[28]

While prominent politicians had some protection from violence, such measures were of little use in saving the average Leaguer from repeated whippings. One freedman reported that most of the members of his council were visited by the Klan before the November, 1868, elections; another observed, "It is at present death all most for a man to ly down in the hous with his family . . . i have to lay out every night i can ha[r]dley stay in the field to pick out my cotton." Local activists might frustrate the Klan by sleeping in the field or the forest, but that only underscored their inability to defend themselves. A freedman recalled the troubles of his scalawag-landlord: "De Ku Klux threat to whup Mr. Nelson 'case he took up fer de niggers. Heap of nights we would hear of the Ku Klux comin' an' leave home. Sometimes us was scared not to go an' scared to go 'way

27. Price to Pierce, April 13, 1868, in Letters Received SAC Demopolis, Box 27, RG 105; KKK Report, IX, 685; Jacksonville *Republican*, October 17, 1868, quoting Columbus (Ga.) *Enquirer*, October 4, 1868; C. C. Colton to Butler, April 10, 1868, in Butler Papers, LC. The Georgia newspaper article refers to events in Bullock County, Alabama.

28. O. L. Sheppard to O. O. Howard, August 1, 1868, in Registers and Letters, M752, RG 105; Morgan, *Yazoo*, 168.

from home." A Mississippi Bureau agent agreed that such tales were typical, and he knew of hundreds of freedmen who were staying in the woods at night. At best, Leaguers could only limit the night-riders' ravages.[29]

They adopted extraordinary expedients. In Talladega, Radicals seemed to believe that violence resulted from misunderstanding League activities. Several black leaders actually invited local Democratic politicians to witness a Saturday-night gathering. One of the Democrats was permitted to address the crowd. According to the Conservative Talladega *Watchtower*, "He was treated, during the most of his speech, with the utmost courtesy and politeness, and was listened to with very respectful attention." The speaker made no converts, but then neither did the Radicals accomplish much with their strategy. Local Democrats continued to laud the nightriders or to excuse Klan activities by alleging Loyal League atrocities.[30]

Replying to force with force often made matters worse. Since Leaguers seldom caught mounted terrorists in the act, any retaliation would have to be against whites generally. In practice, League leaders avoided such reprisals for fear of full-scale race war. Even where blacks predominated, activists appear to have seldom incited violence. As Senator John Pool of North Carolina stated: "The leagues have been the means through which a greater amount of this retaliation has been prevented. If the Colored men had not been under the control, to some extent, under the advice, under the counsel of men of conscience and honor, who advised them against the horrid resort to retaliation, they would have resorted to it in a thousand localities instead of two or three." League activists, however, frequently adopted the threat of retribution, in hopes of deterring Klan depredations. They thus relied on bluff, which proved a most ineffective response.[31]

29. Selma *Times and Messenger*, October 1, 1868, quoting Livingston *Journal*; KKK Report, IX, 686; W. G. Crittenden to Smith, October 10, 1868, in Gov. Smith Papers, ADAH; George P. Rawick (ed.), *The American Slave: A Composite Biography* (Westport, Conn., 1972), Ser. 1, VI, 421; Rawick (ed.), *The American Slave, Supplement Series 1*, VI, 17–18; J. Pierce to T. Eliot, December 9, 1868, No. 1667, in file HR 40A-F10.4, RG 233.
30. Talladega *Watchtower*, August 12, 1868.
31. *Congresional Globe*, 42nd Cong., 1st Sess., Appendix, 102.

Events in Sumter County, Alabama, typified this critical failure. In mid-1868, freedmen marched on the county seat after the murder of a white Radical. Their leader, the black legislator George Houston, told the townspeople, "We have sent for you white men up here to see what you will do, and if you don't do it . . . we will have this town burned." Several nights later, Houston was shot at his home, and violence increased sharply as Klansmen flowed in from surrounding regions. Fully twenty Republicans were slain in all, and every League activist in the county fled or made peace with the Democrats. A similar case occurred in Brooksville, Mississippi, when an altercation developed out of a League procession. After one freedman was shot, Leaguers gathered and demanded an arrest. They threatened to burn the town, but they were dissuaded and the matter settled peacefully. Afterward, though, the Klan mobilized "as a check upon these other [League] organizations," in one Democrat's words. Thirteen killings followed, and the leagues "pretty much stopped parading." Leaguers' direct action met a like response in many rural localities.[32]

Yet Radicals sometimes successfully resisted the Klan. In a scalawag stronghold in mountainous Fayette County, Alabama, white "Mossy-backs" fought the terrorists to a standstill that lasted years. They were eventually overwhelmed only by superior numbers. Since the Unionists had horses, they could mimic Klan tactics and raid the nearby plantation areas. The freedmen also sometimes stopped the regulators. In Hale County, Leaguers established a warning system—buglers to alert them to Klan raiders. A Mississippi league surprised Klansmen in the act of whipping a freedman and inflicted several casualties upon the nightriders, but such successes were likely to be short-lived. In Courtland, Alabama, a black man, learning of a threat against him, gathered some friends and ambushed the regulators. The freedmen killed one, wounded another, and captured several horses. The whites then swore to exterminate them. One participant wrote the Freedmen's Bureau, "Send us a standing army the Clu Kluck is killing us . . . we can not do

32. KKK Report, IX, 1001, X, 1622–23; Fleming, *Civil War and Reconstruction in Alabama*, 705; KKK Report, XI, 556, 234, xxv.

nuthing without your help . . . [send] us sume help jess as quick as you can." The Klan generally could bring overwhelming force to bear upon their opponents.[33]

The regulators operated with impunity in wide regions of Alabama and Mississippi, and they broke up leagues almost at will. A few examples indicate how potent the repression was. In one community, Klansmen warned a teacher that "the first time they found him in the League, or reading newspapers, or in the act of giving instruction to the colored people . . . [they would] fix him well." These same Klansmen later killed the black who was president of the local League. In Columbus, Mississippi, the Klan fell upon an apparent League procession. A later account stated that "no great trouble came of this incident, although three negroes were killed." In Sumter County, an elderly freedman was asked by a Democrat if he was a Leaguer. Receiving an affirmative reply, the Democrat told the freedman to get off his horse "as he did not want to shoot it but him." The old man fled but was pursued and killed, and a mob later freed his murderer from jail. Even those who escaped direct assault suffered tremendous psychological stress. A white Republican ordered from his home wrote: "Neither me nor my family have the fisical durability to go through again the anxiety we have went through the last month. Our healths have already failed and now their is scarsely one of my family able to take care of the rest." Violence and intimidation decimated the League leadership in the countryside.[34]

The number of activists who became Klan victims furnishes one measure of the scope of the repression. Of 362 individuals identified as League activists, at least 15 met violent deaths from the period 1868 to 1871, and another 7 were shot but lived. Twenty-six were assaulted or fired upon, 22 seriously harassed, and 4 driven into exile. These categories together total 74, over one-fifth of the identified activists in Alabama and Mississippi. That figure, however,

33. Trelease, *White Terror*, 268; Hunnicutt, *Reconstruction in West Alabama*, 51–53; KKK Report, XII, 1184; Wager to Smith, August 16, 1870, Irving Allen to [?], August 15, 1870, both in Gov. Smith Papers, ADAH; Huntsville *Democrat*, August 15, 1870.

34. Martin *et al.* to Smith, May 25, 1869, in Gov. Smith Papers, ADAH; KKK Report, VIII, 3; "Reconstruction," in Subject File titled Lowndes County W.P.A., Pt. 1, pp. 278–80, ADAH; Stelzig to Wilson, August 11, 1868, in Letters Received SAC Demopolis, Box 27, RG 105; KKK Report, X, 1002; G. A. Smith to Applegate, September 19, 1868, in Gov. Smith Papers, ADAH.

understates the virulence of the Klan in the backcountry. Many activists resided in larger communities, where they were relatively safe; others lived in places—the overwhelmingly black counties of the Mississippi Delta, for example—the Klan never appeared in force. In strong Klan areas, the toll was proportionally higher. In Greene County, Alabama, for instance, terrorists reportedly drove out every single white who voted for Grant.[35]

These statistics, moreover, do not take into account the impact intimidation had on the League. Many activists experienced repeated Klan warnings—W. T. Blackford received "eleven different notices from the Ku-Klux organization to the leave the country, or that they would go for me." Such pressure had a potent effect, as John Keffer himself admitted. Certainly as physically courageous as any Leaguer, Keffer later stated that if he had his life to live again, "I would not go through the outrages, wrongs and persecutions I have endured . . . for the ownership of an entire county." He advised no one to come to Alabama unless he abandoned all sympathy for the oppressed. Prominent Leaguers clearly were a major target of regulators' attention, and the movement in rural regions suffered severely.[36]

The Ku Klux Klan achieved its most dramatic political success in Alabama, where it swiftly demolished the League. By mid-1868, terrorists roved through the western cotton belt and the entire Tennessee Valley. The Republican administration's cautious policy encouraged this expansion. Governor William H. Smith actually said that "if such an organization [as the Klan] ever existed in this state he was not aware of it." Faced with such attitudes, and unable to stop the Klan themselves, many Republicans concluded that the League had outlived its usefulness. Perhaps disbanding would placate opponents. One Hale County activist informed the press that whatever the League's original design, now it only awakened racial conflict. Republican papers such as the Tuscaloosa *Reconstructionist* agreed,

35. KKK Report, VIII, 9. In compiling these figures, I counted each individual once, in the category of the most serious injury inflicted upon him. Most cases were Klan operations, though some are doubtful. One murder, that of Congressman Haughey, was actually committed by a fellow Leaguer.

36. KKK Report, IX, 1278; Keffer to Howard, September 19, 1868, in Howard Papers, Bowdoin.

proclaiming the group's clandestine character at fault. Eventually even Keffer and other state-level leaders "pronounced themselves in favor of discontinuing that secret organization," according to the Montgomery *Alabama State Journal*. Some leagues, like that in Tuskegee, changed into open Republican clubs, but most appear to have gone into decline by 1869, except perhaps for occasional pre-election rallies. The regular weekly gatherings stopped, and the demise of the leagues hurt the Republicans. A Democrat described the results of the repression in the countryside during the election of 1870: "The League of which I speak was no longer in existence. These carpetbaggers, who had been manipulating the negroes, had left and were gone; and their organization was defective in consequence—not complete. A good many negroes who had quit them had taken an active part in the canvass. The county was canvassed very thoroughly by the white democrats; but there was no canvass on the other side to speak of." The Klan destroyed the Radicals' political network in the plantation region, thus paving the way for eventual Democratic victory.[37]

The Klan also attacked the League in Mississippi, but it developed later and less broadly than was the case in Alabama. Because the state voted down the Radical constitution in the June, 1868, elections, Democrats had less occasion for political violence. The Klan appeared in many interior counties, but intimidation rather than bloodshed was the dominant pattern, at least at the polls themselves. The League had spread only gradually through Mississippi, therefore providing less incentive for political repression. With the inauguration of Republican governor Alcorn in early 1870, however, this changed, and Klan murders became common in the eastern part of the state. Here terrorism was successful. A League activist in Meridian reported that during this period "party organization became a little slack, and the Leagues were pretty well lost sight of since the

37. Montgomery *Alabama State Journal*, February 12, 1870; Montgomery *Mail*, February 19, 1868, quoting Greensboro *Alabama Beacon*; Selma *Messenger*, March 24, 1868; Montgomery *Alabama State Journal*, September 16, 1870; KKK Report, X, 1679. Fleming claims that Keffer tried to reorganize the state League for the 1870 canvass, but this seems to have been crediting a false campaign charge. No real efforts were made in Alabama to restructure the body (Fleming, *Civil War and Reconstruction in Alabama*, 568; Montgomery *Mail*, August 20, 1870; Montgomery *Alabama State Journal*, September 16, 1870).

fall of 1869." With little guidance or assistance from the state organization, local leagues either broke up or made the typical transition to public clubs. Yet the repression seems to have been less widespread than it was in Alabama. One Klansman testified that "in the lower counties, along on the river, and in the Yazoo country, you seldom hear of them [regulators]; the negroes are so largely in the excess of population that they never have anything of that kind down there." Regardless of the practical demise of the state organization by 1870, League-like groups continued to meet in heavily black counties for years. A Conservative paper noted as late as September, 1871, that "the Loyal League is said to be in full blast with diminished attendance since 1869." An offshoot of the Vicksburg Council survived until 1874, when its members were mowed down in the great riot in December of that year. Some few leagues may have endured until the turbulent "Mississippi Plan" campaign of 1875, but the organization as a whole ceased to exist long before the Redeemers' final victory.[38]

The later history of the League in both states is something of a mystery, though the downward trend is clear enough. Democrats deliberately confused later organizations with leagues, hoping to reactivate white fears of the hated secret associations. Democratic papers reported sporadic League activities right up to the end of Reconstruction. Freedmen further complicated the issue by referring to their clubs as leagues, which remained a generic term for black political groups. None of these bodies, however, retained much real connection to any Union League organizational structure. The National Council reported in 1869 that "there has been an amount of intimidation and violence which has seriously interfered with the successful working of the League. . . . By these means, men were kept away from the League meetings, and in most of the States meetings have not been held for months." Despite the survival of vestiges of the League, repression altered the situation drastically in the countryside. A mass movement of freedmen had swept the region in 1867, and the Klan successfully halted this upsurge. Black

---

38. *House Miscellaneous Documents*, 40th Cong., 3rd Sess., No. 53, pp. 51–54, 94, 97; KKK Report, XI, 77, 245; Forest *Register*, September 9, 1871; *House Reports*, 43rd Cong., 2nd Sess., No. 265, pp. 467-68.

support for the Republican party remained strong, but grim determination replaced naïve eagerness and confidence in eventual victory. Black legislator and League activist George Houston described the change. Driven into exile and carrying a Klan bullet in his leg, he breathed defiance at his tormentors:

I had to fly here, and yet I am a republican, and I will die one. I say the republican party freed me, and I will die on top of it. I don't care who is pleased. I vote every time. I was [voter] register of my county, and my master . . . lent me his pistols . . . to protect myself against my enemies. I am a republican to-day, and if the republican party can't do me any good, I never will turn against it. I can work in the cotton-patch and work at my trade, and get along without any benefit from my party, so I will stick to the republican party and die in it.

By abandoning such men, the southern Republican governments sealed their fate as well. With the suppression of the League, the party in the South lost its infrastructure of local activists and members, a loss it could not sustain and long survive.[39]

In addition to its political influence, the Ku Klux Klan had a social and economic impact as well, and these aspects were of great importance in rural areas. The League upsurge had undermined planter dominance, and Klan repression restored that power over laborers. The disappearance of the League removed one check upon the employers' arbitrary conduct. Beyond its general chilling effect on the freedmen's political behavior, the Klan was directly aimed at disciplining agricultural workers. "The overriding purpose of the Ku Klux movement," as Trelease put it, "was the restoration of white supremacy in every walk of life." Klansmen frequently whipped freedmen for owning firearms or for petty theft; impudence of various sorts was the pretext for nightriding. The spreading violence strengthened planters because freedmen became more dependent on their good will. Terror thus halted the initiative freedmen had briefly held in forcing changes in the plantation system. Decentralized tenant farming remained the basic system of production, but it became increasingly coercive.[40]

39. KKK Report, VIII, 240; ULA, *Proceedings, 1869*, p. 11; KKK Report, IX, 1003–1004.
40. Trelease, *White Terror*, xlvi.

Much regulator activity occurred in response to perceived insubordination on the plantations. Klansmen tried to restore the discipline that characterized slavery, and they especially wanted freedmen to fear their employers. In one area, for example, Klansmen allegedly began riding because the League had demoralized the freedmen. Several planters in another community determined that a neighbor's freedmen did not work hard enough, so they whipped several hands to straighten them out. An appreciative Mississippi planter praised the Klan because it "gave notice to White & Black, who did not work, to leave." The regulators took special pains to help planters with unusual discipline problems. One plantation mistress described how the Klan came to her aid: "Four 'Ku Klux' dressed in *black* were at the window, their horses covered with white. They did not stay long, but asked a number of *questions*, if the negroes were humble and respectful and obeyed me & c. . . . They said 'Madam you need not fear to tell us, we will see you are protected.'" Even such transgressions as talking back triggered violence. In Mississippi, one fatal assault occurred for "some insult or impudence to an old man," an explanation that seemed fully adequate to the Democratic politicians discussing the case. This sort of violence occurred frequently, and threats toward whites received especially savage punishment—generally, lynching. The goal of the terror was to cow the freedmen, using extralegal force to place them in a subservient position. One planter recalled affairs in the Mississippi-Tennessee border region: "Had it not been for their deadly fear of the Ku Klux, I do not think we could have managed them as well as we did."[41]

Enforcing labor discipline through repression aided planters in several ways. Sometimes the Klan forbade out-migration. A Lauderdale County, Mississippi, Klan ordered freedmen not to leave, and they took the warning seriously enough to abandon their departure plans. Klansmen in Sumter County, Alabama, not only threatened freedmen with death if they tried to leave but also actually recaptured many who had escaped to Mississippi. In addition to preserv-

41. Hunnicutt, *Reconstruction in West Alabama*, 51; KKK Report, XI, 233; M. Crawford to "My Old School Mates," April 15, 1871, in Cameron Family Papers, UNC; Otey Diary, December 6, 1868 (MS in UNC); Agnew Diary, September 4, 1869, UNC; Barksdale to Humphreys, March 30, 1868, in Gov. Humphreys Papers, MDAH; Robert Philip Howell Memoir, UNC.

ing the local labor supply, the Klan frequently confiscated freedmen's firearms. Even before Military Reconstruction, white militias formed to take away blacks' guns, and this became an important aspect of later regulator activity. A Leaguer observed that around Huntsville the Klan "took the weapons from mighty near all the colored people in the neighborhood." Even years later, he stated, few freedmen possessed firearms. Another freedman complained of Klan threats, and noted he suffered "all this bothery because i . . . take my gun & go out an kiled me a squarrel a[l]so [they] said i am a radicale." A Bureau agent said the purpose was to keep the blacks down, and that indeed seems to have been a major motive.[42]

Landowners also benefited by being better able to stop thefts of livestock. Swine and other animals roamed at large through the region, and poaching by newly armed freedmen became a problem. After the war, losses were so widespread that some whites suspected an organized League plot. The Montgomery *Advertiser* reported that many planters thought League leaders responsible, and a rural Alabama official commented that "after these white persons [Leaguers] I spoke of came to the county, the habits of the colored people changed . . . and the hogs disappeared very much." He thought the freedmen's "moral stamina" deteriorated badly. While there is no evidence that League leaders actually recommended theft, landowners did experience increasing pilferage at a time they could ill afford it. Poor harvests caused intense privation among freedmen, and many preferred shooting some planter's hog to going hungry. Rather than turn to the Republican court system, employers looked to the Klan for relief. Sometimes the regulators held mock trials of suspected felons, but more often they simply whipped the suspects. A landowner near Aberdeen, Mississippi, reported that since Klansmen began punishing theft, farmers had begun raising stock again. "We can't live without them," he wrote. Another planter testified: "[The Klan] has had, in my honest opinion, a good effect in my immediate locality, because the negroes have behaved better there than anywhere I have ever heard of, or better than could be expected. I have thought they were intimidated . . . and that was,

42. KKK Report, XI, 372, X, 1466, IX, 683; Crittenden to Smith, October 10, 1868, in Gov. Smith Papers, ADAH; KKK Report, IX, 935.

perhaps, one of the causes [of their good behavior]. . . . They are working well." This extralegal campaign both put down petty crime and helped planters regain control over the freedmen.[43]

The nature of cotton production reinforced intimidation, for planters often benefited from driving workers away. There was a short-term financial incentive to dismiss freedmen despite the prevailing labor shortage. John Wager, a Bureau agent, reported that "the Ku-Klux always remain quiet during what is called the planting season . . . and remain so until the time they call 'laying by the crop,' and then they would commence again, and so on, until the time to put the crop in the ground again." Planters often overlooked insubordination during heavy planting, said Wager, only to call in their Klan neighbors, once labor needs dropped off. Certainly evidence exists that many freedmen fled violence and left a full field of cotton behind. "Colored men are not allowed any chance," an Alabama Radical wrote. "They are beaten . . . and told that if they vote with the Radicals they shall be deprived of their homes and their crops taken away." Such intimidation was more effective now than evictions had been in parallel circumstances earlier. The Bureau was ceasing operations, so legal redress scarcely existed unless the planter could be proved responsible for the threats. And, as Wager pointed out, nightriders arranged matters so that the landlord would appear not to be involved. A freedman deserting his crop forfeited his share, whatever his reason for leaving. It was all quite legal. The situation gave landowners a bounty for ridding themselves of troublemakers and an economic lever with which to enforce plantation discipline. Eventually many planters tired of the Klan and the disorder it caused, but at least initially the majority welcomed it as a way of controlling the blacks.[44]

The spreading terror halted further concessions to freedmen in their desire for autonomy, yet it did not reverse the changes that

43. Montgomery *Advertiser*, December 18, 1867; KKK Report, X, 1811–12, 1960; Otey Diary, December 6, 1868 (MS in UNC); M. Crawford to "My Old School Mates," April 15, 1871, in Cameron Family Papers, UNC; KKK Report, VIII, 639. See Eric Foner, *Nothing But Freedom*, 58–59, for the impact of theft.

44. KKK Report, IX, 935; J. A. Dexman[?] *et al.* to Smith, August 7, 1869, J. F. Tracy[?] to Smith, July 27, 1869, both in Gov. Smith Papers, ADAH; Rawick (ed.), *The American Slave, Supplement Series 1*, VI, 421; Crittenden to Smith, October 10, 1868, in Gov. Smith Papers, ADAH.

already had occurred. Declining labor militancy indeed stabilized tenant farming as a system of agricultural organization. Repression was doubtless a partial cause, but the freedmen were at first satisfied with the end of the centralized plantation. Pleasure at finally renting land lessened black discontent. The Republican Montgomery *Alabama State Journal* reported that by mid-1869, few freedmen spoke of land redistribution, since they now sought homesteads in other ways. One eyewitness in the Alabama black belt, recalling the February, 1868, elections, attributed the League's diminishing influence to this same agricultural shift: "'The word' went out through the customary channels . . . but its force was lessened by some important recent changes in the management of the great plantations, where the mass of negroes yet lived. With this year, the old plantation plan of 'gang work' . . . yielded to small squads, four to six strong, each squad working for a part of the crop produced and harvested by itself and each member conscious of the importance to him of the steadiness of all the others." In other words, blacks were less restive once gang labor broke up, and organizers were "at a discount" in the new circumstances. The dispersal of freedmen from the old slave quarters also tended to inhibit collective action. Social demobilization on a large scale ensued, the balkanization of the labor force throughout the countryside. As Roark perceptively noted in *Masters Without Slaves*, "Immobilized by share tenancy, terrorized by the Ku Klux Klan, dispirited by the failure of Reconstruction, blacks gradually settled back into behavior which whites found more acceptable."[45]

Not surprisingly, freedmen's enthusiasm for decentralized tenant farming was short-lived. They soon developed misgivings about the workings of the new system. Low land values during the postwar period had made the gradual purchase of farms appear possible, but this expectation proved illusory. Once cotton prices recovered and crops improved in 1868, the cost of land rose. "Lands have greatly increased in value over the past few months," the Gainesville *News* reported, "and we have heard of one or two tracts that rented for as much as they would have sold for a year ago." The impact on blacks

45. Montgomery *Alabama State Journal*, June 19, 1869; DuBose, *Alabama's Tragic Decade*, 90; Roark, *Masters Without Slaves*, 159.

was described by a freedman in wealthy Washington County, Mississippi: "I heave bin riden a rond severel days & in pasting I saw great many of the poor colored peepel out of dors & was naked & did not know ware to go . . . we por colored peepel can not git a liven contracts to live on[.] The land holders Will Rent the land so as we cant live[;] 10 dollars for 1 accar are two much for land & we poor colard peepol can not live on them turms." Black leaders, recognizing what was taking place, became increasingly disillusioned with the emerging plantation regime. James Lynch objected to "the share system" because its results were uncertain and because it subjected "neither laborer nor planter to those necessary restraints that are required for the protection of each." The black Alabama Labor Union also expressed dissatisfaction with how sharecropping worked in practice. There existed, however, a time lag before this recognition set in. Immediately, the transition to tenant farming reduced discontent during the critical period. Thus a combination of co-optation and repression restored order to the plantation system, and planters reasserted coercive control over the freedmen.[46]

The planters' attitude toward these changes was the mirror image of the freedmen's. They demonstrated initial skepticism toward renting out land but rapidly gained an appreciation of its virtues. In a few cases the Klan tried to prevent land rentals. In Noxubee County, Mississippi, regulators whipped many tenant farmers. According to one Klansman, local planters thought "it would be the better plan not to have the negroes rent land at all, so they could always control the labor themselves." The same thing occurred around Tuskegee; in another Alabama location, a freedman recalled that he rented a home, but Klansmen drove him out. He had to move in with a white Republican for protection. Democratic newspapers occasionally denounced tenant farming, or they argued almost nostalgically for a return to hiring hands. These instances, however, grew less common over time. Planters soon learned the advantages the new way offered. "I greatly prefer the renting system and get along very well with it," a Mississippi Klan sympathizer stated. "The negro likes it better, and

46. Montgomery *Alabama State Journal*, January 23, 1869, quoting Gainesville *News*; Fulcher to Alcorn, January 19, 1871, in Gov. Alcorn Papers, MDAH; Forest *Register*, May 13, 1871; Myers, "Black Human Capital," 212–13.

I like it better." Several factors combined to force most planters to similar conclusions. Cotton prices rose, and the weather improved after the disastrous 1867 season. These trends, together with the shift to widespread tenantry, resulted in the first substantial profits for planters since before the war. Moreover, they soon recognized that there was money in furnishing supplies on credit, more than there was in farming themselves with unwilling laborers.[47]

Thus decentralized tenant farming swept the cotton South within a few years, and it remained the norm across the region for over half a century. This took various forms, from sharecropping to more favorable types of tenantry, but the decisive break from gang labor was critical. The role of Klan repression in this outcome is difficult to quantify, but it clearly reimposed a measure of discipline on rural freedmen. The politicization of the blacks had created labor unrest, which itself contributed to the demise of the gang system and other remnants of the old plantation regime; had the mass movement remained intact, it might well have forced further changes. In many postemancipation societies in the New World, the plantation order disintegrated in the face of black hostility, yielding to some form of peasant proprietorship. As Eric Foner observed, "The survival of the plantation . . . ultimately rested on political power." In the South Carolina low country, for example, years of Reconstruction Era labor strife helped doom the great rice estates. Republican rule limped on in both Alabama and Mississippi, but something certainly altered in the countryside, once the Klan put down the League. Extralegal force compensated for the lapse of planters' power at the state level. Intimidation restored employers' control over their plantations, and labor relations became increasingly harsh. The emergence of the Klan was a major turning point, and the coercive features of the regime escalated over time. After Redemption especially, planters regained control of the legal system and rewrote legislation dealing with agriculture to their advantage. The League mobilization had represented the high-water mark of the former slaves' social radicalism, and its suppression largely foreclosed their bringing pressure

47. KKK Report, XI, 233; Rawick (ed.), *The American Slave, Supplement Series 1*, VI, 421; Selma *Messenger*, November 2, 1867; Jackson *Clarion*, April 1, 1868; KKK Report, XI, 388; Ransom and Sutch, *One Kind of Freedom*, 98.

to bear on the agricultural order. The balance of fear shifted dramatically in the planters' favor.[48]

Overall, the rural terror allowed planters to reassert political and social power in the cotton belt. Neither co-optation nor economic intimidation tamed the League insurgency; only massive violence destroyed it. Taking advantage of the dispersal of the freedmen, the nightriders adopted methods that allowed them to take on adversaries one at a time, and neither the League nor the Republican governments devised any effective defense. The partisan impact of the regulators was dramatic: they quickly shut down the League in Alabama and suppressed it across wide sections of Mississippi as well. The destruction of the Republican party's mass base devastated its electoral strength and contributed in particular to the 1870 Democratic sweep of Alabama. The social impact was equally important, and the large landowners were increasingly able to dictate terms to the labor force. The net effect was to help stabilize decentralized tenant farming, in its various forms, as the norm of postbellum agricultural production, an event of critical long-term importance in southern history.

48. Foner, *Nothing But Freedom*, 14–15, 106–10.

Epilogue

The League's national structure survived Klan violence, though its significance declined during the remainder of Reconstruction. The organization's functionaries gradually narrowed operations to lobbying while they watched the southern movement disintegrate. After the final collapse of Reconstruction in 1877, however, the leaders of the Union League of America (ULA) redoubled their efforts. Northern and southern Leaguers pressed Congress for voting rights legislation, hoping that the grass-roots movement would then reemerge. The League also endeavored to reorganize its southern base, but after more than a decade, Republican politicians took no action and repression was too intense. To prosper, the movement needed outside support. Surviving League activists admitted defeat only in the early 1890s, when it finally became clear that the Republican party had abandoned the freedmen to their fate.

After the League's brief heyday in 1867, the National Council's influence eroded. The Republican party proved reluctant to subsidize its continued operation, once the initial organizing drive was completed. Democratic attacks rendered the League an embarrassment, and many Republicans saw no further use for it. By mid-1868, President James M. Edmunds had difficulties funding the organization. "If the National Committee can aid me with money," he wrote the Grant campaign staff, "I can . . . do work in proportion to the means at command, but can do nothing effectively without means."

Edmunds further observed that "the Southern people are too poor to pay for the necessary books[,] Charters[,] Documents[,] clerk hire & c. & c." The Republican party responded with a contribution of one thousand dollars, a subsidy well below that of the previous year.[1] After James Edmunds retired as League president in 1869, troubles intensified. Other southern leaders followed Keffer's example and disbanded their local leagues for tactical reasons, a concession to white hostility that dismembered the national organization. This process did not proceed smoothly. In Texas, when Republicans around Governor E. J. Davis decided to abolish the League, they faced a revolt by the black membership. The insurgents set up a rival state organization, and both sides appealed to headquarters in Washington to settle the dispute. The decision went against the black insurgents. The ULA had lost most of its mass following by the early 1870s, and the national body increasingly occupied itself with jurisdictional disputes and lobbying in Congress. A brief revival occurred during the 1872 presidential canvass, but the organization lapsed into inactivity again by the middle of the decade. "What about the U.L.A.?" one activist inquired during the climactic election of 1876. Indeed, the organization had almost no role toward the end of Reconstruction.[2]

Curiously, Redemption triggered a renewal of League activity. By late 1878, northern revulsion at President Rutherford B. Hayes's conciliatory southern policy created new interest among Republicans in the clandestine order. The League's secrecy might well prove useful in any Republican revival in the South; if Congress passed new Reconstruction measures, the organization might become important once again. A committee in Washington was to oversee southern activities, and one in New York was to tap wealthy members of the Union League Clubs and other groups. The central figure in this effort was Colonel John Emory Bryant of Atlanta, a prominent Georgia carpetbagger. He worked assiduously to rebuild

1. Edmunds to Chandler, June 13, 1868, W. Claflin to W. E. Chandler, July 22, 1868, both in W. E. Chandler Papers, LC.
2. Abbott, *The Republican Party and the South*, 218; William B. Hesseltine, *Ulysses S. Grant: Politician* (New York, 1935), 283; Carl H. Moneyhon, *Republicanism in Reconstruction Texas* (Austin, 1980), 155–59; D. Ullmann to T. Baker, June 26, 1876, in Daniel Ullmann Papers, New-York Historical Society.

the organization during his frequent trips north. As a recent biography demonstrates, Bryant felt a strong sense of mission. "I am still of the opinion," he wrote his wife, "that God has called me to the work of political evangelization in the South, and also in the North. The evidence is so strong that I can not doubt." Other leaders, like national secretary Thomas G. Baker, were perhaps more realistic. He wrote that "the most important point with me is to keep busy at something lest I become demoralized." Baker spent considerable energy trying to secure a patronage post to finance his political activities. For whatever reasons, a cadre of aging politicos and businessmen dedicated themselves to rebuilding the League. Although the ULA's national leaders remained moderate during Reconstruction, they now became thoroughly Radicalized, favoring the sternest possible measures to combat terror in the southern states.[3]

Behind the scenes, the League leadership often had a self-interested agenda, acting as a patronage clique. In 1882 the national organization mobilized to secure the post of consul to Italy for Daniel Ullmann, then a member of the League's executive committee. "You ought to be in Rome today as the representative of American ideas and Protestant opinions," Baker assured Ullmann. The Leaguers organized a full-scale campaign in support of the nomination. "I will rally letters from all our *live* members of the League, and have them write directly to the President," Baker wrote. The effort apparently succeeded, and it can be defended as expanding the patronage—and thus the resources—available to the League. But the leaders often pursued interests far from the needs of the black membership.[4]

League activities took several other forms, many of which bore more directly on black concerns. Publicizing the freedmen's plight was a major focus of the organization. "The chief work of this League is in the nature of political education," proclaimed the National Council in 1881. Leaguers also pressured Republican politicians, urging them not to abandon the freedmen to the mercies of the former Rebels. The League's rhetoric seemed fiery in direct propor-

3. Ruth Currie-McDaniel, *Carpetbagger of Conscience: A Biography of John Emory Bryant* (Athens, Ga., 1987), 167–68, 181; J. E. Bryant to "Darling Wife," December 22, 1878, T. Baker to Bryant, June 16, 1886, both in Bryant Papers, Duke University.
4. Baker to Ullmann, May 13, May 3, July 7, 1882, all in Ullmann Papers, New-York Historical Society.

tion to its powerlessness. For example, one ULA gathering up-braided President Hayes: "In the name of humanity! in the name of a Christian civilization! and in the sacred name of justice! We protest against the continuance of bloodshed and outrage in the Southern States." During the 1880s the ULA urged Congress to take a firmer stand on southern affairs. The main goal was preserving the freed-men's political liberties. There could be no "more imperative work before this League" than to demand that the government "protect the ballot-box and secure the perfect freedom of elections." The League's activities seemed to ebb and flow with the prospects of such a "Force Bill."[5]

While Congress unhurriedly pondered enactment of this pro-gram, the League leadership explored prospects for regaining a foothold in the South. Signs of a latent Republican revival filled them with anticipation. Before the 1882 campaign, Baker, the national secretary, conferred with Republican leaders on the possibility that the League could "do effective work" in Tennessee, Kentucky, and Missouri. In 1886, Baker speculated that the "League could be of immense service, in a quiet way, among the Colored men. In Ken-tucky, for instance, we have two or three Congressional dist[rict]s which might be carried by the help of the colored men's votes. My idea would be, to get hold of the preachers among them, and so get the people." Again in 1887, League President C. H. Grosvenor thought the time ripe for mass expansion, and two years later Colo-nel Bryant reached a similar conclusion. President Benjamin Har-rison was attempting detente with the "old rebel element," and this required vigorous countermeasures. "The National Union League with something like its old power is needed in this emergency," Bryant declared. Despite brave talk, little resulted from these en-deavors except in a few scattered areas of the upper South. Potential Republican contributors regarded a League upsurge unlikely with-out a "Force Bill" and strong administration support. Given the tenor of national politics, they were doubtless more realistic than were the enthusiasts in the ULA leadership. At all events, the lack of

5. ULA, *Twentieth Annual Report of the National Council of the National Union League of America* . . . (New York, 1883), 6; Baker to Hayes, July 27, 1880, in Rutherford B. Hayes Papers, Hayes Library.

funds and of serious party sponsorship halted the organizing drive before it really began.[6]

In spite of this failure, the League's efforts probably had some repercussions in the Deep South. Rumors flew that secret councils functioned long after Redemption. In Louisiana, for example, Leaguers were involved in the Kansas exodus of 1879. Vestiges of the organization survived into the 1880s and even beyond. In 1882 the League reportedly resurfaced at the time of the Jack Turner disturbances near Butler, Alabama. A Democratic editor privately disparaged white fears: "The negroes were inducted into politics through the 'Loyal League,' with its midnight meetings, signs, grips, guards, sentinels, and secrecy, and doubtless in many places they are re-organizing for the approaching election under some of the unforgotten forms of that order. In almost every place when there has recently been a scare, the unsubstantial foundations have been in something not more terrible than this." Blacks increasingly described their organizations as fraternal, since direct political activity was dangerous. According to Wharton's *The Negro in Mississippi*, "These organizations . . . naturally excited for a number of years the distrust and opposition of a large part of the white population." Many reports indicate that such secret clubs composed of freedmen continued to meet in rural areas.[7]

The relationship between these remnants of the League in the South and the National Council's activities is unclear, for most freedmen did not parade their political ties after Redemption. But, as one Alabamian observed, freedmen had "a great many associations of their own" safely hidden from intrusive oversight. Conservatives feared even black social clubs. A white author wrote from Vicksburg that these orders fostered a spirit of resistance and offered means for

6. Baker to Ullmann, Mach 25, 1882, in Ullmann Papers, New-York Historical Society; Baker to Bryant, July 14, 1886, C. H. Grosvenor to Bryant, February 21, 1887, Bryant to Grosvenor, January 15, 1889, Letterbook 1, all in Bryant Papers, Duke University; ULA, *Twentieth Annual Report*, 10; Bryant to "My Darling Wife," December 22, 1878, in Bryant Papers, Duke University.

7. Nell Irvin Painter, *Exodusters: Black Migration to Kansas After Reconstruction* (New York, 1976), 76; Carl H. Moneyhon, "George T. Ruby and the Politics of Expediency in Texas," in Rabinowitz (ed.), *Southern Black Leaders*, 384; R. M. McKee to L. W. Grant, October 22, 1882, in McKee Papers, ADAH; Wharton, *The Negro in Mississippi*, 270; Fleming (ed.), *Documentary History of Reconstruction*, II, 5.

renewed agitation. Such anxieties were not misplaced: considerable evidence suggests that freedmen did indeed discuss political matters at these gatherings. Certainly the possibility existed of a serious Republican challenge, at least as far as the blacks were concerned. A conservative black, describing the situation in Alabama in the 1880s, reported that freedmen saw the Republicans as their salvation, still fearing they would be "put back into slavery, or something of that sort. . . . [Y]ou might as well talk about killing them, as about them not voting the Republican ticket." Clearly, southern blacks had not forgotten the struggle for Radical ideals.[8]

The various clubs eventually did become social in character as memories of Reconstruction faded, but the evolution was gradual. Had circumstances been different, the clubs might have become the basis for insurgency, just as churches and benevolent societies had during Military Reconstruction. Some former Leaguers long hoped for a revival of the movement. A Georgia Unionist stated as late as 1889 that "if the organization had been preserved . . . the Republican party would have continued the *dominant* party of this South land." He urged that steps be taken to "reach *all* of our *old friends* and *reorganize them.*" Many others also awaited congressional action to protect voting rights, hoping to see the Union League spread again through the region.[9]

But that was not to be. In 1890, Congress rejected Lodge's "Force Bill," finally putting to rest hopes of a federal guarantee of suffrage. The vote actually had been close; the bill passed the House but fell victim to the silver controversy in the upper chamber. Egalitarian enactments with respect to race, moreover, were out of phase with the public mood, which was increasingly racist and Social Darwinist. In any case, after this blow the ULA disintegrated. Bryant, for example, spent the remainder of his life in business, finally gaining the financial security that eluded him during his decades in politics. Bryant and his cohorts, who had long tried to persuade or shame Republicans into protecting southern freedmen, now at last

8. Senate Committee on Education and Labor, *Report of the Committee* . . . (Washington, D.C., 1885), V, 103, 118–19; Wharton, *The Negro in Mississippi*, 270; H. S. Fulkerson, *The Negro; As He Was; As He Is; As He Will Be* (Vicksburg, 1887), 96.

9. T. Triplett to National Council of the National ULA, February 12, 1889, in Bryant Papers, Duke University.

surrendered. They recognized that their Republican party was no longer that of Stevens and Sumner, or even of Grant, but had become that of Mark Hanna. A Republican Congress soon would acquiesce to disfranchisement. Freedmen gradually came to the same conclusion, and their secret societies became apolitical clubs in actual fact. By the early twentieth century, those groups were so innocuous that Walter Lynwood Fleming noted that the League was the origin or "model" for many and concluded that the clubs were "on the whole, [a] useful factor in negro life today."[10]

The Union League of America faded from view. The post-Redemption history of the organization does, however, indicate one last point that should be stressed. That a number of leaders remained with the organization so long says something about their motives. Black leaders, such as John R. Lynch, Blanche K. Bruce, John M. Langston, and Henry M. Turner agitated for a League revival. White Republicans too spent years working for the League. For example, Albert Griffin of the *Nationalist* had fled Mobile in 1869, yet twenty years later, as an editor in New York, he was still committed to the old movement. "I have had a talk with him [Griffin] this morning," wrote Bryant, "and he promises to aid us in every way in his power." Perhaps more impressive than such expatriates were those who remained in the South and still lent the ULA their support. Those braving public disapproval included J. J. Giers, one of the original Alabama organizers, and former congressman A. C. Buck from the same state (Buck was then living in Georgia). Of course, Colonel Bryant himself is the outstanding example of such fidelity, having largely run the organization for eleven years, despite threats against him that newspapers kept publishing. While these leaders were but a few of the hundreds who had participated in the movement, it is significant that they clung to their earlier commitments and continued their League affiliation.[11]

Others who did not remain active in the ULA kept to Radical

10. Currie-McDaniel, *Carpetbagger of Conscience*, 176–78; Stanley P. Hirshson, *Farewell to the Bloody Shirt: Northern Republicans and the Southern Negro* (Chicago, 1962), 215–35; Fleming (ed.), *Documentary History of Reconstruction*, II, 5.

11. ULA, *Twenty-Fourth Annual Report of the National Council of the National Union League . . .* (New York, 1889), 17; "Members of the National Executive Committee of the ULA calling upon President Hayes," February 8, 1879, in Hayes Papers, Hayes Library;

principles in different ways. Some did so quietly, as did Alabama activist George Houston, who vowed he would vote Republican till the day he died. James K. Green, once a fiery militant, took a more public stand. In 1883 he testified before a congressional committee that he refused to buy land in Alabama as a protest against ballot fraud. When asked by a Democratic senator if officials tallied his vote, he snapped, "Oh yes, it was counted; but not for my side." Thomas W. Conway, one of the League's traveling organizers, also demonstrated a sustained commitment to Republican beliefs. He spent most of the late 1870s gathering relief funds for the Kansas "Exodusters" and other refugees to the North. Mississippians had prevented emigrants from leaving Vicksburg by steamboat, and Conway led a successful drive to uphold the freedmen's right to leave.[12]

Perhaps the most ironic, and almost pathetic, case was that of General Wager Swayne, chief of the Bureau in Alabama. After Andrew Johnson removed him from military command, he took up the practice of law. He settled first in Toledo and then moved to New York City. He became a successful corporate attorney and a vice-president of New York's patrician Union League Club, the organization that had been so significant in bankrolling the initial League expansion across the South. Here, just before his death in 1902, he fought a last battle for his youthful principles. A management committee determined to evict the club's black servants and replace them with an all-white staff. Outraged, Swayne was "one of a few who got up a petition" to bring the matter to an open vote. "Supported on his crutches," according to the New York *Times*, "he spoke in favor of the negroes, and after several others had talked on the same side the . . . decision was overthrown."[13] One suspects that the outcome resulted from deference to the ailing general. Even so, the episode could have given him little comfort. The same upper-class Republicans who had

Bryant to Grosvenor, January 15, 1889, Letterbook 1, "Resolutions Adopted by the Executive Committee of the ULA at a Meeting Held at the Ebbitt House, Washington D.C., March 13, 1879," and undated clipping, all in Bryant Papers, Duke University.

12. KKK Report, X, 1003–1004; Senate Committee on Education and Labor, *Report*, V, 450; Hirshson, *Farewell to the Bloody Shirt*, 70–77.

13. New York *Times*, December 19, 1902.

once ardently supported Reconstruction sponsored openly racist policies. These vignettes suggest that the movement failed in the South, not because of the Leaguers' unwillingness to struggle, but because the North would not sustain them.

What conclusions can be drawn about the League's political character and about its treatment in the historical literature? One obvious conclusion is that the League has not been examined adequately. As we have seen, historians of the Dunning school generally deprecated the organization. Even many recent historians have regarded using the League as an error in judgment, contending that it failed because it unnecessarily alarmed whites and therefore triggered Klan violence. Yet Radicals selected the League precisely because they believed that it was the safest way to reach freedmen on plantations. What evoked hostility was the League's effectiveness in mobilizing blacks to vote Republican. Radical leaders could have avoided incurring the resentment of planters, and of most southern whites, only by abandoning their political goals.

The argument that the League failed because of its tactical indiscretion dates back to Reconstruction. For example, the Selma *Messenger* claimed in 1868 that many whites initially had cooperated with Radicals and were only turned away by "the excesses of the loyal league." After 1869, the Republican party distanced itself from the secret clubs. The social tumult and the white hostility the League evoked seemed counterproductive, once Radicalism was firmly entrenched among the freedmen. As a result, a consensus gradually formed that recruiting freedmen through the secret organization had been unwise. The attitude of Albion Tourgée, president of the North Carolina League, was typical. In his novel *A Fool's Errand* (1879), Tourgée wrote of his carpetbagger protagonist: "He quite forgot, in giving his assent to the idea [of joining the League], the fact that he was living at the South, among a people who did not kindly brook differences of opinion among equals, and who would be sure to resent with an implacable hostility . . . any society which encouraged that race to look up to the government as *their* government, *their* guardian, *their* protector. . . . Had he thought of this, it is certain that he would not have consented so readily." Tourgée would remain a principled exponent of civil rights for decades, but even he thought that League drilling, in particular, had alarmed whites unnecessarily and with deplorable results. Second thoughts along these lines became increasingly common as time went on.[14]

Scholars have echoed this appraisal ever since. One historian wrote recently that the League's martial displays inflamed planters. Otis A. Singletary, in *Negro Militia and Reconstruction*, claimed that the League's "clandestine meetings and mysterious initiation rites, shrouded in secrecy . . . gave rise to all sorts of groundless fears." Some historians explicitly blame Republican leaders for enrolling freedmen in the League. In *White Terror*, Trelease argued that under the circumstances "it was dangerous to mobilize Negro support through the agency of a secret society whose full doings could not be known by outsiders. Given the psychopathic fear of Negro insurrection inherited from slavery days, and the explosive attitudes arising from Radical Reconstruction, the League's very existence was provocative and its secrecy unnecessarily so." This assertion, by a historian generally sympathetic to the Radical cause, illustrates the prevalence of such views. If such arguments have any weight, however, they amount to a claim that some alternative manner of mobilizing black voters existed. Using a secret society was an error only if the Republican party could have organized openly. The evidence, I think, refutes this hypothesis. Other available means of Radical activity were at least as dangerous as the Union League was.[15]

Republican leaders could reach rural freedmen either openly or surreptitiously. Since any form of secret agitation would have met much the same reception as the League did, the only real alternative was holding public rallies throughout the cotton belt. Radicals would have had to tour the region, addressing large crowds, to spread the message efficiently. Speed was essential, given the finan-

14. Selma *Messenger*, April 18, 1868; Albion Winegar Tourgée, *A Fool's Errand* (1879; rpr. Cambridge, Mass., 1961), 117–18. Tourgée explained his view of the League's difficulties at greater length in another novel, *Bricks Without Straw*. Tourgée argued that League-related drilling and processions spread rumors of insurrection; this fear deprived white southerners of their senses and left "only an abiding desire to kill" (p. 132). Tourgée clearly indicts the Leaguers for insensitivity toward whites' irrational fears of racial violence (*Bricks Without Straw* [1879; rpr. Baton Rouge, 1969], 126–39).

15. Harris, *The Day of the Carpetbagger*, 98; Singletary, *Negro Militia and Reconstruction*, 10; Trelease, *White Terror*, xxx.

cial and temporal constraints under which they operated. The Republicans could indeed have made this attempt, but it seems unlikely they would have had much success. Freedmen feared attending political gatherings without firearms, and while this was understandable from their point of view, whites always found it objectionable. Open rallies, in short, created an explosive situation, since the locality was then at the mercy of its least stable—or sober—residents of either race.

That public gatherings were perilous is an established fact; many Republican rallies ended in bloodshed. The notorious Eutaw riot in Greene County, Alabama, is a striking example. In October, 1870, a large crowd gathered to hear speeches by Governor Smith and Congressman Hays. Democratic spectators pulled Hays off the platform, and in the struggle, someone fired. There was a gunfight, and fifty-eight freedmen were shot, four fatally; two whites sustained injuries. A disturbance in Clinton, Mississippi, in 1875 led to the indiscriminate slaughter of local blacks. More than twenty freedmen were killed, including one prominent legislator. Such episodes often resulted from deliberate provocation. Violence could effectively deter black voting, and Klansmen frequently plotted such incidents in advance.[16]

Whites saw public gatherings and political activity by blacks as threatening, and they often reacted recklessly. A newspaper account of trouble in Greenville, Alabama, illustrates this problem: "A riot occurred last night! About two hundred negroes went through the principal streets about 8 O'Clock singing and yelling political songs. The whites attempted to put down the disturbance and the riot commenced." Neither the town's citizens, apparently, nor the Democratic paper could see black partisan activity as legitimate. Radical speakers were routinely harassed, and they were afraid to answer for fear of being shot down. Many leaders wore pistols while addressing their followers. Under such circumstances, it seems implausible that public meetings would have been more effective than secret council gatherings. Any organizing was certain to evoke hatred, given the

16. Trelease, *White Terror*, 271–72; Harris, *The Day of the Carpetbagger*, 663.

partisan tension, and separating the contending sides may have been the wisest course.[17]

The Mobile riot in May, 1867, emphasized this point for the Republican leadership at the outset of Military Reconstruction. When Congressman William D. Kelley of Pennsylvania journeyed to the port city to address the freedmen, local Radicals anticipated trouble. Days before the scheduled speech, several Republicans wrote General Swayne about the probability of violence. Ill-feeling ran high after the streetcar demonstrations and strikes in recent weeks, and the Democratic papers egged their readers on to confrontation. Kelley spoke, there was a scuffle with a drunken heckler, and a riot ensued with several casualties. Republicans throughout the region concluded that public meetings were impractical. John Keffer, for instance, turned down a debate set up by rural freedmen; he urged them to abandon the idea because such gatherings invited "disorder and violence." A leading Republican paper concluded that the riot was a strong argument for the League as a form of political agitation. Military officials made the same assessment. General John Pope—a Radical—required that civil officials attend all public meetings in Alabama with sufficient force to keep the peace; Mississippi's General Ord tried to discourage open meetings altogether. Given Democratic hatred of the League, Radicals preferred secret meetings—and with considerable justification in 1867. Even the Vicksburg *Times and Republican*, a paper hostile to the local League machine, admitted that a secret organization had initially been essential: "The proscription and intolerance of the southern people rendered it absolutely necessary to have some close organization . . . for self protection."[18]

In contrast to the sorry record of mass rallies, League councils generally met peacefully prior to the emergence of the Klan. Leagues gathered at secluded locations, and security measures were so extensive that intruders seldom caught the freedmen unawares. Few

17. Talladega *Alabama Reporter*, October 28, 1868.
18. Montgomery *State Sentinel*, May 23, 1867; James E. Sefton, *The United States Army and Reconstruction, 1865–1877* (Baton Rouge, 1967), 125–26; Vicksburg *Times and Republican*, November 11, 1871.

Democrats, moreover, were so foolhardy as to try to assault the councils. The League's technique thus insulated blacks from their opponents, and few casualties resulted directly from council meetings in either Alabama or Mississippi. While clandestine gatherings and drilling did create difficulties, the real objection to the League was that it was a Republican organization. What other method of reaching black voters would have been popular with the Democrats? Historians who see the League as needlessly provocative are probably slipping into wishful thinking.

Another criticism of the League is more substantial. Several historians have stated or implied that the League's Radical stance was counterproductive. In *The Day of the Carpetbagger*, for example, William C. Harris acknowledges that the League's clandestine character has been overemphasized, but he nevertheless is skeptical about the organization. "Ironically," he points out, "the Union League was strongest in the heavily black river counties where the necessity for Republican militancy was least." Harris generally approves Republicans who thought that there was "no real need" for secrecy and that the organization needlessly antagonized whites. Harris makes a point of indicting the League leadership in Vicksburg, which was admittedly flawed: "Furlong spurned the efforts of moderate northerners to build a strong white Republican party, even though the county had a relatively large Union-Whig concentration that might have been amenable to Republican advances." Because Harris defends the moderate Alcorn faction of the Mississippi party, he tends to criticize the League as too Radical. On the whole, his book gives substantial attention to the grass-roots organization's various shortcomings. [19]

Many contemporary historians share Harris' enthusiasm for the moderate or "scalawag" wing of the southern Republican party. For instance, in *Losing the Peace*, Elizabeth Studley Nathans offers a similar interpretation of the Republican defeat in Georgia. Nathans argues that the Republicans needed to conciliate white voters and that some kind of moderate planter-black alliance offered the best chance for the party's survival. Nathans speculates that a natural

19. Harris, *The Day of the Carpetbagger*, 99–100.

majority might have supported a "program of economic and social development . . . similar to that advanced by Henry Grady." The implication is that the civil rights rhetoric of the League and similar groups was misguided, since blacks needed to soft-pedal the movement's Radical politics. Few scholars directly denounce the League as too Radical, but such a view is consistent with this general explanation for the Republican defeat.[20]

This perception of the League does have some validity. The party badly needed white votes, and forthright demands for civil rights discouraged such converts. To the extent that the League mobilized freedmen behind a Radical program, it probably made appeals to yeoman whites or to wealthy Whiggish planters more difficult. The obvious question, then, is whether the freedmen ought to have placated racist allies. Should they have refrained from nominating blacks to office, even though blacks constituted nine-tenths of the Republican electorate? Should they have embraced segregation? In practical terms, that policy might have helped the party, but one can see why freedmen rejected it. They had no desire to redeem the South themselves. The argument that the League was too militant rests on the counterfactual hypotheses that centrist scalawags could have stabilized power, had the blacks supported them uncritically, and that the moderates in power would have acted differently from Bourbon Redeemers. If we consider Governor Alcorn in Mississippi, as well as Governor Smith in Alabama, neither hypothesis seems particularly persuasive. Furthermore, it is inconceivable that freedmen would have followed such leadership for long.

Overall, the political history of the Union League has been distorted even by revisionist scholars. Recent historians have laid too much of the blame for the defeat of Radical Reconstruction at the League's door. Secret meetings certainly troubled planters, but no other form of political activity would have troubled them less. Any organizing activity would have generated tremendous resistance, and Radicals concluded that the least dangerous form of agitation was through clandestine meetings. Without the Radical tendencies

20. Elizabeth Studley Nathans, *Losing the Peace: Georgia Republicans and Reconstruction, 1865–1871* (Baton Rouge, 1968), vi; Wiggins, *The Scalawag in Alabama Politics*; Cash, "Alabama Republicans During Reconstruction."

that doubtless alienated many whites, the League could hardly have succeeded in mobilizing blacks. Any alliance between wealthy planters and their former slaves would necessarily have been unstable, and the idea that blacks would permanently support a Whiggish party seems farfetched. Whatever the League's shortcomings, a balanced appraisal should also take note of its successes. Multitudes of freedmen became politicized through the organization, and in a period of months, the League made the Republican party a major political force in the South. Its tragedy is that this was not nearly enough. The League, in essence, was an overwhelmingly successful mobilization on behalf of a doomed cause.

As has been stressed throughout, the League's social impact rivaled its political significance. While the organization's stated goals were political, the League represented far more than a partisan mobilization. Political, social, and economic grievances fused into a multi-layered mass movement; these elements were so linked that separating them is impossible. Black disaffection with the plantation system fueled political agitation, and rural leagues took on aspects of an agrarian insurgency. They exercised an important, if transitory, impact on the plantation order.

After the war, planters farmed along the general pattern derived from slavery, or at least they tried to do so. They reorganized production under a variety of coercive forms, most notably gang labor with tight supervision. Freedmen recognized the continuity from slavery. What they wanted was control of their own land or, failing that, as much freedom from oversight by their former masters as possible. Two years of collective struggle ensued, which left the region near economic collapse. Planters blamed the freedmen for abysmal crops, and laborers were convinced they had been cheated. Acute tension thus characterized the whole plantation order. Landowners declined to make even the limited concession of renting acreage; they remained adamantly opposed to any further erosion of their former authority. That was the situation when Military Reconstruction began, and frustration among freedmen contributed to their enthusiastic response to the Radical evangel. The explosive politicization of the freedmen, occurring through the League, grew out of their deep-seated sense that semi-slavery still existed on the plantations.

Despite its short duration, the League played an important part in the transition to decentralized tenant farming by empowering freedmen to resist planter control. Drilling and direct action by freedmen sapped plantation discipline, and in many areas, League-related boycotts of the contract process pressured planters to rent land. Political disorder combined with other troubles to push landowners to the recognition of a crisis: the freedmen would never get back to work without some basic change. In response, vast numbers of planters began renting land to their former slaves. They did so with the deepest misgivings, believing, as did the Mississippi agricultural writer Thomas Affleck, that the freedman had been "deliberately demoralized" until he was worthless as a farm laborer. No choice remained, and as "painful as it may be to the feelings of every planter and land-owner, and destructive of all previous views and habits, there is no alternative left, but to lay off large plantations into small farms, and sell or lease to those who will buy or rent." Further reliance on hired labor would be an "extreme act of folly" under the circumstances.[21]

If political unrest contributed to the emergence of tenant farming, then one would expect that the transformation occurred first in areas of extensive agitation by the League. The evidence is mixed. Because so many economic, social, and political factors were involved, it is difficult to establish the exact timing of any single variable. The force of successful example, moreover, spread decentralized tenant farming throughout the cotton region. The new system's profitability generated considerable publicity by late 1867, and within a short time, most white resistance to renting land collapsed—even in the less politically restive areas. Nonetheless, the evidence tentatively suggests that the shift to decentralized tenant farming occurred first in areas of political and social upheaval, at least in Alabama and Mississippi. The Natchez *Democrat* described the experiment as taking root among "a few planters" around Jackson; another paper commented that the new style of farming was most appropriate for the

21. Typescript copy of article, in Thomas Affleck Papers, p. 4, Department of Archives, Louisiana State University, Baton Rouge.

river counties. Decentralized sharecropping was not generally reported in Mississippi's more isolated interior counties until after 1867. This is broadly consistent with the pattern of the League's gradual expansion; it is also consistent with the widely held view that labor relations remained more repressive, or traditional, in the backwoods away from Bureau agents and political agitators. In Alabama, on the other hand, both the League and decentralized tenant farming spread so rapidly through the entire state that it is hard to point to a geographic pattern. But in places such as Hale, Bullock, and Sumter counties, the evidence indicates that Reconstruction Era political turbulence helped disrupt the old-style plantation.[22]

However, the form of tenantry that would replace gang labor was not settled. This issue is complex, for planters were far more discursive about the painful departure from established practices than they were enlightening about that which followed. Moreover, the whole agricultural system was in flux. As one correspondent reported from the Alabama black belt in 1869, "Negroes are engaged upon almost every conceivable plan, and everything appears experimental."[23] Chaos reigned in rural labor arrangements in the late 1860s, and it took several years for a new standard to become accepted.

Ralph Shlomowitz and Gerald David Jaynes have argued that the "squad system" of multifamily voluntary work groups often immediately succeeded gang labor. Jaynes contends that "the gang system's replacement, the small scale collective contract, was far from being dominated by family-based sharecropping." There is a great deal of evidence to sustain that statement. The squad system was common in 1868 and for some time thereafter. On many plantations, gang labor gave way to the squad system, which in turn quickly evolved into one of various forms of family-based tenant farming. But another of Jaynes's arguments, that the freedmen preferred collective labor arrangements, is more questionable. Contemporary testimony that freedmen wanted individual farms for their families seems overpowering.[24]

22. Natchez *Democrat*, June 20, December 31, 1867.
23. Mobile *Register*, May 30, 1869.
24. Shlomowitz, "The Transition from Slave to Freedman"; Jaynes, *Branches Without Roots*, 173, 180.

And what of those freedmen who did secure land for family-based tenant farming? After the demise of gang labor, most freedmen who were not farming as part of multifamily squads became sharecroppers. The more favorable forms of family-based tenantry, such as "standing rent" or "Thirds and Fourths," required substantial capital from the lessee—at least as contract terms became standardized in the 1870s. If Joseph Reidy's calculations for central Georgia are typical of the cotton South, then only a tiny minority, perhaps 5 percent, of all black agricultural households had fifty dollars' worth of personal property in 1870. The destitute freedmen could hardly have opted for anything but sharecropping, which did not require that the laborer contribute capital. But sharecropping was not yet as oppressive as that institution would become. As Harold D. Woodman makes clear, the revision of southern laws to deprive sharecroppers of traditional legal rights occurred after Redemption. Sharecroppers eventually were reduced to the legal status of hired hands, with no control over the disposal of the crop, but this only happened once the Democrats regained power.[25]

Freedmen's initial satisfaction with the demise of gang labor is thus entirely understandable. The squad system, and especially sharecropping, looked like a substantial improvement. Family-based sharecropping enabled freedmen to escape many of the specific grievances associated with the slave regime, and because the new system had not yet developed its full legal rigor, freedmen were pleased with it—though planters and merchants gradually reasserted some right to supervise sharecroppers through the crop lien.[26] Furthermore, freedmen initially had reason to hope that they would be able to buy land at the low prices that then prevailed. After the planters abandoned gang labor, some dissipating of agricultural unrest was probably inevitable, at least for the short term.

Once this change occurred, the wave of agricultural discontent subsided as the League rapidly disintegrated. A combination of re-

25. Joseph Patrick Reidy, "Masters and Slaves, Planters and Freedmen: The Transition from Slavery to Freedom in Central Georgia, 1820–1880" (Ph.D. dissertation, Northern Illinois University, 1982), 385; Ransom and Sutch, *One Kind of Freedom*, 90–91; Woodman, "Post–Civil War Southern Agriculture and the Law," 319–37.

26. Thomas J. Edwards, "The Tenant System and Some Changes Since Emancipation," *Annals of the American Academy of Political and Social Science*, IL (September, 1913), 38–46.

pression and the simultaneous concession of widespread land rental demobilized the freedmen. Tenant farming rendered the now isolated freedmen more vulnerable to nightriding; Klan terror broke up the Leagues and restored plantation discipline. The freedmen went back to work, production improved, land prices rose, and the new sharecropping system stabilized in the essential form that would last for decades. Sharecropping soon proved unsatisfactory and often economically disastrous for the freedmen, but because it had appeared to be a significant advance over the gang labor system, it reduced mass protest at a critical moment. But once production stabilized and land prices recovered, further progress toward independent proprietorship became vastly more difficult. What freedmen had hoped would be a temporary stage became a permanent condition of tenantry; the trap, as it were, snapped shut. The politicization of the freedmen, which occurred through the League, was critical. By contributing to the final disruption of the old-style centralized plantation, the League paved the way for the transition to tenant farming, and, ironically, for the survival of the plantation system in an altered form.

Bibliography

Primary Sources

Newspapers

ALABAMA

Athens *Post*, 1865–68.
Carrollton *West Alabamian*, 1866–69.
Choctaw *Herald*, [1867].
Clarke County Democrat (Grove Hill), 1867–68.
Clarke County Journal (Grove Hill), [1866].
Demopolis *New Era*, [1867].
Demopolis *Southern Republican*, 1869–70.
Elmore Standard (Wetumpka), 1867–68.
Eufaula *Bluff City Times*, [1869].
Eutaw *Whig and Observer*, [1867].
Florence *Journal*, [1866–67].
Gadsden *Times*, [1867].
Greensboro *Alabama Beacon*, 1867–69.
Greenville *Advocate*, 1867, 1869–71.
Grove Hill *Democrat*, 1867.
Henry County Register (Abbeville), [1867–69].
Huntsville *Advocate*, 1865–68.
Huntsville *Independent*, [1868].
Jacksonville *Republican*, 1867–68.
Livingston *Journal*, 1867–69.
Marengo Reporter (Linden), [1867–68].

Marion *Commonwealth*, [1867–70].
Mobile *Advertiser and Register*, 1865–68.
Mobile *Nationalist*, 1865–69.
Mobile *Register*, 1869–70.
Mobile *Republican*, [1870].
Mobile *Times*, 1866–68.
Monroe Eagle (Claiborne), 1868–71.
Monroe Journal (Monroeville), 1867.
Montgomery *Advertiser*, 1867–68.
Montgomery *Alabama State Journal*, 1869–71.
Montgomery *Mail*, 1865–70.
Montgomery *Picayune*, 1868.
Montgomery *State Sentinel*, 1867–68.
Moulton *Advertiser*, 1867, 1868–69.
Moulton *Christian Herald*, 1866.
Moulton *Union*, 1867.
Notasulga *Universalist Herald*, 1867–70.
Opelika *East Alabama Monitor*, [1868–69].
Opelika *Era and Whig*, [1870].
Opelika *Locomotive*, [1869].
Opelika *New Era*, 1869.
Opelika *Union Republican*, [1869].
St. Clair County Eagle (Ashville), [1869].
Selma *Messenger*, 1867–68.
Selma *Press*, 1869.
Selma *Southern Argus*, 1869.
Selma *Times and Messenger*, 1868–69.
Shelby County Guide (Columbiana), 1868–70.
Talladega *Alabama Reporter*, 1866–69.
Talladega *Sun*, 1869–70.
Talladega *Watchtower*, 1867–70.
Troy *Messenger and Advertiser*, 1869.
Troy *Southern Advertiser*, 1867.
Tuscaloosa *Monitor*, 1867–70.
Tuskegee *News*, 1866–67.
Union Springs *Times*, 1867–69.
Wilcox County News (Camden), 1867–68.
Wilcox News and Pacificator (Camden), 1868–70.

MISSISSIPPI

Aberdeen *Examiner*, [1869–70].
Bolivar Times (Beulah), [1870].

Canton *Mail*, [1868–70].
Chickasaw Messenger (Okalona), [1866].
Columbus *Mississippi Index*, 1865–66.
Columbus *Southern Sentinel*, [1865, 1867].
Corinth *News*, [1868].
Forest *Ku Klux*, [1871].
Forest *Register*, 1868–71.
Friar's Point *Cohomian*, 1865–66.
Friar's Point *Delta*, 1869–71.
Hazlehurst *Copiahan*, [1865, 1867].
Hinds County Gazette (Raymond), 1867–70.
Holly Springs *Reporter*, [1871].
Jackson *Clarion*, 1865–71.
Jackson *Pilot*, 1869–70.
Jackson *State Leader*, [1872].
Lexington *Advertiser*, [1866, 1868, 1870].
Liberty *Advocate*, [1866].
Liberty *Southern Herald*, 1866–71.
Macon *Beacon*, 1867–71.
Meridian *Chronicle*, [1868].
Meridian *Gazette*, 1867, 1869–70.
Natchez *Courier*, [1867].
Natchez *Democrat*, 1867–70.
Oxford *Falcon*, [1866–67].
Panola *Star*, [1867–70].
Vicksburg *Herald*, 1867–68, 1869.
Vicksburg *Times*, 1866, 1868.
Vicksburg *Times and Republican*, 1869–72.
Vicksburg *Vicksburger*, 1874.

OTHER PAPERS AND PERIODICALS

Memphis *Post*, 1867.
Nation, 1865–68.
National Anti-Slavery Standard, 1867–69.
New York *Times*, 1867–69.
New York *Tribune*, 1867.
Philadelphia *Christian Recorder*, 1865–68.
San Francisco *Elevator*, 1873–74.
Southern Cultivator, 1865–69.
Washington *Chronicle*, 1866–70.
Washington *New National Era*, 1870–73.
Washington *Great Republic*, 1866–68.

Manuscripts

Alabama Department of Archives and History, Montgomery
 Blue, M. P. Papers.
 Browne, William Phineas. Papers.
 Cooper, William. Diary.
 Cummings, Kate. Diary.
 DuBose, J. W. Papers.
 Dustan, C. W. Papers.
 Felder, Adam C. Papers.
 Gorgas, Josiah. Journal.
 Hall Family. Papers.
 Houston, George S. Papers.
 Lindsay, Governor R. B. Papers.
 Lowndes County W.P.A. File.
 McKee, Robert. Papers.
 Maxwell, J. R. Diary.
 Moore, J. B. Papers.
 Parsons, Governor Lewis E. Papers.
 Patton, Governor R. M. Papers.
 ———. Letterbooks.
 Perry, Sally Randle. Diary.
 Smith, Governor William Hugh. Papers.
 Swayne, [Military] Governor Wager. Papers.
University of Alabama, Tuscaloosa
 Curtis Family. Papers.
 Jemson, Robert. Papers.
 Mobile City Police. Records.
 Peck, E. W. Papers.
Boston Public Library, Boston
 Moody, Loring. Papers.
Bowdoin College Library, New Brunswick, Maine
 Howard, O. O. Papers.
The Bancroft Library, University of California at Berkeley
 Ord, Edward Otho Cresap. Papers (C-B 479).
University of Chicago, Chicago
 Lincoln Collection.
Clarksdale Public Library, Clarksdale, Mississippi
 Robinson, Nancy McDougall. Diary.
Rare Book and Manuscript Library, Columbia University, New York
 Sprague, William. Papers.
William R. Perkins Library, Duke University, Durham
 Bryant, John Emory. Papers.

Bunting, Sarah W. Papers.
Caldwell, Eliza F. Papers.
Campbell Family. Papers.
Clarke, Lewis. Papers.
Clay, Clement Claiborne. Papers.
Crydenwise, Henry M. Papers.
Dimitry, John Bull Smith. Papers.
Dimon, Charles Augustus Ropes. Papers.
Ellet, Alfred Washington. Papers.
Houston, George Smith. Papers.
Johnson, Andrew. Papers.
Lewis, Burwell Boykin. Papers.
Peck, Elijah Wolsey. Papers.
Smith, Washington M. Papers.
Watson, Henry, Jr. Papers.
ITC Gammon Theological Seminary Archives, Woodruff Center Library,
Atlanta University, Atlanta
Freedmen's Aid Society. Correspondence.
Fisk University, Nashville
American Missionary Association. Papers.
Rutherford B. Hayes Memorial Library, Fremont, Ohio
Hayes, Rutherford B. Papers.
Schenck, Robert C. Papers.
State Historical Society of Iowa, Des Moines
Dodge, Grenville. Papers.
Library of Congress, Washington, D.C.
Bingham, John A. Papers.
Bromberg, Frederick G. Papers.
Butler, B. F. Papers.
Chandler, William E. Papers.
Chandler, Zachariah. Papers.
Chase, Salmon P. Papers.
Covode, John. Papers.
Forney, John Wien. Papers.
Fowler, Joseph S. Papers.
Gillette Family. Papers.
Grant, Ulysses S. Papers.
Johnson, Andrew. Papers.
Lincoln, Abraham. Papers.
Montgomery, Benjamin. Papers.
Schofield, John. Papers.
Sherman, John. Papers.
Sherman, William T. Papers.

Stevens, Thaddeus. Papers.
Trumbull, Lyman. Papers.
Wade, B. F. Papers.
Department of Archives, Louisiana State University, Baton Rouge
Affleck, Thomas. Papers.
Farrar, Alexander K. Papers.
Mercer, William Newton. Papers.
Mississippi Department of Archives and History, Jackson
Alcorn, Governor J. L. Papers.
Alexander, Robert B. Diary.
Ames, Governor Adelbert. Papers.
Barksdale, E. Papers.
Dantzler, A. F. Papers.
Darden, Susan Sillers. Diary.
Davis, Joseph. Papers.
Garner, James W. Papers.
George, James Z. Scrapbook.
Harper, Annie E. Manuscript.
Humphreys, Governor Benjamin G. Papers.
Lamar, L. Q. C. Papers.
McCardle, William H. Papers.
McNabb, Eliza. Letters.
Matthews, S. Papers.
Mayes-Dimitry-Stuart. Papers.
Middleton, Ellis Scattergood. Papers.
Nicholson, Flavellus G. Diary-Journal.
Sharkey, H. Clay. Papers.
Stuart, Oscar J. E. Papers.
Whitfield, Henry B., and Company. Papers.
University of Mississippi, Oxford.
Brown, Juanita. Collection.
Museum of the History of Mobile
Horton Family. Papers.
New-York Historical Society, New York
Southern Famine Relief Commission. Papers.
Ullman, Daniel. Papers.
Rare Books and Manuscripts Division, New York Public Library, New York
Fleming, Walter L. Papers.
Greeley, Horace. Papers.
Southern Historical Collection, Library of the University of North Carolina at Chapel Hill
Agnew, Samuel Andrew Diary.

Alcorn, J. L. Papers.
Arrington, A. H. Papers.
Baker, Everard G. Diary.
Bragg, John. Papers.
Bromberg, Frederick G. Papers.
Cameron Family. Papers.
Caruthers, Robert. Papers.
Forwood, W. S. Papers.
Fowler, Joseph S. Papers.
Gorgas, J. Papers.
Hairston and Wilson Family. Papers.
Haywood, Ernest. Papers.
Herbert, Hilary A. Papers.
Howell, Robert Philip. Memoir.
King, Thomas Butler. Papers.
Mallory, James. Diary.
Niles, Jason. Diary.
Nisbet, J. Papers.
Polk Family. Papers.
Slack Family. Papers.
Wyche and Otey Family. Papers.
Samford University, Birmingham, Alabama
    Randolph, Ryland. Papers.
Schomburg Center for Research in Black Culture, New York Public Library, New York
    Carpenter, John. Papers.
Tennessee State Archives, Nashville
    Warner, Willard. Papers.
Manuscripts Department, University of Virginia Library, Charlottesville
    Cabell Family. Papers (acc. no. 38–111).
    White Family. Papers (acc. no. 9372-b).

Local Government and Federal Agency Records

Bullock County Courthouse, Union Springs, Alabama
    Bullock County Trial Records, 1866–70.
Lauderdale County Courthouse, Meridian, Mississippi
    Docket Books, 1866–71.
National Archives, Washington, D.C.
    Records of the Bureau of Refugees, Freedmen and Abandoned Lands. Record Group 105.
    Records of the United States Army, Continental Command. Record Group 393.

Records of the U.S. House of Representatives. Record Group 233.
Vicksburg City Hall, Vicksburg, Mississippi
 Minutes of the Council of City of Vicksburg, 1866–72.
Warren County Courthouse, Vicksburg, Mississippi
 Board of Police, Minute Book, 1867–70.

Federal and State Government Publications

Congressional Globe. 42nd Cong., 1st Sess., Appendix.
House Executive Documents. 40th Cong., 1st Sess., No. 20.
House Executive Documents. 40th Cong., 2nd Sess., No. 238.
House Executive Documents. 40th Cong., 2nd Sess., No. 303.
House Miscellaneous Documents. 40th Cong., 2nd Sess., No. 111.
House Miscellaneous Documents. 40th Cong., 3rd Sess., No. 53.
House Reports. 42nd Cong., 2nd Sess. No. 22.
House Reports. 43rd Cong., 2nd Sess., No. 262.
House Reports. 43rd Cong., 2nd Sess., No. 265.
Report of the Commissioner of Agriculture for the Year 1866. Washington, D.C.,
 1867.
Senate Committee on Education and Labor. Report of the Committee of the
 Senate upon the Relations Between Labor and Capital and Testimony Taken by
 the Committee. 5 vols. Washington, D.C., 1885.
Senate Executive Documents. 39th Cong., 2nd Sess., No. 6.
Senate Executive Documents. 40th Cong., 1st Sess., No. 20.
State of Alabama. Official Journal of the Constitutional Convention of the State of
 Alabama Held in the City of Montgomery, Commencing on Tuesday,
 November 5th A. D. 1867. Montgomery, 1868.
———. Report of Joint Committee on Outrages. Montgomery, 1868.
State of Mississippi. Journal of the Proceedings in the Constitutional Convention
 of the State of Mississippi, 1868. Jackson, 1871.

Books, Recollections, and Other Published Primary Sources

Alcorn, James Lusk. Views of the Honorable J. L. Alcorn on the Political Situa-
 tion of Mississippi. N.p., [1867].
American Missionary Association. The American Missionary, XIX–XXIII
 (1865–69).
———. The Twenty-First Annual Report of the American Missionary Association,
 and the Proceedings at the Annual Meeting, Held at Homer, New York,
 October 17th and 18th 1867. . . . New York, 1867.
Appleton's Annual Cyclopaedia and Register of Important Events. 15 vols. New
 York, 1865–1871.
Beard, James Melville. K. K. K. Sketches, Humorous and Didactic, Treating the

More Important Events of the Ku Klux Klan Movement in the South. Philadelphia, 1877.

Bellows, Henry W. *Historical Sketch of the Union League Club of Philadelphia: Its Origin, Organization, and Work, 1863–1879.* New York, 1879.

Berlin, Ira, Joseph P. Reidy, and Leslie S. Rowland, eds. *The Black Military Experience.* Freedom: A Documentary History of Emancipation, 1861–1867, Series 2. Cambridge, Mass., 1982.

Biddle, Ellen McGowan. *Reminiscences of a Soldier's Wife.* Philadelphia, 1907.

Brewer, Willis. *Alabama: Her History, Resources, War Record, and Public Men from 1540 to 1872.* 1872; rpr. Tuscaloosa, 1964.

Bromberg, Frederick G. *The Reconstruction Period in Alabama.* Iberville Historical Society Papers, Nos. 3 and 4. N.p., 1905.

Browning, Orville H. *The Diary of Orville Hickman Browning.* 2 vols. Springfield, Ill., 1933.

Chronicle of the Union League Club of Philadelphia. Philadelphia, 1902.

Dennett, John Richard. *The South as It Is, 1865–1866.* 1866; rpr. New York, 1965.

Fleming, Walter Lynwood, ed. *Documentary History of Reconstruction: Political, Military, Social, Religious, Educational and Industrial: 1865 to 1906.* 2 vols. 1906–1907; rpr. Gloucester, Mass., 1960.

———, ed. *Union League Documents.* Documents Relating to Reconstruction, No. 3. Morgantown, W.V., 1904.

———, ed. *The Union League of America.* Documents Relating to Reconstruction, No. 4. Morgantown, W.Va., 1904.

Foner, Philip S., and George E. Walker, eds. *Proceedings of the Black National and State Conventions, 1865–1900.* Philadelphia, 1987.

Forney, John Wien. *Anecdotes of Public Men.* 2 vols. New York, 1899.

Fulkerson, H. S. *The Negro; As He Was; As He Is; As He Will Be.* Vicksburg, 1887.

Furlong, Charles E. *Origin of the Outrages at Vicksburg: Speech of Hon. Chas. E. Furlong, Senator from Warren County, in the Senate of Mississippi, December 18, 1874.* Vicksburg, 1874.

Gibson, J. M. *Memoirs of J. M. Gibson: Terrors of the Civil War and Reconstruction Days.* N.p., 1966.

Grayson, Claude C. *Yesterday and Today, Memories of Selma and its People.* New Orleans, 1948.

Hardy, William H. "Recollections of Reconstruction in East and Southeast Mississippi." *Publications of the Mississippi Historical Society,* IV (1901), 105–32, and VIII (1904), 137–51.

Howard, Oliver Otis. *Autobiography of Oliver Otis Howard, Major General, United States Army.* 2 vols. New York, 1907.

Hunnicutt, John L. *Reconstruction in West Alabama: The Memoirs of John L. Hunnicutt.* Edited by William Stanley Hoole. Tuscaloosa, 1959.

[Keffer, John C.]. *Alabama: A Few Reflections Upon her Resources and the Advantages she Possesses as Inducement to Immigration.* Montgomery, 1869.

King, Edward. *The Great South* . . . . Edited by W. Magruder Drake and Robert R. Jones. 1875; rpr. Baton Rouge, 1972.

Lynch, James D. *Kemper County Vindicated, and a Peep at Radical Rule in Mississippi.* rpr. New York, 1969.

Lynch, John Roy. *Reminiscences of an Active Life: The Autobiography of John Roy Lynch.* Edited by John Hope Franklin. Chicago, 1970.

Moore, Glover. *A Calhoun County, Alabama, Boy in the 1860s.* Edited by Glover Moore, Jr. Jackson, Miss., 1978.

Morgan, Albert T. *Yazoo; or, on the Picket Line of Freedom in the South.* Washington, D.C., 1884.

Nordhoff, Charles. *The Cotton States in the Spring and Summer of 1875.* rpr. New York, n.d.

Palmer, Beverly Wilson, ed. *Papers of Charles Sumner.* Microfilm. London, 1987.

Powers, Stephen. *Afoot and Alone: A Walk from Sea to Sea by the Southern Route.* . . . Hartford, 1871.

Proceedings of the Colored National Labor Convention Held in Washington, D.C. on December 6th, 7th, 8th, 9th, and 10th, 1869. Washington, D.C., 1870.

Proceedings of the National Union Republican Convention Held at Chicago, May 20 and 21, 1868. Chicago, 1868.

Rawick, George P., ed. *The American Slave: A Composite Autobiography.* 19 vols. Westport, Conn., 1972.

———, ed. *The American Slave: A Composite Autobiography: Supplement Series 1.* 12 vols. Westport, Conn., 1977–.

Reid, Whitelaw. *After the War: A Tour of the Southern States, 1865–1866.* 1866; rpr. New York, 1965.

Robuck, J. E. *My Own Personal Experience and Observation as a Soldier in the Confederate Army During the Civil War, 1861–1865, Also During the Period of Reconstruction.* . . . Birmingham, 1911.

Royall, William L. *A Reply to "A Fool's Errand, by One of the Fools."* New York, 1881.

Shuften, John T. *A Colored Man's Exposition of the Acts and Doings of the Radical Party South From 1865 to 1876.* . . . Jacksonville, 1877.

Smith, William R. *The History and Debates of the Convention of the People of Alabama Begun and Held in the City of Montgomery, on the Seveṛ th Day of January, 1861.* 1861; rpr. Spartanburg, S.C., 1975.

Somers, Robert. *The Southern States Since the War, 1870–71.* rpr. University, Ala., 1965.

Sylvis, James C. *The Life, Speeches, Labors and Essays of Williaṃ H. Sylvis.* rpr. New York, 1968.

Tourgée, Albion Winegar. *Bricks Without Straw.* 1879; rpr. Baton Rouge, 1969.
————. *A Fool's Errand.* 1879; rpr. Cambridge, Mass., 1961.
Trowbridge, J. T. *A Picture of the Desolated States; and the Work of Restoration, 1865–1868.* Hartford, 1868.
————. *The South: A Tour of Its Battlefields and Ruined Cities, A Journey Through the Desolated States, and Talks with the People.* Hartford, 1866.
Union League of America. *Proceedings of the Annual Meeting of the Grand National Council, Union League of America, Held at Washington, December 13th, 1865.* Washington, D.C., 1865.
————. *Proceedings of the National Council of the Union League of America, at its Sixth Annual Session, Held in the City of Washington, D.C., on Tuesday and Wednesday, March 2d and 3d 1869.* N.p., [1869].
————. *Twentieth Annual Report of the National Council of the National Union League of America.* . . . New York, 1883.
————. *Twenty-Fourth Annual Report of the National Council of the National Union League.* . . . New York, 1889.
Warren, Henry W. *Reminiscences of a Mississippi Carpetbagger.* Holden, Mass., 1914.
Welles, Gideon. *Diary of Gideon Welles.* Edited by Howard K. Beale. 3 vols. rpr. New York, 1960.
Wells, James M. *The Chisolm Massacre: A Picture of "Home Rule" in Mississippi.* 1877; rpr. New York, 1969.

Secondary Sources

Books

Abbott, Richard, H. *The Republican Party and the South, 1855–1877.* Chapel Hill, 1986.
Alexander, Thomas B., and Richard E. Beringer. *The Anatomy of the Confederate Congress: A Study of the Influences of Member Characteristics on Legislative Voting Behavior, 1861–1865.* Nashville, 1972.
Ames, Blanche. *Adelbert Ames, 1835–1933: General, Senator, Governor.* New York, 1964.
Amos, Harriet E. *Cotton City: Urban Development in Antebellum Mobile.* University, Ala., 1985.
Aptheker, Herbert. *To Be Free: Studies in American Negro History.* New York, 1948.
Barney, William L. *The Secessionist Impulse: Alabama and Mississippi in 1860.* Princeton, 1974.

Benedict, Michael Les. *A Compromise of Principle: Congressional Republicans and Reconstruction, 1863–1869.* New York, 1974.

Bentley, George R. *A History of the Freedmen's Bureau.* 1944; rpr. New York, 1970.

Berlin, Ira. *Slaves Without Masters: The Free Negro in the Antebellum South.* New York, 1974.

Biographical and Historical Memoirs of Mississippi. 2 vols. Chicago, 1891.

Blue, Frederick J. *Salmon P. Chase: A Life in Politics.* Kent, Ohio, 1987.

Boles, John B., and Evelyn Thomas Nolen, eds. *Interpreting Southern History: Historiograhical Essays in Honor of Sanford W. Higginbotham.* Baton Rouge, 1987.

Bond, Horace Mann. *Negro Education in Alabama: A Study in Cotton and Steel.* Washington, D.C., 1939.

Bowers, Claude G. *The Tragic Era: The Revolution after Lincoln.* New York, 1929.

Branfon, Robert L. *Cotton Kingdom of the New South: A History of the Yazoo Mississippi Delta from Reconstruction to the Twentieth Century.* Cambridge, Mass., 1967.

Brodie, Fawn. *Thaddeus Stevens: Scourge of the South.* New York, 1959.

Burton, Orville Vernon, and Robert C. McMath, Jr., eds. *Toward a New South? Studies in Post–Civil War Southern Communities.* Westport, Conn., 1982.

Carter, Dan T. *When the War Was Over: The Failure of Self-Reconstruction in the South, 1865–1867.* Baton Rouge, 1985.

Cochran, Fan Alexander. *History of Old Tishomingo County, Mississippi, Mississippi Territory.* Oklahoma City, 1969.

Cox, LaWanda F., and John H. Cox. *Politics, Principle, and Prejudice, 1865–1866: Dilemma of Reconstruction America.* New York, 1963.

Current, Richard Nelson. *Old Thad Stevens: A Story of Ambition.* Madison, 1942.

Currie, James T. *Enclave: Vicksburg and Her Plantations, 1863–1870.* Jackson, Miss., 1980.

Currie-McDaniel, Ruth. *Carpetbagger of Conscience: A Biography of John Emory Bryant.* Athens, Ga., 1987.

Davis, David Brion. *The Problem of Slavery in the Age of Revolution, 1770–1823.* Ithaca, 1975.

Davis, Ronald L. F. *Good and Faithful Labor: From Slavery to Sharecropping in the Natchez District, 1860–1890.* Westport, Conn., 1982.

Dearing, Mary R. *Veterans in Politics: The Story of the G.A.R.* Baton Rouge, 1952.

DeCanio, Stephen J. *Agriculture in the Postbellum South: The Economics of Production and Supply.* Cambridge, Mass., 1974.

Drago, Edmund L. *Black Politicians and Reconstruction in Georgia: A Splendid Failure.* Baton Rouge, 1982.

Du Bois, W. E. B. *Black Reconstruction in America: An Essay Toward a History of the Part Which Black Folk Played in the Attempt to Reconstruct Democracy in America, 1860–1880.* 1935; rpr. New York, 1971.

DuBose, John Witherspoon. *Alabama's Tragic Decade: Ten Years of Alabama, 1865–1874.* Edited by James K. Greer. Birmingham, 1940.

Dunning, William Archibald. *Reconstruction: Political and Economic.* New York, 1907.

Fite, Gilbert C. *Cotton Fields No More: Southern Agriculture, 1865–1980.* Lexington, Ky., 1984.

Fleming, Walter Lynwood. *Civil War and Reconstruction in Alabama.* New York, 1905.

——. *The Sequel of Appomattox.* New Haven, 1919.

Foner, Eric. *Free Soil, Free Labor, Free Men: The Ideology of the Republican Party before the Civil War.* London, 1970.

——. *Nothing But Freedom: Emancipation and Its Legacy.* New York, 1970.

——. *Politics and Ideology in the Age of the Civil War.* New York, 1980.

——. *Reconstruction: America's Unfinished Revolution, 1863–1877.* New York, 1988.

Foner, Philip S. *From Colonial Times to the Founding of the American Federation of Labor.* New York, 1947. Vol. I of *History of the Labor Movement in the United States,* 5 vols.

Fox-Genovese, Elizabeth, and Eugene D. Genovese. *Fruits of Merchant Capital: Slavery and Bourgeois Property in the Rise and Expansion of Capitalism.* New York, 1983.

Franklin, John Hope. *Reconstruction: After the Civil War.* Chicago, 1961.

Garner, James Wilford. *Reconstruction in Mississippi.* 1901; rpr. Baton Rouge, 1968.

Gillette, William. *Retreat from Reconstruction, 1869–1879.* Baton Rouge, 1979.

Glymph, Thavolia, and John J. Kushma, eds. *Essays on the Postbellum Southern Economy.* College Station, Tex., 1985.

Going, Allen Johnson. *Bourbon Democracy in Alabama, 1874–1890.* University, Ala., 1951.

Gutman, Herbert. *The Black Family in Slavery and Freedom, 1750–1925.* New York, 1976.

Hahn, Steven. *The Roots of Southern Populism: Yeoman Farmers and the Transformation of the Georgia Upcountry, 1850–1890.* New York, 1983.

Hamilton, Peter J. *Mobile of the Five Flags.* Mobile, 1913.

Hardy, Toney A. *No Compromise with Principle: Autobiography and Biography of William Harris Hardy in Dialogue.* New York, 1946.

Harris, William C. *The Day of the Carpetbagger: Republican Reconstruction in Mississippi.* Baton Rouge, 1979.
————. *Presidential Reconstruction in Mississippi.* Baton Rouge, 1967.
Herbert, Hilary A. *Why the Solid South? Or, Reconstruction and Its Results.* 1890; rpr. New York, 1969.
Hermann, Janet Sharp. *The Pursuit of a Dream.* New York, 1981.
Hesseltine, William B. *Ulysses S. Grant: Politician.* New York, 1935.
Higgs, Robert. *Competition and Coercion: Blacks in the American Economy, 1865–1914.* Cambridge, England, 1977.
Hine, Darlene Clark, ed. *The State of Afro-American History: Past, Present, and Future.* Baton Rouge, 1986.
Hirshson, Stanley P. *Farewell to the Bloody Shirt: Northern Republicans and the Southern Negro.* Chicago, 1962.
Hobsbawm, Eric J. *The Age of Capital, 1848–1875.* New York, 1979.
————. *The Age of Revolution, 1789–1848.* London, 1962.
Holt, Thomas C. *Black Over White: Negro Political Leadership in South Carolina During Reconstruction.* Urbana, 1977.
Hoole, William Stanley. *Alabama Tories: The First Alabama Cavalry, U.S.A., 1862–1865.* Tuscaloosa, 1960.
Howard, Gene L. *Death at Cross Plains: An Alabama Reconstruction Tragedy.* University, Ala., 1984.
Jaynes, Gerald David. *Branches Without Roots: Genesis of the Black Working Class in the American South, 1862–1882.* New York, 1986.
Jones, Jacqueline. *Labor of Love, Labor of Sorrow: Black Women, Work, and the Family from Slavery to the Present.* New York, 1985.
Kirwan, Albert D. *Revolt of the Rednecks: Mississippi Politics, 1876–1925.* New York, 1964. Paper. Lexington, Ky., 1951.
Klement, Frank L. *Dark Lanterns: Secret Political Societies, Conspiracies, and Treason Trials in the Civil War.* Baton Rouge, 1984.
Klingburg, Frank W. *The Southern Claims Commission.* Berkeley and Los Angeles, 1955.
Kolchin, Peter. *First Freedom: The Responses of Alabama's Blacks to Emancipation and Reconstruction.* Westport, Conn., 1972.
Kousser, J. Morgan. *The Shaping of Southern Politics: Suffrage Restriction and the Establishment of the One-Party South.* New Haven, 1974.
Kousser, J. Morgan, and James M. McPherson, eds. *Region, Race, and Reconstruction: Essays in Honor of C. Vann Woodward.* New York, 1982.
Lathrop, George Parsons. *History of the Union League of Philadelphia.* Philadelphia, 1884.
Leverett, Rudy H. *Legend of the Free State of Jones.* Jackson, Miss., 1984.
Litwack, Leon F. *Been in the Storm So Long: The Aftermath of Slavery.* New York, 1979.

Loewen, James W. *The Mississippi Chinese: Between Black and White.* Cambridge, Mass., 1971.
Lonn, Ella. *Desertion During the Civil War.* New York, 1928.
Lynch, John R. *The Facts of Reconstruction.* Edited by William C. Harris. rpr. Indianapolis, 1970.
McFeely, William S. *Yankee Stepfather: General O. O. Howard and the Freedmen.* New York, 1968.
McKitrick, Eric. *Andrew Johnson and Reconstruction.* Chicago, 1960.
McLemore, Richard A., ed. *A History of Mississippi.* 2 vols. Hattiesburg, 1973.
McMillan, Malcolm Cook. *Constitutional Development in Alabama, 1798–1901.* Chapel Hill, 1955.
————. *The Disintegration of a Confederate State.* Macon, Ga., 1986.
McPherson, James M. *The Struggle for Equality: Abolitionists and the Negro in Civil War and Reconstruction.* Princeton, 1964.
Magdol, Edward. *A Right to the Land: Essays on the Freedmen's Community.* Westport, Conn., 1977.
Mandel, Jay R. *The Roots of Black Poverty.* Durham, 1978.
Mantell, Martin E. *Johnson, Grant, and the Politics of Reconstruction.* New York, 1973.
Miller, L. D. *History of Alabama Adapted to the Use of the Schools and for General Reading.* Birmingham, 1901.
Moneyhon, Carl H. *Republicanism in Reconstruction Texas.* Austin, 1980.
Montgomery, David. *Beyond Equality: Labor and the Radical Republicans.* New York, 1967.
Moore, Albert Burton. *History of Alabama.* University, Ala. 1934.
Murphy, James B. *L. Q. C. Lamar: Pragmatic Patriot.* Baton Rouge, 1973.
Nathans, Elizabeth Studley. *Losing the Peace: Georgia Republicans and Reconstruction, 1865–1871.* Baton Rouge, 1968.
Nieman, Donald G. *To Set the Law in Motion: The Freedmen's Bureau and the Legal Rights of Blacks, 1865–1868.* Millwood, N.Y., 1979.
Olsen, Otto H. *Reconstruction and Redemption in the South.* Baton Rouge, 1980.
Osthaus, Carl R. *Freedmen, Philanthropy, and Fraud: A History of the Freedmen's Savings Bank.* Urbana, 1976.
Oubre, Claude F. *Forty Acres and a Mule: The Freedmen's Bureau and Black Land Ownership.* Baton Rouge, 1978.
Owen, Thomas McAdory. *History of Alabama and Dictionary of Alabama Biography.* 4 vols. Chicago, 1921.
Owens, Susie Lee. *The Union League of America: Political Activities in Tennessee, the Carolinas and Virginia, 1865–1870.* Ann Arbor, 1947.

Painter, Nell Irvin. *Exodusters: Black Migration to Kansas After Reconstruction.* New York, 1976.

Pereyra, Lillian A. *James Lusk Alcorn: Persistent Whig.* Baton Rouge, 1973.

Perman, Michael. *Reunion Without Compromise: The South and Reconstruction, 1865–1868.* Cambridge, England, 1973.

————. *The Road to Redemption: Southern Politics, 1869–1879.* Chapel Hill, 1984.

Powell, Lawrence N. *New Masters: Northern Planters During the Civil War and Reconstruction.* New Haven, 1980.

Rabinowitz, Howard N. *Race Relations in the Urban South, 1865–1890.* New York, 1978.

————, ed. *Southern Black Leaders of the Reconstruction Era.* Urbana, 1982.

Rable, George C. *But There Was No Peace: The Role of Violence in the Politics of Reconstruction.* Athens, Ga., 1984.

Rachleff, Peter J. *Black Labor in the South: Richmond, Virginia, 1865–1890.* Philadelphia, 1984.

Randall, James G., and David Donald. *The Civil War and Reconstruction.* Boston, 1969.

Ransom, Roger L., and Richard Sutch. *One Kind of Freedom: The Economic Consequences of Emancipation.* Cambridge, England, 1977.

Reid, Joseph D. *Agriculture in the Postbellum South.* New Haven, 1975.

Richardson, Harry V. *Dark Salvation: The Story of Methodism as It Developed Among Blacks in America.* Garden City, N.Y., 1976.

Roark, James L. *Masters Without Slaves: Southern Planters in the Civil War and Reconstruction.* New York, 1977.

Robinson, Armstead L. *Bitter Fruits of Bondage: The Demise of Slavery and the Collapse of the Confederacy, 1861–1865.* Forthcoming.

Rogers, William Warren. *The One-Gallused Rebellion: Agrarianism in Alabama, 1865–1896.* Baton Rouge, 1970.

Schweninger, Loren. *James T. Rapier and Reconstruction.* Chicago, 1978.

Sefton, James E. *Andrew Johnson and the Uses of Constitutional Power.* Boston, 1983.

————. *The United States Army and Reconstruction, 1865–1877.* Baton Rouge, 1967.

Seip, Terry L. *The South Returns to Congress: Men, Economic Measures, and Intersectional Relationships, 1868–1879.* Baton Rouge, 1983.

Sellers, James Benson. *Slavery in Alabama.* University, Ala., 1950.

Shore, Laurence. *Southern Capitalists: The Ideological Leadership of an Elite, 1832–1885.* Chapel Hill, 1986.

Silvestro, Clement Mario. *Rally Round the Flag: The Union Leagues in the Civil War.* [Lansing, 1967].

Singletary, Otis A. *Negro Militia and Reconstruction.* 1957; rpr. Austin, 1963.

Smith, Charles Spencer. *A History of the African Methodist Episcopal Church.* . . . Philadelphia, 1922.

Stampp, Kenneth M. *The Era of Reconstruction, 1865–1877.* New York, 1965.

Stover, John F. *The Railroads of the South, 1865–1900.* Chapel Hill, 1955.

Suggs, Henry Lewis, ed. *The Black Press in the South, 1865–1979.* Westport, Conn., 1983.

Summers, Mark W. *Railroads, Reconstruction, and the Gospel of Prosperity: Aid Under the Radical Republicans, 1865–1877.* Princeton, 1984.

Sydnor, Charles S. *Slavery in Mississippi.* New York, 1933.

Tatum, Georgia Lee. *Disloyalty in the Confederacy.* Chapel Hill, 1934.

Thomas, Benjamin P., and Harold M. Hyman. *Stanton: The Life and Times of Lincoln's Secretary of War.* New York, 1962.

Thornton, J. Mills, III. *Politics and Power in a Slave Society: Alabama, 1800–1860.* Baton Rouge, 1978.

Trefousse, Hans L. *Impeachment of a President: Andrew Johnson, the Blacks, and Reconstruction.* Knoxville, 1975.

———. *The Radical Republicans: Lincoln's Vanguard for Racial Justice.* New York, 1969.

Trelease, Allen W. *Reconstruction: The Great Experiment.* New York, 1972.

———. *White Terror: The Ku Klux Klan Conspiracy and Southern Reconstruction.* New York, 1971.

Unger, Irwin. *The Greenback Era: A Social and Political History of American Finance, 1865–1879.* Princeton, 1964.

Walker, Clarence E. *A Rock in a Weary Land: The African Methodist Episcopal Church During the Civil War and Reconstruction.* Baton Rouge, 1982.

Walton, Gary M., and James F. Shepard, eds. *Market Institutions and Economic Progress in the New South, 1865–1900: Essays Stimulated by "One Kind of Freedom: The Economic Consequences of Emancipation."* New York, 1981.

Wayne, Michael. *The Reshaping of Plantation Society: The Natchez District, 1860–1880.* Baton Rouge, 1983.

Wharton, Vernon Lane. *The Negro in Mississippi, 1865–1890.* Chapel Hill, 1947.

Wiener, Jonathan M. *Social Origins of the New South: Alabama, 1860–1885.* Baton Rouge, 1978.

Wiggins, Sarah Woolfolk. *The Scalawag in Alabama Politics, 1865–1881.* University, Ala., 1977.

Woodman, Harold D. *King Cotton and His Retainers: Financing and Marketing the Cotton Crop of the South, 1800–1925.* Lexington, Ky., 1968.

Woodward, C. Vann. *Origins of the New South, 1877–1913.* Baton Rouge, 1951.

————. *Reunion and Reaction: The Compromise of 1877 and the End of Reconstruction.* Boston, 1951.

Articles and Essays

Abney, M. G. "Reconstruction in Pontotoc County." *Publications of the Mississippi Historical Society,* XI (1910), 229–69.

Alexander, Thomas B. "Persistent Whiggery in Alabama and the Lower South." *Alabama Review,* XXV (1948), 35–52.

Bailey, Hugh C. "Disloyalty in Early Confederate Alabama." *Journal of Southern History,* XXIII (1957), 525.

Barney, William L. "The Ambivalence of Change: From Old South to the New in the Alabama Black Belt, 1850–1870." In *From the Old South to the New: Essays on the Transitional South,* edited by Walter J. Fraser, Jr. and Winfred B. Moore, Jr. Westport, Conn., 1981.

Bartley, Numan V. "In Search of the New South: Southern Politics after Reconstruction." *Reviews in American History,* X (1982), 150–63.

Bethel, Elizabeth. "The Freedmen's Bureau in Alabama." *Journal of Southern History,* XVI (1948), 49–92.

Blain, William T. "'Banner' Unionism in Mississippi: Choctaw County, 1861–1869." *Mississippi Quarterly,* XXIX (Spring, 1976), 206–20.

Braden, W. H. "Reconstruction in Lee County." *Publications of the Mississippi Historical Society,* X (1909), 135–46.

Brock, Euline W. "Thomas W. Cardozo: Fallible Black Reconstruction Leader." *Journal of Southern History,* XLVII (1981), 183–206.

Brown, Julia C. "Reconstruction in Yalobusha and Grenada Counties." *Proceedings of the Mississippi Historical Society,* XII (1912), 214–82.

Browne, Fred Zollicoffer. "Reconstruction in Oktibbeha County." *Publications of the Mississippi Historical Society,* XIII (1913), 273–98.

Cooper, Forrest. "Reconstruction in Scott County." *Publications of the Mississippi Historical Society,* XIII (1913), 99–221.

DeCanio, Stephen J. "Sharecropping in History and Theory." *Agricultural History,* XLIX (1975), 426–40.

Donald, David. "The Scalawag in Mississippi Reconstruction." *Journal of Southern History,* X (1944), 447–60.

Edwards, Thomas J. "The Tenant System and Some Changes Since Emancipation." *Annals of the American Academy of Political and Social Science,* IL (September, 1913), 38–46.

Ellem, Warren A. "Who Were the Mississippi Scalawags?" *Journal of Southern History,* XXXVIII (1972), 217–40.

Fitzgerald, Michael W. "Radical Republicanism and the White Yeomanry During Alabama Reconstruction." *Journal of Southern History,* LIV (1988), 565–96.

Fleming, Walter Lynwood. "The Formation of the Union League in Alabama." *Gulf States Historical Magazine*, II (1903), 73–89.

Foner, Eric. "Reconstruction Revisited." *Reviews in American History*, X (1982), 82–100.

Genovese, Eugene D. "Yeoman Farmers in a Slaveholders' Democracy." *Agricultural History*, XLIX (1975), 331–42.

Harris, William C. "James Lynch: Black Leader in Southern Reconstruction." *Historian*, XXXIV (1971), 40–61.

Hume, Richard L. "The Freedmen's Bureau and the Freedmen's Vote in the Reconstruction of Southern Alabama: An Account by Agent Samuel S. Gardner." *Alabama Historical Quarterly*, XXXVII (1975), 217–24.

Jones, J. H. "Reconstruction in Wilkinson County." *Publications of the Mississippi Historical Society*, VIII (1904), 153–75.

Kendel, Julia. "Reconstruction in Lafayette County." *Publications of the Mississippi Historical Society*, XIII (1913), 223–72.

Kincaid, Larry. "Victims of Circumstance: An Interpretation of Changing Attitudes Toward Republican Policy Makers and Reconstruction." *Journal of American History*, LVII (1970), 48–66.

King, J. Crawford, Jr. "The Closing of the Southern Range: An Exploratory Study." *Journal of Southern History*, XLVIII (1982), 53–70.

Krebs, Sylvia H. "Will the Freedmen Work: White Alabamians Adjust to Free Black Labor." *Alabama Historical Quarterly*, XXXVI (Summer, 1974), 151–63.

Kyle, John W. "Reconstruction in Panola County." *Publications of the Mississippi Historical Society*, XIII (1913), 9–98.

McNair, Cecil E. "Reconstruction in Bullock County." *Alabama Historical Quarterly*, XV (Spring, 1953), 75–125.

McNeily, John S. "War and Reconstruction in Mississippi, 1863–1890." *Publications of the Mississippi Historical Society, Centenary Series*, II (1918), 135–535.

Magee, Hattie. "Reconstruction in Lawrence and Jeff Davis Counties." *Publications of the Mississippi Historical Society*, XI (1910), 163–204.

Moore, A. B. "Railroad Building in Alabama During the Reconstruction Period." *Journal of Southern History*, I (1935), 421–41.

Nathans, Sydney. "Fortress Without Walls: A Black Community after Slavery." In *Holding On to the Land and the Lord: Kinship, Ritual, Land Tenure, and Social Policy in the Rural South*, edited by Robert L. Hall and Carol Stack. Athens, Ga., 1982.

Nichols, Irby C. "Reconstruction in DeSoto County." *Publications of the Mississippi Historical Society*, XI (1910), 295–316.

Puckett, Ernest F. "Reconstruction in Monroe County." *Publications of the Mississippi Historical Society*, XI (1910), 103–61.

Robinson, Armstead L. "Beyond the Realm of Social Consensus: New Meanings of Reconstruction for American History." *Journal of American History*, LXVIII (1981), 276–97.

Rogers, William Warren. "'Politics is Mighty Uncertain': Charles Hays Goes to Congress." *Alabama Review*, XXX (1977), 163–90.

Schweninger, Loren. "Alabama Blacks and the Congressional Reconstruction Acts of 1867." *Alabama Review*, XXXI (1978), 185–86.

————. "Black Citizenship and the Republican Party in Reconstruction Alabama." *Alabama Review*, XXIX (1976), 88.

Shlomowitz, Ralph. "The Transition from Slave to Freedmen's Labor Arrangements in Southern Agriculture, 1865–70." *Journal of Economic History*, XXXIX (1979), 333–36.

Stearx, H. E. "William C. Jordan and Reconstruction in Bullock County, Alabama." *Alabama Review*, XV (1962), 61–73.

Watkins, Ruth. "Reconstruction in Newton County." *Publications of the Mississippi Historical Society*, XI (1910), 205–28.

Wells, W. Calvin. "Reconstruction and its Destruction in Hinds County." *Publications of the Mississippi Historical Society*, IX (1906), 85–108.

White, Kenneth B. "Wager Swayne: Racist or Realist." *Alabama Review*, XXXI (1978), 92–109.

Wiener, Jonathan M. "Class Structure and Economic Development in the American South." *American Historical Review*, LXXXIV (1979), 970–1006.

Witty, Fred M. "Reconstruction in Carroll and Montgomery Counties." *Publications of the Mississippi Historical Society*, X (1909), 115–34.

Woodman, Harold D. "Post–Civil War Southern Agriculture and the Law." *Agricultural History*, LIII (1979), 319–37.

————. "Sequel to Slavery." *Journal of Southern History*, XLII (1978), 523–54.

Woodward, C. Vann. Review of *From the Old South to the New*, edited by Walter J. Fraser, Jr., and Winfred B. Moore, Jr. *American Historical Review*, LXXXVIII (1983), 188.

Wright, Gavin. "The Strange Career of the New Southern Economic History." *Reviews in American History*, X (1982), 164–80.

Theses and Dissertations

Bailey, Richard. "Black Legislators during the Reconstruction of Alabama, 1867–1878." Ph.D. dissertation, Kansas State University, 1984.

Bell, William Dudley. "The Reconstruction Ku Klux Klan: A Survey of the Writings on the Klan with a Profile and Analysis of the Alabama Klan Episode, 1866–1874." Ph.D. dissertation, Mississippi State University, 1973.

Bhurtel, Shyam Krishna. "Alfred Eliab Buck: Carpetbagger in Alabama and Georgia." Ph.D. dissertation, Auburn University, 1981.

Cash, William McKinley. "Alabama Republicans During Reconstruction: Personal Characteristics, Motivations, and Political Activity of Party Activists, 1867–1880." Ph.D. dissertation, University of Alabama, 1973.

Cook, Marjorie Howell. "Restoration and Innovation: Alabamians Adjust to Defeat, 1865–1867." Ph.D. dissertation, University of Alabama, 1968.

Davis, Barbara Joan. "A Comparative Analysis of the Economic Structure of Mobile County, Alabama, Before and After the Civil War, 1860 and 1870." M.A. thesis, University of Alabama, 1963.

Drake, Richard Bryant. "The American Missionary Association and the Southern Negro, 1861–1888." Ph.D. dissertation, Emory University, 1957.

Ganus, Clifton L., Jr. "The Freedmen's Bureau in Mississippi." Ph.D. dissertation, Tulane University, 1953.

Gibson, Guy James. "Lincoln's League: The Union League Movement During the Civil War." Ph.D. dissertation, University of Illinois, 1957.

Gilmour, Robert Arthur. "The Other Emancipation: Studies in the Society and the Economy of Alabama Whites During Reconstruction." Ph.D. dissertation, Johns Hopkins University, 1972.

Hume, Richard L. "The 'Black and Tan' Constitutional Conventions of 1867–1869 in Ten Former Confederate States: A Study of Their Membership." Ph.D. dissertation, University of Washington, 1969.

Morris, Robert C. "Reading, 'Riting and Reconstruction: Freedmen's Education in the South." Ph.D. dissertation, University of Chicago, 1976.

Morrow, Ralph E. "The Methodist Episcopal Church, the South, and Reconstruction." Ph.D. dissertation, Indiana University, 1954.

Myers, John Benjamin. "Black Human Capital: The Freedmen and the Reconstruction of Labor in Alabama." Ph.D. dissertation, Florida State University, 1974.

Owens, Susie Lee. "The Union League of America: Political Activities in Tennessee, the Carolinas, and Virginia, 1865–1870." Ph.D. dissertation, New York University, 1943.

Rabinowitz, Howard N. "The Search for Social Control: Race Relations in the Urban South, 1865–1890." 2 vols. Ph.D. dissertation, University of Chicago, 1973.

Reidy, Joseph Patrick. "Masters and Slaves, Planters and Freedmen: The Transition from Slavery to Freedom in Central Georgia, 1820–1880." Ph.D. dissertation, Northern Illinois University, 1982.

Rogers, William Warren, Jr. "Scalawag Congressman: Charles Hays and

Reconstruction in Alabama." Ph.D. dissertation, Auburn University, 1983.

Ryan, John Burkett, Jr. "Willard Warner: Soldier, Senator, and Southern Entrepreneur." M.A. thesis, Auburn University, 1971.

Scudder, John Ralph, Jr. "The Alabama and Chattanooga Railroad Company, 1868–1871." M.A. thesis, University of Alabama, 1951.

Shlomowitz, Ralph. "The Transition from Slave to Freedman: Labor Arrangements in Southern Agriculture, 1865–1870." Ph.D. dissertation, University of Chicago, 1978.

Silvestro, Clement Mario. "None But Patriots: The Union Leagues in Civil War and Reconstruction." Ph.D. dissertation, University of Wisconsin, 1959.

Thomas, James D., Jr. "The Alabama Constitutional Convention of 1867." M.A. thesis, Auburn University, 1947.

Virts, Nancy Lynn. "Plantations, Land Tenure and Efficiency in the Postbellum South: The Effects of Emancipation on Southern Agriculture." Ph.D. dissertation, University of California, Los Angeles, 1986.

Woods, William Leon. "The Travail of Freedom: Mississippi Blacks, 1862–1870." Ph.D. dissertation, Princeton University, 1979.

Index

Abbott, Richard H., 14
Aberdeen, Miss., 228
Affleck, Thomas, 249
Agricultural system: freedmen's dissatisfaction with, 9, 70, 126–27, 129, 135–37, 139, 141, 145–48; legal and financial matters pertaining to, 104–107; Black Codes and, 137–38; during early postwar period, 137–39; rental of land to freedmen, 137, 139–40, 146–49, 152–53, 159–61, 174–76, 204, 230–32, 249; black women's withdrawal from, 138–39, 141, 145, 147; freedmen's militancy and, 138, 153–59, 166–70; erosion of plantation discipline, 143–46, 160, 162–66; Union League's impact on, 148–49, 150–69, 173–76, 248–52; labor contracts, 149–50, 162–63, 165, 170–75, 192, 209–10, 249; city Leagues' concerns for, 192–93, 194; planters' economic pressures on freedmen, 207–13; Ku Klux Klan's impact on, 226–33; squad system, 250–51. See also Planters; Sharecropping; Tenant farming
Alabama: Union League activists in, 13–14; antebellum period in, 16–17; white yeomanry in, 16–23, 42, 73–74, 82; economic difficulties in, 18–21; Black Codes, 29, 137–38; rejection of Fourteenth Amendment, 39; voter registration of freedmen, 43, 52n; defeat of constitution, 82, 83; corruption in, 98; railroad legislation in, 98; agricultural

conditions in, 137–69, 250; during Civil War, 137; readmission to Union, 164; violence in, 214–15. See also names of specific counties and towns
Alabama Constitutional Convention, 79–81, 96–97
Alabama Labor Union, 168–69, 231
Alabama League: establishment of, 12; State Council of, 12, 44, 46, 79, 115, 123; membership of, 23, 43; leadership of, 31, 107–10; segregation of local leagues, 34, 184, 187; organization and structure of, 37–46, 71; freedmen's involvement in, 42–43; disbanding of, 46, 56, 83, 86, 224; Radicalism of, 73–76; Republican party and, 76–79; and Alabama Constitutional Convention, 79–81; factionalism in, 80–86, 90–91; later progression of, 90–91; limitations of League activists, 91–100; legal assistance to freedmen, 100–102, 105–107, 109; social service roles of, 102–104; impact on agricultural system, 104–107, 148–69; confiscation of land, 123–24; labor organization tactics of local leagues, 166–69; Ku Klux Klan's impact on, 223–24
Albright, G. W., 128
Alcorn, James Lusk, 59–60, 69, 89, 99, 198, 224, 246, 247
Alcorn Clubs, 89
Alexander, Allen, 169, 186
Alston, James H., 44, 152, 169, 193
ALU. See Alabama Labor Union

275